The BETOOTA ADVOCATE

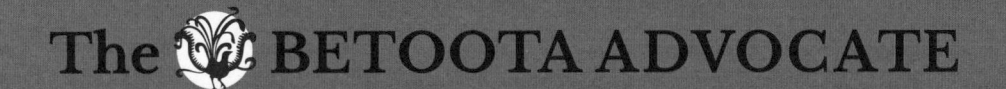

AUSTRALIA 2020

A COLLECTION OF STORIES
TO TIE A BOW ON THIS NIGHTMARE.

MACMILLAN
Pan Macmillan Australia

THE BETOOTA ADVOCATE is a small and independent regional newspaper from far west Queensland. We pride ourselves on reporting fair and just news with an authenticity that rivals only the salt on the sunburnt earth that surrounds us here in the Queensland Channel Country.

Having been established in the mid-1800s, we are arguably Australia's oldest newspaper and have always taken pride in our ability to walk in both worlds: regional and metropolitan news. In recent times, our popularity has grown immensely as a result of a bold move to create an online revival for our publication.

CLANCY OVERELL

Born on V-J Day in 1945 to a staunchly Methodist temperance-league-organiser mother and a lapsed Catholic newspaper-baron father, Clancy Overell was a result of his family's last crack at a male heir – in an effort to protect four generations of blatant patriarchal media nepotism that had proven fruitful for them since the first barrel of ink.

Luckily for the Overells, their son showed no interest in law, medicine or Duntroon and was ready for a reporting cadetship shortly after confirmation.

Despite the promise of a job for life, Clancy took several brief sabbaticals from the media publishing game in his early adulthood. First, he explored the possibility of playing professional rugby league, before a disgusting compound fracture to both his tib and fib during the Betoota Dolphins 1965 grand final loss to the Cunnamulla Rams steered him back to the less physically-exerting brand of alcoholism known as journalism. He took off again to join Jimmy Sharman's Boxing Tent, building a résumé through the grog and head knocks that eventually landed him a job as lead media advisor for the Sir Joh government. This career tangent wrapped up after Overell's then-fiancée's house was raided as part of the sensationalist left wing witch-hunt known as the Fitzgerald Inquiry.

He then returned to the Channel Country to take up the editor role left empty by his retiring father. He has remained in that role ever since.

ERROL PARKER

Born in Hong Kong on 2 April 1977 into a middle-class family in Wan Chai, the only child of Gigi Lau, a Cathay Pacific stewardess and Schalk Parker, a Namibian arms dealer and Namibian War of Independence veteran.

Following high school at Sheng Kung Hui Tang Shiu Kin Secondary School, Parker found work as a copy boy at the *South China Morning Post* in 1995. At age 20, Parker met esteemed Australian journalist Murray Sayle at the 1997 Handover Ceremony, who urged him to take a position at *The Sun* in the United Kingdom.

After close to ten years at *The Sun*, Parker was recruited to its sister paper, *News of the World*. It was at this paper that the high-water mark of Parker's career was recorded until he was indicted with a string of criminal offences during the 2011–12 Leveson Inquiry, which ultimately brought an end to his time in the United Kingdom.

In 2014, after working as a keeper at West Falkland lighthouse and sailing around the South Pacific, Parker arrived in Australia, which led him to answer an ad in *The Courier-Mail*. The ad was written by Dr Clancy Overell OAM, who was looking for a senior journalist with 'tabloid experience'.

CONTENTS

FOREWORD 9

INTRODUCTION 10

2020 BC – BEFORE CORONA 13

THE CRUCIFIXION OF SCOTTY FROM MARKETING 33

SPORTS RORTS 57

COLLAPSE OF SOCIETY 75

LIFE IN ISO 105

COMRADE DUTTON 127

PRIME MINISTER ALBO 149

THE BIRTH OF SCOCIALISM 163

THE SHOW GOES ON 181

GLOBAL UNREST 209

LIKE NOTHING HAPPENED 231

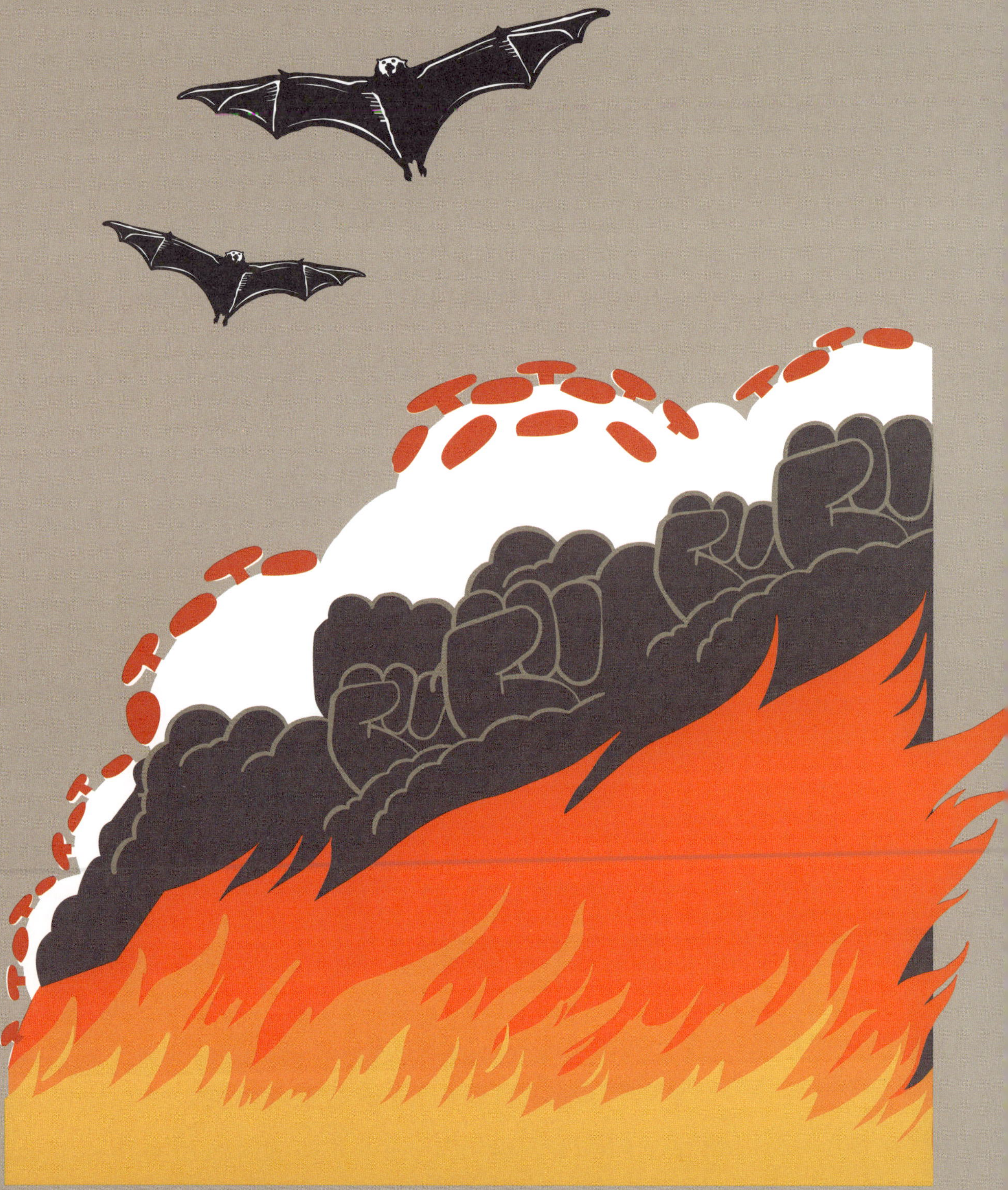

FOREWORD

WE LIKE TO THINK IN JOURNALISM that the truth will out. Call it a secular faith – like believing News Corp is vigorously independent and people are basically decent. There is a degree to which keeping up the fight can't happen without a smidgeon of sustained belief. So, I declare myself with relief, a *Betoota* believer.

My career in journalism, begun in the cretaceous era, stretched half a century. I now emerge an impossibly ancient and emaciated survivor. Nine of us in the SS Media lifeboat with rations enough for four. It turned ugly. I prefer not to go on.

Then *Betoota* sailed into view. Amazing. And a testament to the merits of desperation. The *Betoota* boys created a job for themselves, which seemed to work without handouts from Howard Hughes-like billionaires or a parsimonious government. And yes, like the finally-arrived lukewarm Uber Eats Pad Thai, they found a way.

I realise the stock-in-trade is truthiness rather than truth, but as you know, post-truth is upon us. People like me, who understood the remoteness of absolute truth, in our naivety, continued the pursuit anyway. We now know better. You are now your own information gatekeeper. That means *you* rather than the media shoulder the blame.

I am grateful *Betoota* is here to keep me in touch and in check – and all you other bastards honest. Australian class-based humour ranges wide between the self-loathing Barry Humphries stuff and the innocent affection of Working Dog's, *The Castle*. I reckon *Betoota* settles sensibly in middle ground, between the French Quarter and the Flight Path District – tough but fair with an intermittent burst of evil genius, 'Scotty from Marketing' now firmly in the lexicon.

Sometimes, best of all is the reader's feedback – insightful, piss-taking and revelatory. One of the worst features of the digital age is having the stage handed to so many morons. The notion that what we have is an electronic democracy accessible to more than the inside few property developer party members who used to show up at the Town Hall in the Old City District, is offset by the collective IQ. How good are *Betoota* readers for being you and being there.

The oldest trick in the media playbook, employed more prolifically as rations diminish, is the tabloid one of flattering the public. You tell them it is fine, indeed honourable to be a racist, misogynist, disillusioned and angry turd.

The best we can do is the opposite and take the turds on. The noblest fight (leaving aside State of Origin), embraced by this champion publication is between ourselves, full-on turd-on-turd.

Sincere regards to all Betoota Advocates.

**Chris Masters,
Australian investigative journalist**

INTRODUCTION

IN LATE 2019, the same people who wrote this book were in the process of publishing its prequel.

Before Australia 2020, there was *How Good's Australia*. A similar style of book, but with a much different tone.

At the time, the publishers, book stores, and critics all asked the same question. Why didn't *The Betoota Advocate* include a question mark at the end of the title. Why wasn't it *How Good's Australia?*

The answer, at the time, was that the title was more of a statement than a question. At least, it was when that term entered the Australian vernacular on the evening of the 2019 Federal Election.

Prime Minister Scott Morrison, the unexpected winner, stood on stage at The Wentworth Hotel in Sydney's CBD to claim victory in an election that the entire media caste was convinced he would lose.

His first words were 'How Good's Australia' – there was no question mark. No upward inflection. It was a statement.

It was an election that was fought in the trenches. His opposition entered the race with the momentum and upper hand of a political party that hadn't needed three different leaders to get through two parliamentary terms.

With nothing more than a multibillionaire from New York who owns 70% of the Australian media landscape in his corner, as well as an army of spin doctors who were able to turn slight changes to wealth-hoarding tax loopholes into a 'retiree tax' – Scott Morrison defied what seemed already written and won himself another 3 years.

However, the 12 months that followed that fateful evening would truly test him as a leader, and leave many Australians wondering if maybe we *should* have put a question mark at the end of our last title.

It started with a drought. And not one of those droughts that Range Rover-owners complain about on the sidelines of private school rugby matches. This was one of those rotting livestock droughts – and one that our government seemed rather apathetic towards.

The Prime Minister appeared more interested in running water at novelty rugby league and cricket matches than visiting these crippled rural towns. The issues of rain and water were left to his rural allies in the National Party, but they seemed to be too busy hiding the emails and spreadsheets that linked them to $100 million dollars' worth of pork-barrelled sports grants.

As someone who had up until that point spent his life bouncing between public service jobs that had been handballed to him by his mates, Morrison looked to be in over his head in the role of Prime Minister – a position that has traditionally been associated with some sort of air of accountability. In response to the early cracks in the new Liberal government, both the media and the Federal cabinet began to counter all criticism with the tried and true method of culture warmongering.

Australia Day, cancel culture, religious freedoms, refugees. All that shit that doesn't enter the average Australian's mind unless it's on the front page of a NewsCorp rag.

But, it didn't matter how loud they complained about gender-neutral bathrooms in Parliament House, their constituents, particularly those in the bush, were pissed off.

Then came the fucken bushfires.

You couldn't go too hard on any man or woman who had to oversee such an unprecedented natural disaster like that.

Unless that man or woman decided to take a week long holiday to Hawaii in the middle of it. As hundreds of millions of native animals perished, and thousands of homes and businesses were lost, Scotty From Marketing insisted on finishing his leave of absence with Jenny and the girls. He argued that he was entitled to a holiday as much as any other fair dinkum Aussie, except the firefighters who were dying trying to stop the blaze. But as Scotty argued, 'I don't hold a hose, mate'.

These fires were without precedent not only because of how bad they were as a natural disaster, but also by how terribly they were handled. The images of a Prime Minister being told to fuck off on live television remain vivid. The nation is also left wondering how a man, having spent over half a century on this spinning celestial prison, could ever think it was appropriate to force a handshake on another man. To grab his hand and put your other hand in his.

Thankfully for Australians, the rains came. Thankfully for our political class, they came before they had to confront and discuss the role climate change might have played in the blaze that scorched 21 per cent of all bushland on the eastern seaboard.

But the good times never came.

At the same time the bushfires were being extinguished by the big wet, another disaster was brewing.

This has arguably been the toughest year in recent history. Untold death and destruction. Market corrections. Guy Sebastian's brother winning The Voice.

The other big news story of the year was coronavirus, which may or may not be still going on right now as you're reading these words. We don't have a crystal ball; we're writing this in July because books take a long time to print and lawyers need to make sure our publisher doesn't get taken to court over something in this collection of newspaper clippings.

How the coronavirus pandemic differs from the bushfires is that it's something that a man sitting on the electric trolleybus whizzing through the French Quarter can help fix. He can wear a mask, he can wash his hands. He can download the COVIDSafe app and do what the government tells him to do.

Stay inside, don't go to the pub. Make sure to keep a metre and a bit away from everyone else. Don't go and visit your Nan if you don't have to.

What makes it worse was that we almost had it fucked. In terms of pandemics, it was a Gold Coast-based sporting team. It was sixty points down at half time.

And then it scored a soft try – or goal.

It scored another, then a few more before the second half of the second half was over. All of a sudden, that pathetic Gold Coast-based sporting team was winning.

Again, it's probably worth saying that when this book finally reaches the shelves, coronavirus might be fucked again. The pangolin might've kissed the last Australian. It's also worth noting here that our publisher didn't think enough of you knew what a pangolin looked like, so they asked us to remove it from the front cover. Now you know.

So here we are, at the end of 2020. Well, you are. Right now, it is July and this so-called deadly pandemic changes every day.

From our base here in the Queensland Channel Country, we hope this book introduction finds you and your family well. We hope that this year hasn't been too hard on you and hasn't dampened your spirits. That is hasn't stolen any of the usual panache that you enjoy moving from goal to goal.

Just remember, every day is sunny in Betoota.

The Betoota Advocate Editorial Team

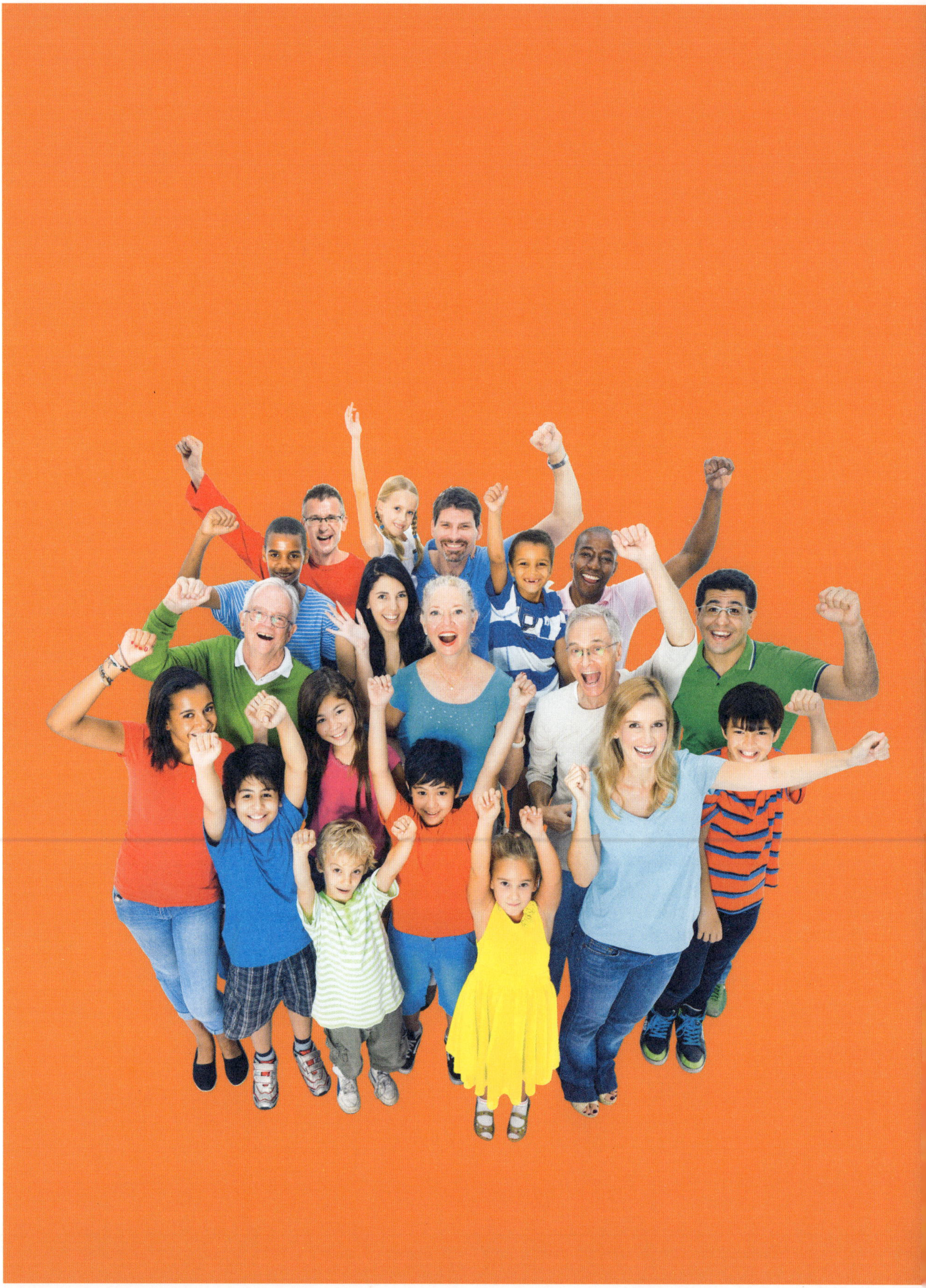

2020 BC – BEFORE CORONA

If 2020 had been a motor vehicle, it would have been recalled to Detroit within the first week.

And that was before anyone got a really good look at what was going on in Wuhan at that time.

First, there were the unprecedented Australian bushfires that ravaged over ten per cent of the nation's east coast with 60 metre high fires billowing across drought-stricken bushlands and whole cities shrouded in smoke for weeks on end.

When all was said and done, 10,000 buildings were destroyed, including 3000 homes, over a billion animals perished, and at least 34 people died as a result of the unstoppable blazes.

Then there were the escalating tensions and threats exchanged between Donald Trump and Iranian President Hassan Rouhani. It was the closest our planet has come to World War III since the Cuban missile crisis.

Unsurprisingly, the US President's poor interpersonal skills were not well received by the volatile military forces in the Persian Gulf. This led to both Iran and USA classifying each other as terrorist organisations, and to both countries skirting as closely as they possibly could to bombing each other's bases without actually doing it. In a bizarre and cruel twist of fate, this very close encounter with a major global conflict was defused when Iran's Islamic Revolutionary Guard Corps (IRGC) accidentally shot down a Ukrainian passenger plane in Tehran on 8 January, just as things were about to boil over. 176 innocent civilians were killed and both Trump and Rouhani quickly pulled their heads in after the much scarier Vladimir Putin started asking questions.

Still, even though it felt like both the natural environment and human civilisation were on their final lap, none of this felt as inconvenient as the global pandemic that was to follow. That was as normal as things got in 2020.

The following chapter covers what else was happening in the Australian news cycle for that brief moment in time where it seemed like things couldn't get worse: BC.

Relative With Pool Selfishly Refuses To Host Christmas

A BETOOTA GROVE MAN who converted his privileged private school background into a successful career in business has refused to host Christmas this year just because he can.

The main reason why Mark Roland doesn't want to have Christmas at his place again is that his less successful relatives take the piss and stay there until after dark, eating and making the tiles beside the pool all wet.

He said he's been hit up by his brother, sister and brother-in-law about celebrating some imaginary sky man's kid's birthday more than once this month. Each time he has outright refused.

Mark spoke to this reporter over our shared fence this morning.

'I'm just not up to it this year,' he said. 'They're like a pack of locusts. Last year, they ate two kilos of wasabi peas before lunch! They treat my place like a resort. Getting towels out, leaving them on the floor. Expecting my wife to prepare the lunch *and* pay for it. I'm just not up to it.

'This year, I want to make the potato salad, get in the MG and put the top down. Drive over to my brother's place. Shoot the shit for a few hours then drive home, get in the spa and have a Dunhill. Maybe a bowl of spaghetti alfredo and a Splice for dessert. Who gives a fuck. I'm 65 years old.'

Our reporter nodded along and waited for a pause in the conversation to ask if he could use the pool while Mark's at Whistler next week.

> *'They're like a pack of locusts. Last year, they ate two kilos of wasabi peas before lunch!'*

Man About To Head Through Airport Security Looks For Line With Least Number Of Boomers In It

A LOCAL MAN ARRIVED at the airport this morning cutting it a little more finely, timewise, than he might have preferred.

Darcy Rollins told *The Advocate* this afternoon via telephone that he'd checked in on his phone and wasn't carrying any checked luggage.

'The only thing that stood between me and the Virgin Lounge was security,' he said.

As the morning rush was at its peak, all six security lanes at the Remienko Memorial Airport were open and the lines snaked back almost to the bag drop desks.

He was at a critical juncture in his trip, Darcy was. It was critical because the line he picked needed to be one that moved quickly.

'You see, I wasn't there late enough to get ushered through the business class line and I wasn't early enough to waste time,' he said.

'So I had to pick the right line.'

He scrutinised each line for the number of baby boomers queuing.

Their terrified, confused faces. Their sausage fingers clutching their printed itineraries. The loud clanging of bangles and rustling of beads. The attempts to strike up a conversation with the security staff.

'All things I didn't have time for,' said Darcy.

He picked a line with three up the front, because the rest looked like business travellers like him.

The first boomer thought the 'take all laptops out of your bag' rule didn't apply to him. Then he tried to walk through the metal detector with a belt on. His partner kicked up a fuss about having to take her shoes off. She glared at the security worker and asked him if she looked like a terrorist. Her bangles set the metal detector off. The third one in line forgot to take his Glock 23 out of his hand luggage and tried to laugh it off as six AFP officers surrounded him. Security then closed the lane just as Darcy was about to put his MacBook down on the conveyor.

He joined another queue at the back behind a Probus group.

> *She glared at the security worker and asked him if she looked like a terrorist. Her bangles set the metal detector off.*

Anti-Racing Protestors Urged To Try And Imagine How Good It Feels To Land A Boxed Trifecta

#NUPTOTHECUP ACTIVISTS HAVE today been urged to try their hand at a boxed trifecta this week.

A trifecta is the selection of the first three runners to finish a race, in the correct order. A boxed trifecta is a type of trifecta bet where the bettor selects three or more runners to fill the first, second and third places in any order.

This comes as calls to boycott the Melbourne Cup and the horseracing industry in general grow across the country, particularly in inner-city pockets like West End, Brunswick and Newtown.

However, the far greater number of people who look forward to a day – or at least a few hours – off tomorrow, have pleaded with the protesters to have a crack at a trifecta with a big payout.

'Could just be a boxed one with four or five horses in it, something big enough to win you an overseas holiday if it comes off, you know,' explained one Melbourne resident planning to give it a nudge tomorrow.

'Honestly, I get where they are coming from, but a couple of brekky beers topped off by a big win a few hours later is pretty good,' he continued.

'Might make them reconsider their position a little bit, and potentially be happy to allow the industry its many and appalling indiscretions.'

2020 BC – BEFORE CORONA 17

Cafe Phases Out Cups By Pouring Hot Coffee Directly Into Customers' Mouths

TONGUES ARE LITERALLY wagging in the Betoota CBD this morning as trendy cafe Caff.Hey! implements a new environmentally friendly zero-waste policy that eliminates the need for disposable cups and even reusable coffee vessels.

'It's all about leaving the smallest possible environmental footprint,' explained Caff.Hey! owner, barista and part-time clerical assistant Terry Salt, 22.

'We found that people who use reusable coffee vessels are periodically being gifted new reusable coffee vessels by their family and workmates, thereby negating any environmental saving.

'To get around this we take the coffee directly to the consumer by asking them to rest their head under the espresso machine and pouring their drink straight into their open mouths.

'We have saved over 50 cups this morning alone.'

One unnamed customer approached our reporter to share her excitement about the new scheme.

'Dar bur ma farkar marf wa hart karfay! Ar car arven farl ma tarnge arnie mare! [sic]' she enthused in an unknown language while waving her arms around.

'Ars sarn ars ar gut bark fra da barn yarnit ar garna garv ma lawyer a carl sar ar carn takk thars farkan arjet far arl hars gut!'

'It's great to see everyone so enthusiastic about our new initiative,' grinned Terry as he waved her goodbye.

'There's been lots of fervent shouting going on here this morning and no complaints, as far as I can tell. Plus we are selling heaps of our new Aloe Vera Choc Chip Muffins.'

> *'Ars sarn ars ar gut bark fra da barn yarnit ar garna garv ma lawyer a carl sar ar carn takk thars farkan arjet far arl hars gut!'*

Function Waiter Silently Judges Woman Coming Back For Fourth Arancini Ball

A LOCAL FUNCTION WAITER, Jess Fernsby, has today revealed that she does, in fact, judge people for helping themselves to multiple rounds of finger food.

Jess says that she was particularly perturbed by one recent incident, in which a woman gorged herself silly on arancini balls after having a few too many glasses of bubbly.

'In my industry, arancini balls are the gold standard,' says Jess. 'You can barely get out of the kitchen before they're all gone. And of course, because they're so popular, we only ever serve them once. Then it's all vegetable quiches and spring rolls.

'That's why it's particularly bad form to hoard them. The person-to-ball ratio is already too high.'

The woman, who would not be named, had helped herself to a number of balls, stating that 'the rest of them are for my friends'.

Jess says she later saw the woman devouring the balls like a python unhinging its jaw.

'Honestly, being a function waiter is like being in a David Attenborough doco,' says Jess. 'You see humans at their most primal. You miss one part of the room and they'll stalk you like a lion tracking down a gazelle.'

Jess says it gets particularly bad when a tray of chicken Kievs pops up after a dry run of the shit stuff.

'It's like dropping blood into a vat full of sharks,' shudders Jess.

'Once one notices it, there's a shift of energy in the air.'

The woman reportedly resurfaced for a fifth ball but at least had the decency to look slightly ashamed.

Centrelink Under Fire For Blasting 'Work, B**ch' By Britney Spears In Waiting Rooms

LOGAN CENTRELINK HAS reportedly been investigated by local authorities for blasting Britney Spears' 2013 smash hit 'Work B**ch' in the waiting area.

The initiative, spearheaded by the Morrison Government, was being tested as a way to motivate Centrelink dependants to ditch Newstart and 'gain employment' – an idea the government obviously thinks hasn't occurred to any of them before.

Now, after dropping their daks for a piss test, recipients are awarded the privilege of hearing 'Work, B**ch' on repeat.

One such person who was privy to Logan's short-lived experiment was ex-accountant Melanie Birdwhistle.

The fifty-five-year-old mother of three had just been given the sack when she begrudgingly attended her local Centrelink. After navigating her way through the long line and tapping what services she needed into the prehistoric office iPad, Melanie found herself in the waiting room.

'At first I was just listening to a couple have a domestic spat,' says Melanie, 'but then I heard what they were playing.'

The Logan office had originally been playing Dolly Parton's '9 to 5', but found that it actually had the opposite effect than they'd hoped.

Torn between the Princess of Pop and adding sad-face emojis to bank statements, the government chose the former, claiming that they are trying to appeal to millennials.

'We'd heard of scientists playing Mozart to rats,' says a Logan City councillor, before pausing and adding, 'I now realise that doesn't sound too good, can you scratch that?'

This new controversy comes shortly after the robodebt scandal, which saw thousands of Australia's most vulnerable people accused of owing money to the government due to clerical errors.

In response to the robodebt scandal, Prime Minister Morrison has reportedly announced plans to switch Britney with Rihanna's 'Bitch Better Have My Money'.

Roo Shooter Not Allowed Near The House, Says Mum

A TRANSIENT MAN WHO Dad has contracted to thin out the wild animals that keep killing themselves on his fences shouldn't be driving around the family property while the kids are awake, and certainly isn't allowed over the cattle grid entrance to the homestead, says Mum.

The nameless vagrant, who comes from Adelaide or somewhere fucking ages away, doesn't seem to reveal much about his personal life – but always seems responsive to Dad offering him a beer and talking about gates.

Like former Greens senator Lee Rhiannon, Mum has never been a big fan of the types of blokes who somehow have government licences to carry some of the most powerful guns allowed in human hands.

But unlike inner-city politicians, it's not because she's worried about Australia's 45 million wild kangaroos going extinct. It's because she thinks this guy's a serial killer.

'I don't want him coming up this way,' says Mum to Dad, who's pretty much given up on the he's-not-a-bad-bloke thing, purely because Mum is right when she says he looks shifty.

The nameless vagrant, who comes from Adelaide or somewhere fucking ages away, doesn't seem to reveal much about his personal life.

Mum has no real basis for these rules, considering half of Dad's mates are equally dodgy, and the manager who lives by himself in the fibro shack in the top paddock has actually admitted to killing someone before.

However, the fact that the dogs can't stop barking at him is a pretty fair indication that he's probably wanted for questioning in a couple of states over some stuff that has gone down at truck stops.

High School Teacher Hides Life Of Sin From Students By Using Her Weird Middle Name On Facebook

THEY TOLD SAMANTHA WILLIAMS during her time at university that she would have to be careful about her behaviour once she qualified as a teacher.

So, when that day came, the 24-year-old regular binge drinker bit the bullet and changed her name on social media to Barbara Williams, substituting her first name with her middle name, a savvy ploy she learnt from some older teachers.

Two years on at Betoota High, young Williams has successfully managed to hide her life of sin from her pupils and the Department of Education.

'It's like joining the police force, you can't allow yourself to be found on socials, otherwise you could compromise your position,' she said to *The Advocate* today.

'I mean, I'm not gonna end up with a stalker if someone finds out who I really am, but it wouldn't be a good look if some of the kids saw what was on my Facebook.

'Look, I haven't exactly got photos of myself dropping elephants on safari, or passed out covered in vomit in a hotel room, but you get tagged in things here and there and stuff gets posted on your wall that can land you in a bit of hot water,' she said.

Williams explained that she has had a few kids she teaches ask her what name she uses on Facebook, but she's been clever enough to swerve the question.

'Some of the kids try and find me, particularly the seedy little Year 9 boys, but they are too stupid and naive to figure out that I'm on there with a fake name,' she said.

Williams said she hopes to navigate through the next few years anonymously, flying under the radar of her pupils and the principal until she becomes old enough that no one really cares about finding her on Facebook anymore because they think she is too old to be up to much.

'Oi, You Should Listen To This Podcast,' Says White Person

SOUTH BETOOTA RESIDENT James Reynolds is one of millions of migaloos worldwide swept up in the podcast revolution.

Close friends of Reynolds report that his love for podcasts has meant he has spent less time socialising lately, something his peers seem unperturbed by as whenever they do see him, all he talks about are his podcasts.

'It's getting a bit much,' said his high school mate Wayne Graves. 'We'll go out for a beer and all he'll want to talk about is if Adnan is innocent or not.'

So great is Reynolds' obsession that after bringing up *S-Town* to his great-aunt at a recent family function, it has been confirmed he has now officially mentioned his podcast habits to every white person he knows, and quite a few others.

'It's interesting but!' Reynolds stated. 'I reckon they should go listen to it themselves so we can discuss! And if they can't, well, I can just explain it to them, I know most of them off by heart anyway!'

Recently, it has also been revealed that Reynolds plans to branch out from being merely a listener, and use his podcast knowledge to start his own.

'There's not really going to be a theme to it. Just me and my guest discussing different issues. Don't want to limit myself with a theme, that way it can be anything.'

When asked about the target audience for his podcast, Reynolds answered that initially it would be his family and friends.

We reached out to Reynolds' family and close friends who politely declined to comment.

> *'It's getting a bit much,' said his high school mate Wayne Graves. 'We'll go out for a beer and all he'll want to talk about is if Adnan is innocent or not.'*

Grill'd Customers Given Option To Cover Wage Theft Of Staff Through Local Matters Initiative

CUSTOMERS OF GRILL'D Healthy Burgers are now being given the option to support the livelihoods of the franchise employees – by donating their charity bottle caps to a separate community fund.

This comes as the upmarket Australian fast-food chain has been accused of using government-subsidised traineeships to keep its young workers on low wages, despite nearly all the employees saying it is a load of shit.

The company is worth about $370 million and has outlets around the country. However, there has been very little trickle-down from the company profits to the overexcited teenagers working the stoves.

With the entire company's business model now in the crosshairs of the unions, Grill'd has today moved quickly to avoid the potential PR disaster faced by Woolies, Dunkin' Donuts, 7-Eleven and a large number of celebrity hospitality groups.

Each franchise around the country is now offering customers the opportunity to donate to a separate charity fund aimed at supplementing the company's wage theft of their employees.

According to the Grill'd website: 'Local Matters began in 2011 as a way for us to give back, to help strengthen and support the communities that have always supported us.'

Local Matters jars are a fixture in all Grill'd restaurants. Each month, in every restaurant, the jars promote three community groups for their guests to support. With every burger ordered, a Local Matters token is handed over for customers to drop into the jar of their choice.

The founder of Grill'd, Simon Crowe, told *The Advocate* that the new scheme will help their poorly paid employees get through Christmas.

'It's a charitable cause that we really believe in,' explained Crowe.

'Instead of paying workers a decent wage for serving up burgers we charge too much for, we are giving customers the chance to kindly donate.

'It's something that people can feel good about leading into the holiday season. So get behind it, everyone!'

130kph Definitely Not Fast Enough To Be In Right Lane, Says Skyline R33 With Red Ps

LOCAL SKYLINE OWNER, BRENDO (19), says he and the boys have got somewhere to be, and they are looking for an off-ramp in the next 40–50 kilometres so if you could fuck off out of the way, that'd be tight.

With some sort of a house party slash gatho happening tonight in the regional outskirts of Betoota, Brendo and Kane, Kyle and Jaxon are not fucking spiders.

This means that everyone in the right lane should clear off because you should only be in there if you are driving fast enough – and according to Brendo, 130 kilometres per hour isn't fast enough.

The 1993 Nissan Skyline, which is currently full to the brim with young cunts drinking Tooheys Extra Dry while listening to Violent Soho, appears to be more than prepared to ride up someone's arse until they either lose their temper or pull left.

Brendo was last spotted sharing his understanding of highway etiquette with other motorists after his R33 spent close to 20 minutes tailgating a local Pajero mum and her two kids, who were rushing to get to Grandma's house before sundown.

'Fucken yewwww,' says Brendo and the boys as they fly past with as many limbs out the window as possible.

Universities To Recognise Netflix Documentaries And Joe Rogan Podcasts As Official Qualifications

IN NEWS THAT MAY upset some properly qualified professionals, universities have today announced that from 2020 onwards they will be recognising Netflix documentaries and Joe Rogan podcasts as acceptable qualifications or credits towards all post-graduate degrees.

A spokesperson from Betoota University explained to *The Advocate* how the move was an attempt to modernise their structure.

'It's where people are getting their education from these days. Libraries and textbooks are a thing of the past. That's why we've decided to recognise these new forms of knowledge. We're opening ourselves up to a whole new demographic. Just think of all the untapped potential that we now have access to because we've made this step. It's only a matter of time before the rest of the world catches on.'

While the university spokesperson was standing by their decision, intellectuals and properly qualified people aren't as convinced.

'It's a terrible idea. Do they really think this will help uncover tomorrow's doctors, lawyers and whatever else?' said one researcher. 'It's a pathetic attempt to get more money.'

While there seem to be some quite differing opinions, one group that will surely welcome the change is the students.

Early reports from social listening indicate that searches for university post-graduate degrees have already increased 30 per cent in just two hours.

'Have You Been To Revolver?' Asks Mate Returning From Melbourne With 1000-Yard Stare

NOTORIOUS LOOSE CANNON TIM Wellsong has just returned from his first ever trip to Melbourne.

The Brisbane local had started his Friday with an obligatory drop into Naked For Satan when all of a sudden he found himself deep in the bellows of Prahran's least exclusive nightclub, Revolver Upstairs.

Despite the night consisting mostly of sinister smokers' area talks and watching a lone man boogie by himself in a corner, Tim cannot stop raving about it.

'Oh man, dude, Revs was so cool,' says Tim, his voice breaking slightly.

'I reckon everyone should go there at least once.'

Tim had been popping his way through the inner-city clubbing scene when the last drink mark loomed.

Off his head and not keen to deal with a comedown, Tim followed the excited calls of 'REVS' and made his way into what appeared to be the seventh dimension of hell.

The 24-hour party hut, known for being the only bar in Melbourne that sells more water than alcohol, proved to be an unforgettable experience.

'It's hard to explain it, really. It's somehow both super energetic and completely soulless at the same time,' says Tim.

Tim ended up spending an entire weekend at the nightclub, which only became clear when he found himself busting out at 8 am on Monday to a sea of city workers. The slightly sobering experience of watching a man buy his morning coffee and bagel sent Tim into a bit of a head spin.

'I had no idea what day it was. It was like being sucked into a black hole where time didn't exist anymore.'

Tim says he'd definitely go again, but needs some time to rethink his life first.

Everyone Shut Up! Hayley Is About To Give A Quite Visual Recount Of Her Most Recent Root

A GROUP OF FIVE girlfriends have been told to shut the fuck up this evening because Hayley is back in the game.

While catching up for their bi-monthly girls' dinner, the group of women, who comprise a fusion of both work and high school friends, have got some serious goss to sink their teeth into.

Most notably, the fact that Hayley's drought has broken, in a big way – with a temporary but fucking hot gym junkie named Colm who she met at the physiotherapist, of all places.

'He's not a physio. But, like, he does something like that,' says Hayley, who will not be marrying this man.

The group alpha, Katie, was the first to pick up on an out-of-place chirpiness vibe at the table – and was almost psychic in her realisation that Hayley had been getting the pipe.

After a bit of drilling, she starts getting some oil.

While the rest of the table continues gasbagging, Katie needs to rein in their attention, because they are gonna wanna hear this.

'SHUT UP, EVERYONE!' says Katie.

Everyone looks, fearing the worst from that end of the table, like a pregnancy or something.

'Hayley has been getting it!'

As the subsequent woohoo sounds echo right across the restaurant, even diners as far as the front door appear to know what these girls are talking about.

It's established quite early on in the retelling of the tale of this explosive and passionate romance that Colm is missing a few roos in the top paddock, but it is also made clear that Hayley wasn't looking to get an intellectual companion out of this relationship.

As the table begins to get rowdier throughout the course of Hayley's quite visual recount of their first root, a cluey restaurant manager realises where he needs to be right now.

'Shots, ladies?' asks Pablo.

'On the house!'

[hysterical girl noises]

Brisbane Man Sends It Into River After Being Unable To Find Station Not Playing 'Dance Monkey'

A BRISBANE ELECTRICIAN HAS treated himself to a dip in the brown snake this afternoon.

The 29-year-old decided to do so after failing to find a radio station not playing 'Dance Monkey' despite trying for a significant period of time.

'I don't know if the fucking thing is on repeat or what, but I couldn't land a frequency not playing the song, so I just decided to send it,' explained the bedraggled local, who certainly smelled like he'd just walked out of the mighty Brisbane River.

'Don't worry, it's the work truck,' the man said, motioning to his ute.

'How's that for a "Dance for you, dance for you, dance for you, oh oh oh."'

The song, written by Melbourne artist Tones and I, who was busking in Byron less than 12 months ago, has risen to prominence over the last few months, reaching the point where it is now at the levels of airplay of Macklemore and Ryan Lewis' 'Thrift Shop' and Daft Punk's 'Get Lucky'.

'Look, I'm not a Triple M rock kinda guy or anything, and I am partial to all different genres of music, but fuck, they've butchered that song now,' explained the tradie.

'I actually used to not mind it. I mean, it's a chart-topper in 27 different countries and has broken the ARIA record for a reason, but it's too much now.

'Anyway, maybe it was a bit rash of me to send it into the river, but I had a rush of blood, and I don't have to pick up the bill, so it is what it is, aye,' he said before trudging off.

Sshhhh, Local Sex Machine Can't Say Too Much About Schoolies Around Mum, But Yeah

A FORMERLY AWKWARD teenager has returned to town after Schoolies Week with a bit of swag and a new pair of sunnies, it has been confirmed.

After pulling back into the driveway of the family home in his dark green 1994 VW Golf, the whole neighbourhood stops for a moment to take in the new man.

Seventeen-year-old James Cleary is now known as Jimmy, and he says words like 'lit' and 'savage' in day-to-day conversations.

'Haha, what-up,' says Jimmy as his younger siblings rush to his car to ask questions about his exciting week away.

'Did you see Damo on the news?' chuckles Jimmy, who also goes by Jimmy C now. 'He was so lit. He'd had like a sixpack in half an hour and then they interviewed him about some guy that got tasered. Haha, such a crack-up.'

Jimmy C's four younger siblings, who range in age from four to 13, have never met Damo before, but want to know more. Jimmy's teenage brother Ryan asks the question on the tip of everyone's tongue.

'Did you meet a girl?'

'Oooooh,' says the crowd of siblings, who have been joined by a few other local neighbourhood kids.

Jimmy C lowers his sunglasses down his nose so that his eyes are just visible.

'Well, haha,' he says, while poking his left index finger through a circle made with his right index finger and thumb.

'Let's just say …

'… I can't say too much around Mum. Haha.'

At time of press, Jimmy was seen checking himself out in the kitchen window with a completely popped collar.

Anxious Millennials Killing The Telemarketing Industry By Not Answering Private Numbers

IN WORRYING NEWS, millennials are under fire again today for ruining yet another industry.

According to some bloke at the *Daily Mail*, the telemarketing industry has taken a huge hit in the last decade, with many young people choosing to ignore calls from an unknown number.

This comes shortly after it was announced that millennials were single-handedly responsible for wiping out everything from napkins to mayonnaise to the use of doorbells.

'Back in my day you'd answer the phone and subject the innocent person on the other end to a torrent of abuse,' says a disgruntled boomer.

'But now young people aren't answering at all. Goes to show how entitled and inconsiderate that lot are.'

A local telemarketing agency, Tellstar, has reported a staggering decline in answered calls, which has resulted in thousands of people losing their jobs.

Rather than placing blame on a parasitic industry that often preys on people, Tellstar has instead pleaded with today's youth to show some empathy and answer the phone.

'I really don't understand why people won't let us waste their time,' says a spokesperson for Tellstar.

'They're on their phones all day anyway. You can spend $10 a month on Stan but you don't want funeral insurance? That's bullshit.'

The Advocate reached out to some young people to see why this was happening.

'I'd literally rather slam my fingers into a door than talk on the phone,' says Liz, a third-year uni student.

'I don't see why people can't just email me. You ever heard yourself on a loudspeaker? I sound like a pre-pubescent goat.'

Liam Fifeman, a twenty-something retail assistant, echoes this statement.

'I keep bleeding out of my ears. Briefly considered calling the doctor but yeah, nah, thanks.'

Multilingual Teenager With Scientific Understanding Of Atmospheric Physics Apparently An Idiot

AN INTERNATIONALLY recognised 16-year-old Swede who is fluent in several languages and responsible for a rapidly changing global consensus towards climatology, is an idiot, according to a lot of old people.

Despite spending a fair amount of time not at school due to her role as an ambassador for the future of humankind, 99 per cent of the world's scientists believe Greta Thunberg has a better grasp of atmospheric physics than any of the world leaders that attended last week's UN summit.

Atmospheric physics is a branch of meteorology and is related to studying the layers of the atmosphere, weather systems, and climatic phenomena.

Atmospheric physicists are usually employed as faculty at universities or as research scientists at national labs, unless that particular institution is being urged by conservative governments and funding bodies to redirect their focus towards Western Civilisation studies, which is a newfound field of study aimed at celebrating what most atmospheric physicists are losing sleep over.

One of the more alarming studies into atmospheric physics was the 'Special Report on Global Warming of 1.5°C' – which was published by the Intergovernmental Panel on Climate Change (IPCC) on 8 October 2018, and subsequently ignored by anyone who had the power to do anything because of the cognitive dissonance that comes with being rich and powerful.

While business leaders and the global political classes are struggling to acknowledge very alarming findings related to carbon emissions and climatology in general, Greta Thunberg (17) has managed to communicate to the masses a relatively accessible summation of the global scientific community's consensus on the man-made effects of climate change.

However, her recent speeches and rapidly echoing rhetoric have been dismissed by media and a lot of old white people, who say she is an idiot.

Her critics, mostly men whose own grandchildren have cut them off because of their inability to love anyone or anything after being exposed to sensationalist media likely linked to the Murdoch family, cite the teenager's notable lack of sympathy and lenience for the fossil fuels and mining sector as a prime example of why she is stupid.

Many then go on to point out as a counter-argument that a lot of young people use iPhones.

> Atmospheric physicists are usually employed at universities or at national labs, unless that particular institution is being urged by governments and funding bodies to redirect their focus towards Western Civilisation studies.

Climate Change Deniers Say Globe Is Only Warming Because There Are So Many Fires Right Now

IN A TIME WHEN Australians are experiencing 'the most dangerous bushfire week the nation has ever seen', which is almost definitely caused by climate change, climate change deniers have taken the opportunity to add yet another excuse to the slew of lies they use to brainwash themselves into thinking climate change isn't real.

Reluctantly, *The Advocate* sat down with the town's biggest climate change denier to hear the latest lie he's peddling.

'I don't know what else you people need to be convinced,' says Bruce McDowd while wiping his sweaty brow with a KFC hand towelette.

'Fossil fuels aren't causing the temperature of the planet to rise, it's these bloody fires.

'Think about how hot a fire makes your living room. Now apply that same thing outside, where there are over 100 fires burning right now. One of them is 370,000 acres big. Now you look me in the eye and tell me a fire that big is not going to heat up the planet.'

The Advocate reached out to the peak scientific body in Australia, the CSIRO, to see if there was any truth in Mr McDowd's statement.

Despite getting through to the CSIRO, our reporter was hung up on after the representative said, 'That is fucking ridiculous, don't waste our time with that bullshit.'

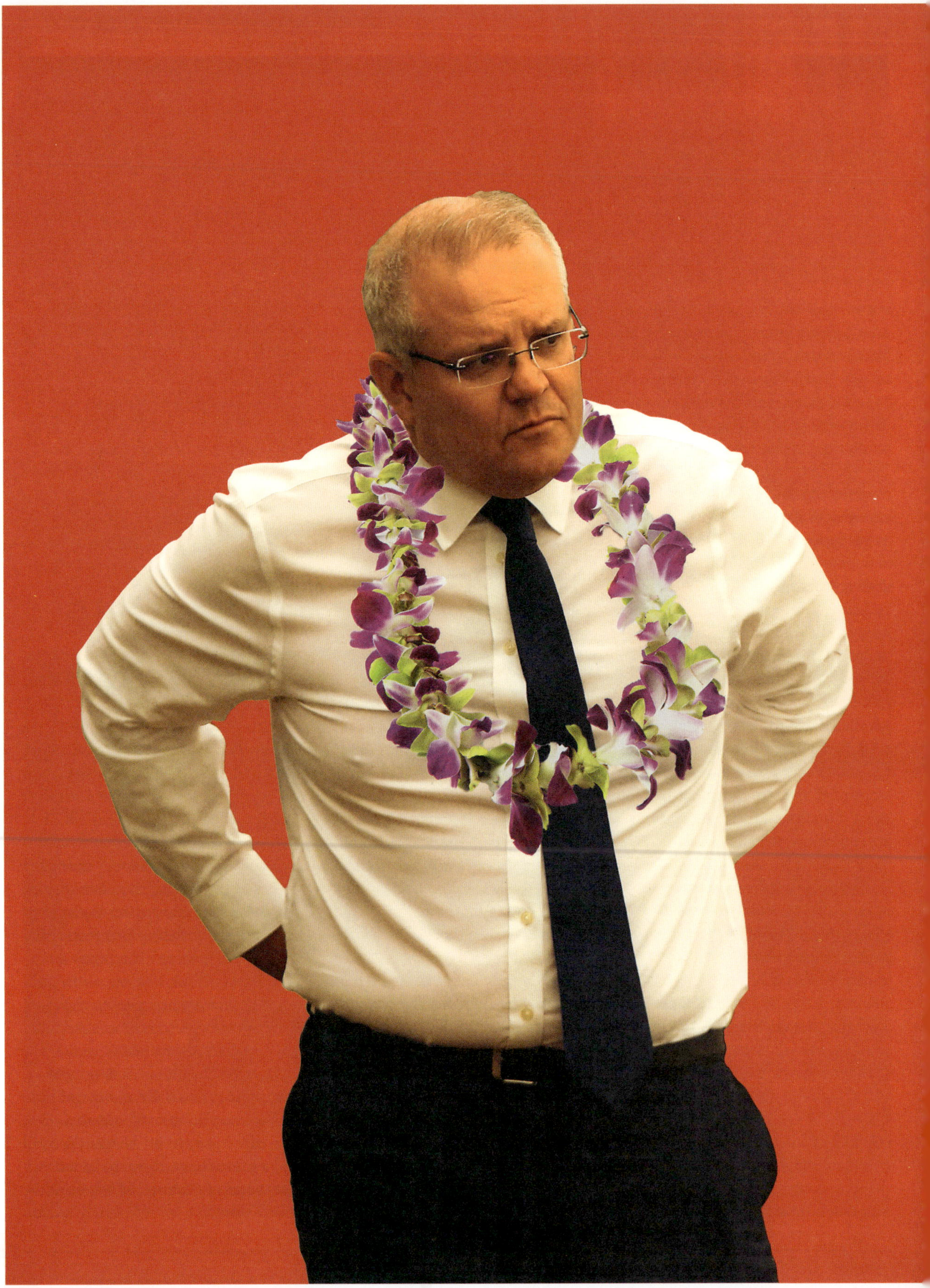

THE CRUCIFIXION OF SCOTTY FROM MARKETING

It is a unique part of the Australian psyche which dictates that when something goes wrong, someone or something must be blamed for it. When the nation caught on fire in the spring of 2019, the person to blame for it was Scott Morrison. If Bill Shorten had won the 2019 election, he would've been to blame. Of course, Scott Morrison didn't cause the bushfires himself, nor was he fully responsible for the complete breakdown in policy that caused the unchecked build-up of fuel, the years-long drought and record-breaking temperatures.

Scotty from Marketing was crucified because of how he handled the bushfires when they arrived. His continued refusal to display leadership. His continuous lies. He was in Hawaii at the time – and he chose to stay there while telling us all he was making every effort to come home as soon as possible.

From there, it was one brain snap after another. The Prime Minister's shine was wearing off. As each day rolled on, it became more and more obvious to Australians that this bloke might actually not be up to the job. Was Scott Morrison just a man who'd been in the right place at the right time his whole life – only to find himself being sacrificed upon the altar of public disgust and anger for something over which he had little control?

Probably.

Scott Morrison spent his professional career up to this point putting positive spins on things. But there aren't many ways to put a positive spin on Australia's worst bushfire season in living memory. Not that he didn't stop trying. Scott is just one man in the Scott Morrison machine. He has teams of advisors, speech writers and support staff. All of whom deserved to be crucified alongside him.

This chapter tells the story of the time a former marketing executive and lifelong bureaucrat was found out at quite possibly the worst moment in Australian history. As a Prime Minister, Scotty took the sins of previous governments, his own government, his own team, and put them on his shoulders – deservedly.

However, all would soon be forgotten when someone in a wet market in Wuhan consumed some undercooked pangolin steak and changed the world forever.

Mate, Do Something, Anything

SCOTTY FROM MARKETING HAS been urged to do something. Address the nation, stand up there next to someone doing sign language, bring in the army, fucken anything.

This comes as rescue services say dozens of fires will burn across Australia for weeks, including a 'mega-fire' – already the size of greater Sydney and too big to put out.

As of last night, more than 100 fires were burning across the state of New South Wales, 18 of which potentially threatened lives and homes in rural and outer metropolitan areas. More than 40 were burning all across Queensland.

However, Prime Minister Morrison is enacting a Soviet-era brand of crisis management, which is to not address anything and keep smiling for photographs that insinuate things are all good in the empire.

When asked by our reporters why he hadn't made a public address, or visited anyone in Ipswich or the Blue Mountains, Morrison responded by telling everyone to calm down because the cricket will be on soon, haha.

Conditions eased on Sunday morning across Australia, allowing firefighters a chance to do critical back-burning and containment work ahead of Tuesday, when the mercury is tipped to soar into the 40s in parts of the state.

Already this fire season, six people have died and more than 1000 homes have been lost across New South Wales and Queensland.

Morrison says now is not the time to discuss climate change. Now is the time to discuss denying detained refugees access to mainland medical treatment. Now is also the time to merge the Arts department with Transport. And the Environment with Agriculture.

Morrison responded by telling everyone to calm down because the cricket will be on soon, haha.

Roman Emperor Urges Pompeii To Avoid Needless Anxiety Over Smoke Coming From Mount Vesuvius

ARCHAEOLOGISTS FOSSICKING in the volcanic rock of Pompeii have today uncovered a stone tablet believed to have been used by Titus Caesar Vespasianus Augustus during his time as Roman Emperor.

The script carved onto the tablet has since been translated from Latin, revealing a speech the leader gave to his nation's academics in mid–79 AD, urging them to stop talking about volcanoes because they were subjecting children to 'needless anxiety'.

Titus, as he was known, served as Roman Emperor between 79 AD and 81 AD – a term that lasted longer than most Australian Prime Ministers. His time as leader was marred by the suffering caused by two disasters, the eruption of Mount Vesuvius and a fire in Rome in 80 AD.

However, he is remembered fondly for his hard work overseeing the completion of the Colosseum – which is recognised as one of the great feats of the Roman Empire, and often compared to Australia's National Broadband Network.

The unearthing of the ancient stone tablet appears to show another side to this short-lived political legacy.

The script includes Titus' response to the scientists and activists of the time – who had accused the political class of failing the younger generations by not taking any action towards the smoke and fiery shit coming out of the top of Mount Vesuvius.

Titus said he acknowledged 'how deeply people feel about this issue' but said the public debate was replete with misinformation about the Roman Empire's volcano evacuation and preparation policies.

'It often comes as news to people when I share with them that the Roman Empire has the highest per capita investment in evacuation chariots of any country in the world,' Titus said.

'I do understand that people feel strongly about this, but I think we also have to take stock, we have to ensure we get a proper context and perspective,' Titus continued.

'I want children growing up in our empire to feel positive about their future, and I think it is important we give them the confidence that they will not die from being melted by lava, and that they will have an economy to live in as well.'

Mount Vesuvius, a stratovolcano in modern-day Italy, erupted later that year in one of the deadliest volcanic eruptions in European history.

NRL Tells Players To Head Down To Bondi Now And Squeeze In A Few Benders While No One Can See

EARLIER TODAY, New South Wales health officials recommended that Sydney residents stay indoors between 11 am and 4 pm if possible, as the combination of a 30–40 degree day and severe air pollution may present serious health risks for the elderly and those with respiratory issues.

While dense bushfire smoke has been a near-permanent fixture in Sydney for the last few weeks, the air in Sydney today is regarded as both visibly and officially the worst quality in recorded history.

Sydney ferries have been cancelled until the smoke clears, Transport for NSW has confirmed. Buses are now replacing F1 Manly services but there are no replacement buses on other routes.

The Rural Fire Service (RFS) headquarters in Homebush was even evacuated after smoke alarms went off inside the building.

Sydney's air quality index (AQI) skyrocketed due to bushfires, particularly those on the city's outskirts. The AQI in some areas reached 12 times hazardous levels today as the city was blanketed in thick smoke.

However, while these conditions pose immediate health concerns for senior citizens and infants, the National Rugby League appears to have taken full advantage of the lack of visibility.

'Get down to Bondi, boys. Now's your chance,' said NRL CEO Todd Greenberg, in a 1500-person group chat of all players, coaches and bender mentors (ex-players) within the competition.

'Corey, Burgo, Victor … Get your arses down there. No one can see shit. Now's your chance to get a big old session out of your system.'

It is believed that with the sand of Bondi currently invisible due to the thick bushfire smoke lingering over the eastern suburbs of Sydney, the waterfront has this afternoon played host to an apocalyptic beach party of drill rap and pineapple Cruisers.

'It's like the "California Love" video clip down there,' said one lifeguard, who appeared rattled after stumbling into the self-contained NRL off-season blow-out as he was packing up for the day. 'Except instead of Dre and Tupac it's Tedesco and Napa.

'Willie Mason is down there banging a Japanese gong in a gas mask. I could tell by the tatts. I think I even saw Gus Gould doing the worm.'

Scotty From Marketing Treats Himself To A Sunset Not Smothered By Apocalyptic Bushfire Smoke

AS THE GOSPERS MOUNTAIN bushfire continues to move rapidly towards western Sydney, Prime Minister Morrison has decided he doesn't want his daughters exposed to the thick bushfire smoke in Cronulla.

According to the RFS, the current bushfire encroaching on metropolitan Sydney is bigger than Wales.

The Prime Minister's Office has repeatedly refused to confirm Mr Morrison's whereabouts this week, but the mystery appeared to be solved on Thursday night after his photograph with Aussie tourists in Hawaii was posted on Instagram.

'Not in my wildest dreams did I ever imagine I would have the opportunity to share a few bevvies and chat about many things with the Prime Minister of Australia,' the Instagram post said.

'Contrary to belief, he's actually a bit of a legend.'

The Prime Minister is enjoying a seven-night break in Hawaii with his wife and two daughters before a busy schedule of official overseas travel during the school holidays.

Morrison is yet to even stand next to a sign language translator, let alone a fire and rescue official, for fear that he might have to make mention of the very well documented evidence that suggests these fires are being ferociously accelerated by climate change.

However, his office says that a seven-day break in Hawaii with his family is just what the Pentecostal fundamentalist needs.

'He's loving the opportunity to enjoy a sunset with his wife and kids without having to worry about such dense grey bushfire smoke,' said a spokesperson.

'It's almost like being in Cronulla when there isn't a few megatonnes of burnt shit going into the air.'

Top 29 Prime Ministers Who Didn't Go On A Holiday To Hawaii During A National Emergency

IT'S A WONDERFUL TIME of the year for everyone, even the pundits at Sky News and the *Herald Sun* who are convinced that political correctness is stealing Christmas from us.

The annual 'War on Christmas' is once again dominating the headlines – and conveniently nabbing front pages from the national bushfire emergency currently ravaging three states.

However, one proud Christian who won't let the PC Police win is Prime Minister Morrison, more commonly known as Scotty from Marketing.

As an area of land half the size of two United Kingdoms put together, is destroyed by out-of-control bushfires which, according to a conglomerate of emergency and rescue response professionals, have been aided by the very real effects of climate change, Prime Minister Morrison has been accused of turning down countless meetings with fire chiefs in an effort to get through a federal election without mentioning the words 'climate change'.

While October and November were dominated by Extinction Rebellion rallies and climate school strikes, Scotty from Marketing was forced to confront the uneasy national sentiment that indicated a lot of people were quite concerned that burning fossil fuels at an accelerating rate for 300 years might not be that good for our planet.

Morrison urged Australians to please stop blocking CBD intersections and taking their kids out of school with their needless anxiety.

But now, as ten per cent of our continent is faced with uncontainable wildfires and two state capital cities have been choked with smoke for nearly two months, it seems that tens of thousands of rural kids are missing out on a lot more than a day of learning.

Scotty from Marketing has, however, refused to let the hysterical bushfire alarmism get in the way of the business class flights to Hawaii that he had booked for Jenny and the girls – before he returns to spend Christmas bouncing between Pentecostal churches, followed by a trail of sympathetic Murdoch journalists.

This begs the question: If a Prime Minister can't take a holiday with his family in another country during a few measly little unprecedented and record-breaking bushfires, when can he?

We compiled a list of former Prime Ministers who decided against taking holidays during a national emergency, just to see if this is actually a standard we should hold our current leader to – or is it just the Canberra Bubble making noise again?

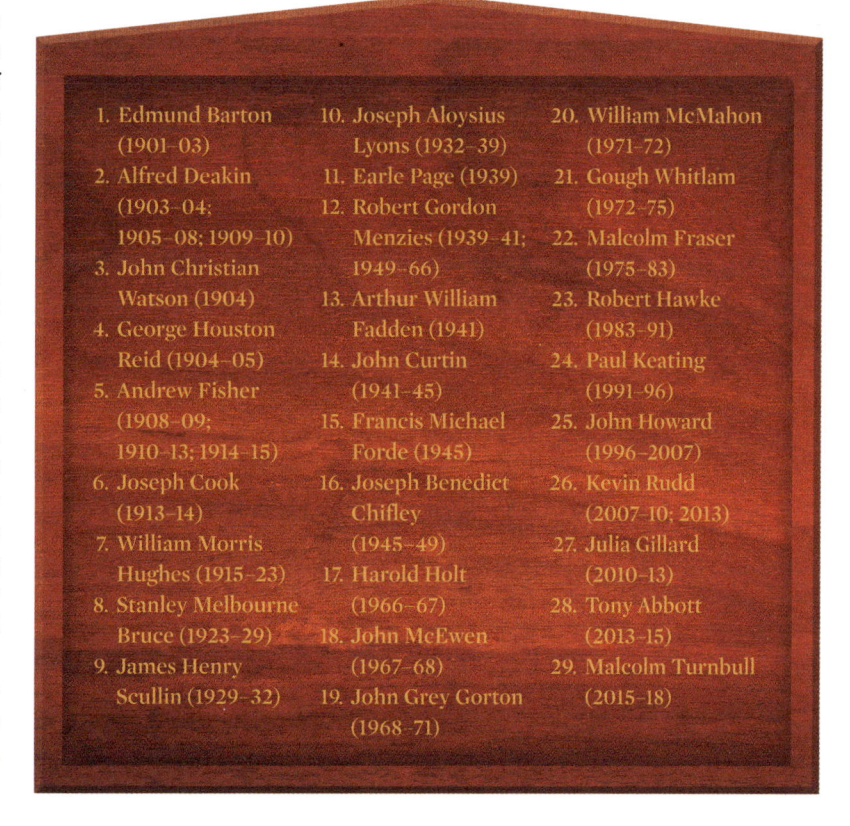

1. Edmund Barton (1901–03)
2. Alfred Deakin (1903–04; 1905–08; 1909–10)
3. John Christian Watson (1904)
4. George Houston Reid (1904–05)
5. Andrew Fisher (1908–09; 1910–13; 1914–15)
6. Joseph Cook (1913–14)
7. William Morris Hughes (1915–23)
8. Stanley Melbourne Bruce (1923–29)
9. James Henry Scullin (1929–32)
10. Joseph Aloysius Lyons (1932–39)
11. Earle Page (1939)
12. Robert Gordon Menzies (1939–41; 1949–66)
13. Arthur William Fadden (1941)
14. John Curtin (1941–45)
15. Francis Michael Forde (1945)
16. Joseph Benedict Chifley (1945–49)
17. Harold Holt (1966–67)
18. John McEwen (1967–68)
19. John Grey Gorton (1968–71)
20. William McMahon (1971–72)
21. Gough Whitlam (1972–75)
22. Malcolm Fraser (1975–83)
23. Robert Hawke (1983–91)
24. Paul Keating (1991–96)
25. John Howard (1996–2007)
26. Kevin Rudd (2007–10; 2013)
27. Julia Gillard (2010–13)
28. Tony Abbott (2013–15)
29. Malcolm Turnbull (2015–18)

THE CRUCIFIXION OF SCOTTY FROM MARKETING

Scotty From Marketing Selflessly Cuts Week-Long Hawaiian Holiday Short By 45 Minutes

SCOTT MORRISON IS BELIEVED to be on his way back from Hawaii after buying the last seat on a flight from Honolulu. The Prime Minister is expected to land in Sydney this evening, from where he will likely get another flight to as many photo ops as possible after covering his eyes and ears to this national emergency for an entire month.

This comes just after Mr Morrison was pictured relaxing in Hawaii mere hours after he said he would come home 'as soon as I can'. Presumably it took longer than expected to organise a flight from one of the biggest airports in the Pacific.

As of this afternoon, one person has been killed in the Cudlee Creek bushfire in the Adelaide Hills, and the Gospers Mountain 'mega-blaze' continues to close in on western Sydney.

Meanwhile a fire-generated thunderstorm has formed over two emergency-warning-level fires in the Shoalhaven region. The RFS warns a similar thunderstorm could form over the Gospers Mountain fire.

While the firefighters' union, and literally every other emergency service, is calling for leadership from the Prime Minister, so far all the nation has been granted is an abundance of his creepy Hillsong 'thoughts and prayers'.

However, Murdoch's newspapers and Sky News are tonight reporting a very different story, and have praised the Prime Minister for finding the empathy to cut his resort holiday short by 45 minutes to come back to Australia and meet with the plebs.

PM: Privatisation Of ABC On Hold Until Rural Areas No Longer Need Crucial Bushfire Updates

PRIME MINISTER SCOTTY FROM Marketing has today continued his 'herculean' efforts to provide the federal support to bushfire response and recovery that he should have provided around the time he went to Hawaii before Christmas.

This comes as close to 4000 homes have been lost and nearly a billion native animals have perished in the climate change–aided bushfire season that started in September last year.

Despite the highly commendable rescue efforts of emergency services staff and volunteers, 29 people, including four firefighters, have tragically died in the fires that continue to ravage five states.

Right across the country, tourists and locals have been evacuated from firegrounds by land and sea, with the RFS website and public broadcaster providing those affected with round-the-clock bushfire updates.

The laudable efforts of ABC Radio to help bring citizens to safety have been praised by fire chiefs and politicians alike, with the Federal Minister for National Disaster and Emergency Management, David Littleproud describing the journalists on the ground as 'lifesavers'.

However, their crucial work in saving Australians for months on end has thrown a spanner in the works for the Liberal Party amid their efforts to silence any form of criticism of the government.

The 2018 Liberal Party vote to privatise the ABC was backed by at least four of the party's top federal officials and gained support from at least one federal Liberal MP.

Liberal members applauded the result at a federal council meeting just over 18 months ago, with a final vote that showed at least 39 council delegates voting in favour of the sale while 10 delegates voted against.

'Obviously I can't go selling it off right now,' explained Scotty from Marketing today.

'But don't worry, as soon as the fires that have raged for the better part of three months calm down a little bit and the latte-sipping lefties push the button on *Q&A* for a year, we'll be going straight to market.

'We'll see how many opinion pieces ABC Online will write about climate change then.'

Party That's Been In Power For 18 Of The Last 24 Years Frustrated With Greens Fire Policy

THE COALITION GOVERNMENT has today reiterated its stance on what it believes is one of the major causes of the bushfires currently ripping through New South Wales, Queensland and Western Australia.

Rather than the fact that it's extremely fucking hot, there's little to no rain about, and experts have been warning about aggravated bushfire seasons as a result of climate change for a few years now, Barnaby Joyce and the Coalition Government have stated it's actually the Greens who have a case to answer.

This comes after Barnaby and a few of the Coalition Government MPs saw a post on Facebook that did the rounds blaming 'greenies' for limiting the amount of back-burning and hazard reduction that can be done to prevent horrendous bushfires like those we are currently seeing.

The popular online claim is that the Greens/greenies have prevented authorities from implementing hazard reduction burns and other measures to prevent the build-up of fuel, causing more severe fires.

However, while experts like former 13-year-tenure New South Wales Fire Chief Greg Mullins have been quick to point out that 'blaming "greenies" for stopping these important measures is a familiar, populist, but basically untrue claim', some within the government are still pointing the finger at the Greens for their role in the bushfires.

Despite the fact that the Greens have had little to no say in politics apart from the time they blocked the ETS for some unrealistic pie-in-the-sky idea of what climate policy should have been at the time, the Coalition has assured the nation that the minor party have crippled them on this critical bushfire policy that hadn't been mentioned before some bloke in Queensland posted about it on Facebook.

'It's been a major issue for us, I just haven't had time to campaign on it in between trying to prevent vulnerable young women in New South Wales having control over their own bodies and advocating for giant tax-dodging multinational companies,' explained embattled MP Barnaby Joyce.

'So we don't want to play the blame game at this time, but you can point your index fucking finger at the Greens for this issue,' explained the fired-up politician, who should probably just shut the fuck up and do whatever he can to help out the emergency services battling around the clock in his electorate.

> *Despite the fact that the Greens have had little to no say in politics apart from the time they blocked the ETS, the Coalition has assured the nation that the minor party have crippled them on this critical bushfire policy.*

THE CRUCIFIXION OF SCOTTY FROM MARKETING

Bombing Panels To Be Legalised As Government Merges Arts Department With Transport Department

THE ART FORM FORMERLY known as 'graffiti vandalism' is expected to be legalised in 2020, following a decision by Prime Minister Scott Morrison to axe the federal Arts department.

On Thursday, Mr Morrison announced dramatic changes to the public service, cutting the number of departments from 18 to 14.

The arts community initially mobilised against the decision, but have since decided that legalising graffiti on train panels is necessary for the arts to survive in a country that only has one high-profile artist in the shape of Anh Doh.

'Basically any form of getting up will be legalised going into the new year,' said Morrison. 'Bombing panels, throwies, scratchies. Whatever you want. There'll be no more ID checks at Bunnings. I'm of half a mind to scrap the GST on Ironlak.'

The current Department of Communications and the Arts is set to be scrapped after Prime Minister Morrison decided there has been no need for it ever since the successful rollout of the NBN and the funding that was tipped into filming *The Great Gatsby* in Joe Hockey's electorate.

Instead, Mr Morrison said Arts will fall under the new Department of Infrastructure, Transport, Regional Development and Communications, which among other things will oversee road and rail and not doing anything about the ice plague currently ravaging rural Australia.

This decision has resulted in a wave of forced redundancies for the very people employed by the state to explore solutions to Australia's cultural deficit that was most visibly on display during the Sydney Olympics Opening Ceremony.

Malcolm Turnbull briefly added 'Arts' to the title of the Department of Communications and the Arts, however, the word 'Arts' will no longer exist in public policies moving forward – like every other legacy left behind from Turnbull's brief time as Prime Minister, except for the same-sex marriage laws – and even they aren't safe from repeal under Morrison.

Morrison has today announced that notorious Brisbane graffer 'Sofles' will step up as the minister in charge of the new department of Arts and Transport – after proving his mettle in the early 2000s when he was bombing every Queensland Rail car in the south-east corner while successfully evading arrest for over a decade.

'This man used to have entire task forces chasing him,' said Morrison.

'Now he will be chasing up on task forces.'

Morrison says hiring Sofles as the Scotty Cam of tagging trains is a perfect example of getting a go after having a go.

'I have full confidence in this new department,' he said. 'If you have a go bombing panels, you'll get a go slashing budgets to art schools and re-selling off land that was rezoned for the Australian speed-rail project that will never exist until they can get the stupid idea of running it on renewable energy out of their proposals.

'Arts and transport go together quite naturally.'

Prime Minister Tells Nation He Deeply Regrets Using Up All Of His Prayers On The Election

PRIME MINISTER SCOTTY FROM Marketing has today acknowledged that he caused 'great anxiety in Australia' by taking a family holiday in Hawaii as bushfires that have been killing people and destroying homes burned across the nation.

Mr Morrison had announced he would cut his trip short on Friday, after the deaths of two volunteer firefighters in New South Wales.

His selfless actions have been praised by the Murdoch newspapers as heroic and completely unnecessary but much appreciated. The rest of the country appears to have made it clear they think he's a fake bogan toff who runs from responsibility.

Morrison says with the benefit of hindsight he would have made a different decision.

'I thought I could just bunker down in the resort with Jenny and the girls and really focus on some high-quality thoughts and prayers.

'This looks a lot like the Rapture. Forget climate change policy, forget Paris agreements. We need to pray our way out. This is God. He's telling us something. I always thought a Royal Commission into the church would upset him.'

However, as Morrison went on to point out, his own prayers weren't really achieving much – he puts it down to the fact that he used up all of his most effective praying on the 2019 election win.

'I'm standing with the three biggest miracles in my life here tonight – and tonight we've been delivered another one,' a jubilant Scott Morrison said while standing next to his daughters and wife after the Coalition's 2019 Australian election win. The Prime Minister made multiple references to his faith in his victory speech, ending by saying: 'We are an amazing country of amazing people. God bless Australia.'

Fast-forward eight months, and Morrison landed in Sydney just before 8 pm on Saturday on a Hawaiian Airlines flight from Honolulu, 48 hours after he said he would get back from the holiday he decided to take during the most unprecedented bushfires in recorded history.

The period of leave was not formally announced, and the Prime Minister's Office refused to confirm the location or dates of leave and in some cases openly lied to the media.

Mr Morrison spent Sunday morning receiving a briefing on the current fire situation in New South Wales at Rural Fire Service (RFS) headquarters.

At a press conference, he said he accepted the criticism about his holiday, and apologised for any upset caused. But not many people asked that many questions because the media isn't very interested in holding him to account.

Scotty From Marketing Furious That They Don't Serve Mai Tais In The Mudgee Evacuation Centre

PRIME MINISTER MORRISON WAS reportedly seething with rage at a central west New South Wales emergency evacuation centre.

Not because he has finally got his head around the scale of the 257 bushfires currently ravaging rural Australia.

Not because his family holiday in Hawaii was cut short after he was photographed chilling on the beach, drinking beer and chucking up shakas while said bushfires destroyed thousands of Aussie homes.

It wasn't because he'd just learnt that small businesses throughout these towns are being crippled because they're losing their staff to the volunteer fire service.

And it wasn't because these volunteers haven't seen their own families in months and are experiencing extreme financial pressures, in some cases being forced to pay for supplies out of their own pockets.

It was because, after everything, he couldn't get a decent tiki-themed white rum–based cocktail at knock-off yesterday.

'Oh, come on!' said Scotty from Marketing, before letting out a guttural sigh.

'Moccona?!! Blend 43? I know I'm still in holiday mode, but is this all that's on offer?'

The PM says he knows he doesn't have it as bad as some, but, you know, these community groups could at least try to pretend they care about him having to cut his holiday short by 45 minutes.

'Let me guess. They don't even have Milo. I've gotta have Ovaltine or some shit like that. Fuck me. Get it together, people. Whose cock do I have to suck to get a decent Mai Tai in this one-horse town?!'

The PM says he knows he doesn't have it as bad as some, but, you know, these community groups could at least try to pretend they care about him having to cut his holiday short by 45 minutes.

THE BETOOTA ADVOCATE | AUSTRALIA 2020

BA Falcon Ute Claims We've Always Had Bushfires As Big As These Ones

AUSTRALIA ALWAYS GETS bushfires at this time of year, and the fact that an area of land the size of California has been destroyed in Southern Queensland and rural New South Wales is nothing new.

That's according to a photograph of a blue 2004 BA Falcon.

Launched in November 2002, the BA was the lesser successor to the wildly-popular AU Falcon.

The Ford Falcon ute has a special place in Australian automotive history, given it was invented by young Ford designer Lew Bandt.

His creation came after a letter had arrived at company headquarters requesting a dual-purpose vehicle that was smart enough to drive to church, but practical enough to cart livestock to market. The humble Barossa entrepreneur obliged and created the iconic vehicle.

It did its job, and was cherished by many until the Abbott Government destroyed the Australian auto industry for good after refusing to invest in the changing world of motor vehicles which has since been dominated by Silicon Valley.

However, in recent years the humble Falcon ute, especially the BA, is most commonly associated with climate denialism and rude comments about Clementine Ford.

Each day, tens of thousands of late-90s through to mid-2010s Falcon utes dominate social media comment threads with their outspoken scepticism of the commonly-held scientific theories that suggest burning carbon emissions into the atmosphere at an accelerating rate for three centuries isn't good for the planet.

They are also known for subscribing to the theory that 'feminism is cancer' – even sometimes going as far as saying, 'Pell did nothing wrong'.

However, the current trend for irate Falcon utes is to insist that Australia always has to deal with catastrophic bushfires that destroy upwards of 2000 homes across the eastern seaboard.

Rural Fire Service brigades have been facing off against 60-metre-high flames in the Blue Mountains for weeks, as the 'mega-blaze' continues to swallow other spot fires in its 200-kilometre journey south from Singleton.

This mega-fire at Gospers Mountain, where this reporter has spent several 16-hour shifts, has been raging for weeks and has burned through more than 380,000 hectares. There are 117 bushfires blazing in New South Wales alone and with extreme heat forecast to arrive at the end of the week, there is no end in sight. Ten people have been killed.

This is business as usual according to the nation's Falcon utes, who are yet to redirect their outrage to the multinational corporations that say 'happy holidays' instead of 'Merry Christmas'.

In recent years the humble Falcon ute, especially the BA, is most commonly associated with climate denialism and rude comments about Clementine Ford.

Scotty From Marketing Holds Focus Group To Suss Out If He'll Get Booed At The Sydney Test

AFTER CATASTROPHICALLY misreading the national sentiment over Christmas, the Prime Minister is today hosting qualitative data surveys among 'everyday Australians' to see if he'll be able to get away with visiting a sporting arena in the next couple of months.

While confident that he'd be able to pull off a Sharkies home game, Scotty from Marketing isn't quite sure of the reception he'd get if he showed his face outside of his electorate following his form over the last two months.

Since spring, out-of-control bushfires have raged in both Queensland and New South Wales, resulting in every national park south of Tenterfield currently being ablaze. Ecologists estimate around a billion mammals, birds and reptiles have been killed so far, directly or indirectly.

As the fires crept from Queensland's Sunshine Coast down to the Southern Highlands of New South Wales, an area the size of Iraq has been left uninhabitable as volunteer firefighters resort to taking leave from work to continue battling this cataclysmic climate change-aided disaster.

Bushfires have since begun ravaging Western Australia, South Australia and Victoria, with the iconic Lorne Falls Festival cancelled yesterday due to the extreme weather conditions.

These same conditions are causing endless grief for Prime Minister Scott Morrison, who disappeared on a Hawaiian holiday with his family at the peak of an east coast heatwave that triggered the merging of two megafires in rural New South Wales, resulting in Sydney being smothered by an apocalyptic haze of smoke. During this time, Australia's most populous city suffered from air pollution that was measured at a lower quality than Beijing on their worst day ever recorded.

Scotty from Marketing has attempted to rectify his standing with the Australian population by announcing a new scheme, which has in fact always existed, where Australian volunteer firefighters are able to get access to up to $6000 if they have suffered financially from not being able to go to work for the two months during which these fires have destroyed their regional communities.

This news has also been received poorly, after it was revealed that Scott Morrison earns an annual salary of $549,229 and secured three pay rises in just a year – with his total annual pay increase since 1 July 2018 being $141,229. In June alone, just under a month after winning the 2019 election, he got another $11,000-a-year pay rise.

According to furious meme pages from both sides of the political spectrum, the Prime Minister's post-Honolulu knee-jerk approach to quelling anxieties over the 2019 Climate Fires has failed to win the public over, with the nation now pointing to the thousands of homes lost and the tragic number of Australians dead.

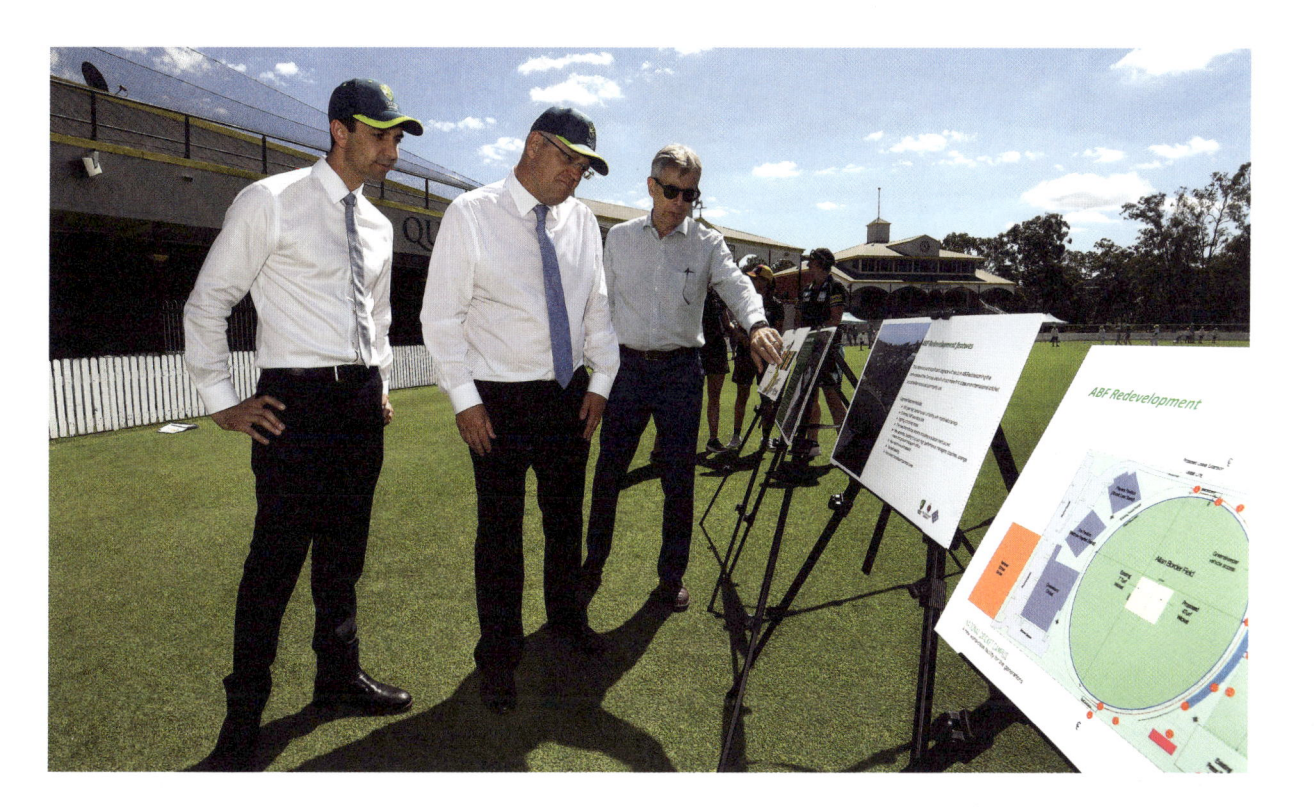

This means Scotty from Marketing must now begin in-depth focus group research to identify whether he can indulge in one of his favourite perks of the job and hit a corporate box at the Sydney cricket test, without being booed mercilessly by a sold-out SCG.

'So hit me, guys,' said Morrison during a market research survey with a select crowd of everyday Australians from his own electorate. 'I wear an all-pink tuxedo and do a shoey while the stadium plays "The Horses" by Daryl Braithwaite, you reckon I'll be able to win over these plebs in their Richie Benaud outfits?'

His question was immediately met with awkward silence by the focus group.

'Okay, no good. I understand. Yeah, all the people losing all their livelihoods has hit the bush pretty hard, yada yada. I get it.

'What If I dab while wearing a Sharkies scarf and begin yelling exaggerated claims about Labor coming to steal franking credits from the boomers and forcing us to sell our fourbys as part of their war on the weekend?'

Morrison was again met with no solid answers.

'What if I just do nothing and don't show my face at any point during my prime ministership unless some skinhead low-breed from Grafton slaughters fifty innocent Muslims in their place of worship and then I can accuse the media of treating me in a similar way because everyone finds it kind of weird that I speak in tongues every Sunday and openly meet with paedophile apologists from the biggest tax-evading mega-church in the southern hemisphere?'

The focus group goes quiet again before Morrison is finally met with a positive response from one of the subjects.

'I think that's your best idea yet,' says a single mother who can't afford childcare and is staring down the barrel of having to piss in a cup in the Centrelink office to gain access to any form of social security.

Another respondent agrees.

'That'll work,' said a silica dust–riddled tradie, who's been thinking a lot about politics recently given the fact that his family's savings account is now under threat of suddenly disappearing because the Banking Royal Commission that Morrison voted against 28 times has since found that Westpac has committed 23 million breaches of the law by funding terrorists and child sex tourists in South East Asia, resulting in the bank now facing a corporate fine the size of one-third of Australia's GDP.

'Just don't go to the cricket. They'll boo the fuck out of you. You aren't Hawkey, mate.'

THE CRUCIFIXION OF SCOTTY FROM MARKETING   47

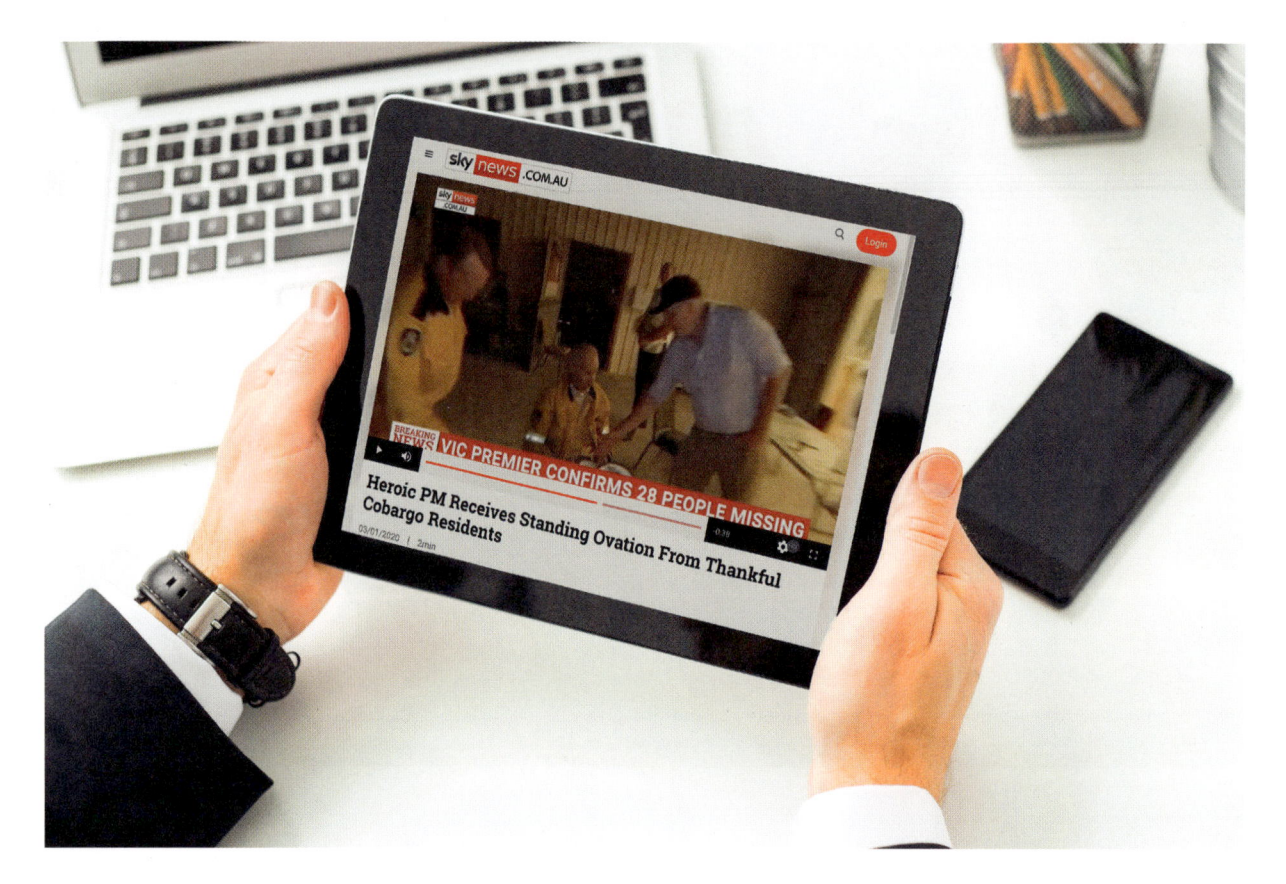

Heroic PM Receives Standing Ovation From Thankful Cobargo Residents, Say Murdoch Newspapers

SKY NEWS AND THE Murdoch newspapers are today reporting that Scott Morrison was forced to abandon a meet-and-greet in a bushfire-ravaged New South Wales town after being overwhelmed by extremely excited and thankful residents.

On Thursday the Prime Minister visited the Bega Valley township of Cobargo, which was engulfed by flames on Tuesday morning. Three people died and many others lost homes, businesses, livestock and pasture when the out-of-control fires hit the community.

However, according to the *Herald Sun* and *Daily Telegraph*, the tragedies faced by this community appeared to be a thing of the past as residents excitedly flocked to the Prime Minister's luxury BMW four-wheeler as it arrived in town.

The Prime Minister was reportedly given a guard of honour as he arrived into Cobargo, and then of course a standing ovation as he stepped out of the car.

'How are you?' Morrison asked as he approached one woman who had her hands by her sides. He then reached out and took her hand and started shaking it.

The seemingly starstruck woman was lost for words at being in the presence of her selfless but very humble Prime Minister; again, this is according to the New York–based multibillionaire media dynasty that owns 70 per cent of all Australian media publications, with a concentration in swinging rural seats.

The same thing happened to a lucky firey who got to meet our heroic and perfectly competent leader. He was so excited that he had to leave the room!

The townsfolk appeared to cheer as the Prime Minister left their town, greatly moved by all of the love he was being shown by the residents who will remember this moment for the rest of their lives.

According to the Murdoch newspapers, it is not known when these perfectly normal and totally expected bushfires that were not caused by climate change will end – but to blame anything other than arsonists and greenies is just making things political and not helping at all.

Scotty From Marketing Forces Bushfire Victim To Watch The Cricket

FRESH FROM MAKING A fool of himself, the Prime Minister has put his hands on another bushfire victim this morning.

Scott Morrison is currently at a bushfire relief centre near Batemans Bay, where he's talking to people affected by the fires as well as the teams tasked with getting these fires under control.

Local member David Littleproud is also down there to provide supportive head nods and quite a few pensive handshakes.

His team, who have honestly shit the bed big time over the past few weeks, rolled a medium-sized flat-screen television into the middle of the relief centre's canteen and turned on Channel Seven.

As the first ball of the last test match of the summer was bowled this morning in Sydney, Scott Morrison grabbed the head of a bushfire victim and forced them to watch it.

'How good is this?' hissed the Prime Minister.

'Don't look away! Look at David Warner watching the ball onto the bat! Look how he shows us the stickers! That's the hallmark of a great cover drive, showing the camera the stickers.'

Scott grunted.

'Keep watching! It's only going to get better. Will Wagner get Smith out again? Who knows! Keep watching! How good's this fucking cricket! I don't even know the rules but I fucking love it!'

Littleproud started to look visibly nervous, perhaps wondering if now was the time to step in and stop the Prime Minister putting his hands on another bushfire victim without consent.

Ultimately, he looked at the Prime Minister's head of security, who read the room enough to move Scott on before he had a repeat of his visit to Cobargo.

David Littleproud agreed to speak to *The Advocate* 'off the record' upon his return to our state's west later in the week.

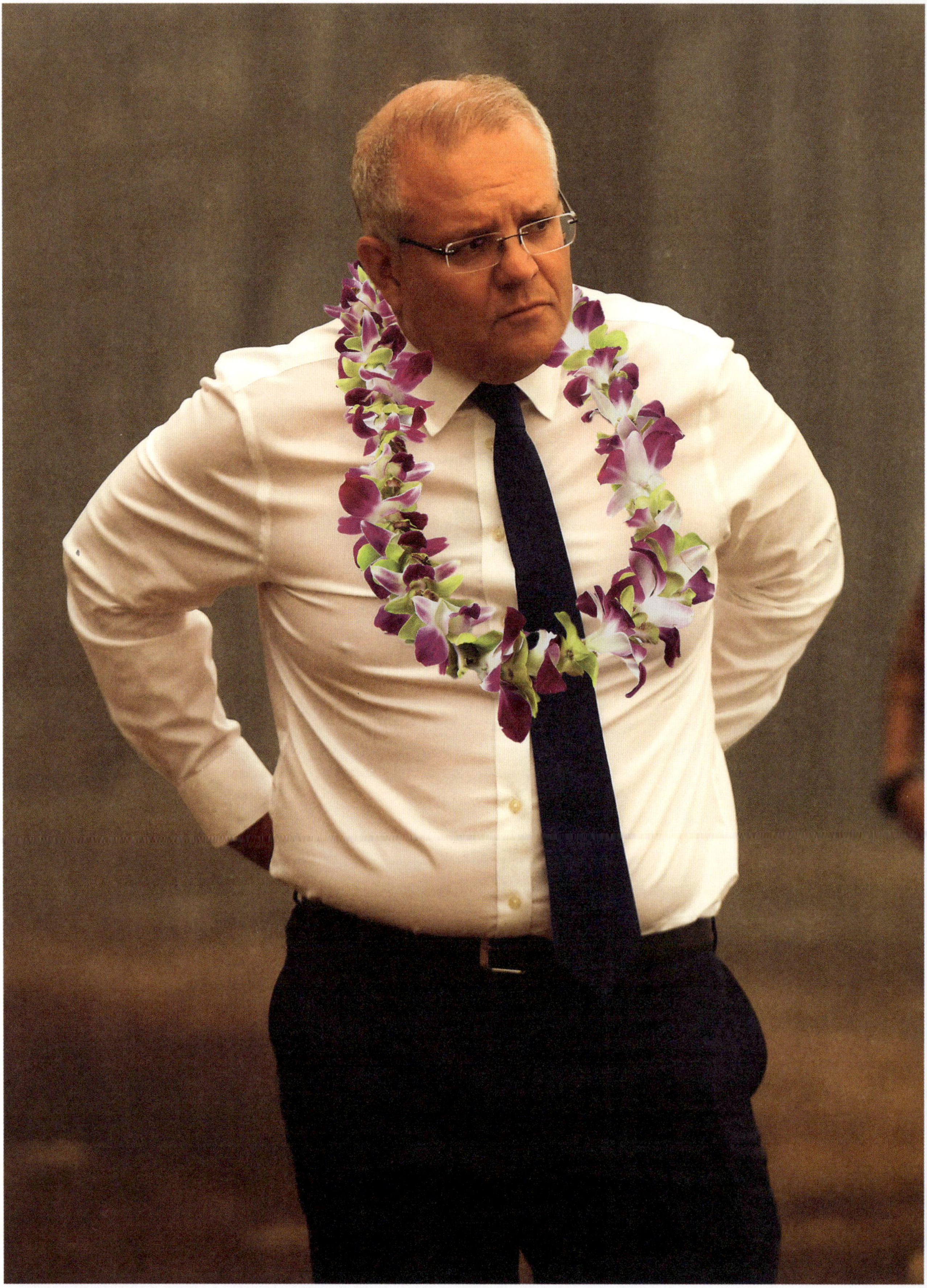

Distraught Prime Minister Wondering If Anyone Will Ask Him How Hawaii Was

AS BUSHFIRES CONTINUE TO take the lives and homes of people across the nation, the ash-covered media landscape seems to have forgotten who the real victim is.

Although uncontained fires are clearly the destructive force in this situation, the majority of the blame seems to be directed at Prime Minister Scott Morrison, all because he denies that climate change is making the fires worse and went on holidays while the nation burned.

'I try not to take it personally,' stated the Prime Minister, still wearing a decorative lei he purchased at Sydney Airport before boarding his international flight.

'But seriously, I went to Cobargo and not one of them asked me how Hawaii was. I was asking them how they were, sort of, I mean, why wouldn't they do the same?'

During his trip to the New South Wales town of Cobargo, the Prime Minister was forced to leave early after being denied handshakes and a photo opportunity, exacerbating his already low self-esteem.

'It's really tragic. I'm back at work and no one has asked me one question about the trip. Seriously, not even a "How was it?"

'Do you know I had pineapple every morning? Kona cut it fresh for me every day. He was our assistant but by the end of it, he was just a mate. Would have loved to have spent more time with him but I had to come home early for *some reason*.'

> *'Seriously, I went to Cobargo and not one of them asked me how Hawaii was. I was asking them how they were, sort of, I mean, why wouldn't they do the same?'*

THE CRUCIFIXION OF SCOTTY FROM MARKETING

Scotty From Marketing Surprises Cobargo Residents With Two Tickets To Gold Class

AFTER TRYING UNSUCCESSFULLY to steal a handshake from Cobargo residents who had next to nothing else left to steal, the PM has finally admitted defeat.

Instead of trying to steal their hands, the PM is instead trying to steal their hearts by sending two Gold Class cinema tickets to the two residents who didn't shake his hand, even if their house isn't there anymore.

Early next week, Scotty from Marketing will be heading back to Cobargo in the big blue bus with bulletproof windows with the two golden tickets which will be hand-delivered to each letterbox.

The bus is also carrying a number of letterboxes which will be pre-installed to drop the vouchers in if the original letterbox has been obliterated like much of the rest of the town.

'I think they'll be pretty impressed,' said a smiling ScoMo at a press conference this morning.

'When I've had a rough time it's nice to be able to kick back and take in a movie, especially if it's in Gold Class; how good are those fancy recliners?

'I reckon if I had lost everything I owned in a devastating inferno caused in part by an incompetent, self-serving government more concerned with short-term showboating than long-term solutions to serious scientifically-proven problems, it would make me feel heaps better.'

> *The bus is also carrying a number of letterboxes which he will drop the vouchers in if the original letterbox has been obliterated like much of the rest of the town.*

A Handful of Drug-Addicted Ferals Cause Scenes In Nation's State Capitals, Report Murdoch Papers

A HANDFUL OF DRUG-ADDICTED low-income waste-of-oxygen junkie cockroaches caused incredibly inconvenient roadblocks in CBDs around the country yesterday, according to the Murdoch newspapers and Sky News.

The piece-of-shit low-breed no-hoper ice addicts were protesting the Federal Government's alleged mishandling of the alleged bushfire crisis and its attitude towards the made-up climate change hoax – again, according to the Murdoch journalists who once dreamed of breaking important stories on *Four Corners*.

The event in Sydney's CBD was set up a few weeks ago by Uni Students for Climate Justice, in conjunction with Extinction Rebellion.

This comes as a senior employee at News Corp has resigned from the Australian news monopoly, sending out a company-wide email accusing them of 'misrepresenting facts' when it comes to the climate change debate.

She accused the media arm of the Morrison Government of running a 'misinformation campaign' and using reports of arson to try to divert attention away from the real cause of our current bushfire crisis.

'I find it unconscionable to continue working for this company, knowing I am contributing to the spread of climate change denial and lies,' she wrote.

'The reporting I have witnessed in *The Australian*, the *Daily Telegraph* and the *Herald Sun* is not only irresponsible but dangerous and damaging to our communities and beautiful planet that needs us more than ever now to acknowledge the destruction we have caused and start doing something about it.'

However, the editors and executives from News Corp insist they only provide balanced debate regarding the ailing health of planet Earth – with Andrew Bolt, Miranda Devine, Prue MacSween and all of those other widely-read conservatives offering both sides of the undebatable cold hard facts surrounding climate change.

Today the papers have reported that while the months of sky-smothering smoke is hard to deny, the protests being made by the two dozen or so worthless leftards who are probably drugged-up immigrants from those fucked-up countries with heaps of terrorists will likely achieve nothing because there were so few of them and the government doesn't listen to large groups of angry people anyway – unless they are surrounding the boardroom table of a tax-evading fossil fuels corporation.

Over a billion animals have perished in the last four months, thousands of homes have been lost and close to 30 people have died, including those two that Scotty said hadn't died.

Scotty From Marketing's Media Team Brief Him To Not Publicly Thank His Church For The Rain

IN THE MOST RECENT example of erratic weather patterns caused by the phenomenon that has seen the climate appear to possibly change, bushfire-devastated communities in both New South Wales and Victoria are today making preparations ahead of heavy rain that could potentially result in flooding.

Rainfall totals of 30–80 millimetres have been forecast for today, with strong falls possible for firegrounds in the Snowy Mountains, south-western Sydney and South Coast regions.

While Southern Queensland, the Blue Mountains, and the mid-north and far-north coasts of New South Wales haven't been as lucky as the south with rain on their firegrounds, the news has eased a lot of anxiety for all Australians as photos of perished koalas and wallabies are replaced by photos of thunderstorms on social media newsfeeds.

However, the immediate risk of floods will now only cause further disruptions to the bushfire recovery efforts that have been stimulated by a $2 billion package that Prime Minister Morrison offered when he realised that everyone hated him for going to Hawaii and turning his phone off during a national emergency.

With rain peppering the smouldering firegrounds, and many of the brave RFS and CFA volunteers given a slight reprieve, the equally exhausted media advisors for the Prime Minister are yet to clock off. In fact, they now face their biggest challenge yet: minimising the gaffes and distasteful comments made by the PM throughout his post-crisis media conferences.

Dressed in a Cronulla Sharks flat-brim that was turned slightly off-centre, Scotty from Marketing was today sternly briefed on how to talk about these fires.

'Now, Scotty. Remember…' says one millennial from the Prime Minister's Office named Clyde Poncington-Smythly (26, son of some cunt from the minerals council). 'Listen carefully here. The cameras have been all over you since the forced handshakes. Whatever you do, don't bring up your church. Horizon Church has done nothing to help in the eyes of these pleb voters.'

As Clyde points out, Morrison's go-to response, which is to offer thoughts and prayers after any form of tragedy, is highly controversial with the public, and growing more so as it becomes apparent that he actually believes communicating with God through sterilised rock music is the best way to survive the imminent climate challenge and widening wealth disparity in Australian society.

Another advisor, Deborah, who is also a millennial who knows how to use Instagram but has a name like Deborah because she's from a born-to-rule Liberal-voting family, takes over from Clyde.

'Scotty, I know this is exciting, and I know you really wanna say "I told you so" to the experts from the CSIRO, but for all intents and purposes, this rainfall was caused by the heat from the sun which turns moisture from plants and leaves, as well as oceans, lakes and rivers, into water vapour, which disappears into the air. This vapour rises, cools, and changes into tiny water droplets, which form clouds. That's how this rain came about, okay?

'I don't care what Brian Houston has been telling you on Wickr. You need to appear to believe the experts on this one. Rain comes from the sky, not from the heavens.'

'Seriously?!' asked Scotty.

'Who takes credit for this then? If it can't be me and it can't be Him … who gets to be the hero?

'I don't think He has forgiven us for the plebiscite yet. But we should thank Him for the generous rain He sent our way,' said Scotty.

'I guess I'll just have to do it in private, like politicians used to.'

PM's Emergency Thoughts And Prayers Package Finally Arrives At Cobargo After Long Drive From Cronulla

SEVERAL RHS (RURAL HILLSONG SERVICE) volunteers have been injured this afternoon attempting to deliver the vapid Pentecostal thoughts and prayers of Scott Morrison to bushfire victims.

The vehicle transporting the care package, which was one of those creepy buses that float around the outer suburbs of major cities, experienced a flat tyre, resulting in immediate evacuation of the volunteer pastors in Morrison's Prime Ministerial jet, SharkOne.

It is believed the Hillsong volunteers were injured, not physically but spiritually, after being told to fuck off and bother God elsewhere by a distressed farmer.

One asexual 20-something happy-clapper says he's surprised he wasn't met with more gratitude, considering how much effort it took to drive all the way down from Cronulla.

While the politicians continue to offer nothing but divisive rhetoric surrounding who caused this disaster, flames continue to tear through large parts of New South Wales and Queensland, and firefighters, volunteers and real charity workers are providing round-the-clock support for those devastated by the ongoing disaster.

> *It is believed the Hillsong volunteers were injured, not physically but spiritually, after being told to fuck off and bother God elsewhere by a distressed farmer.*

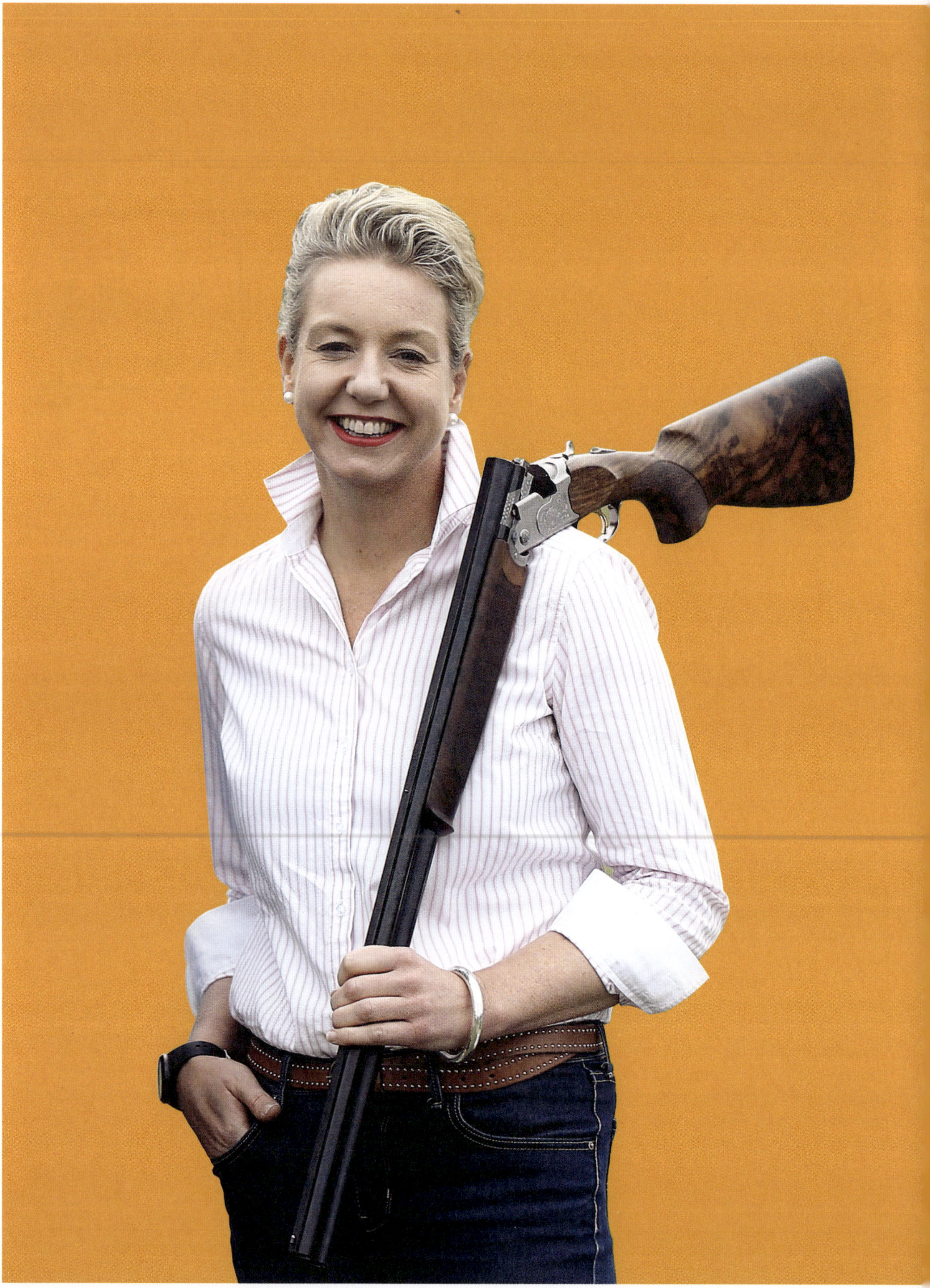

SPORTS RORTS

There's nothing Australians hate more than a rorter. The only time a red-blooded Australian should ever rort is when they're filling out their tax return.

On the pyramid of dishonesty, cheating in sport is right at the top. Australians (especially the media, but not including this newspaper) effectively destroyed Cameron Bancroft's career because one extremely talented teammate told him to tamper with the ball while his polite Don-clone robot skipper tried to spot animal shapes in the clouds above South Africa (or something). In reality, the act of tampering with the ball like that wasn't so serious in the scheme of things. Many, many players have been caught doing it in recent years. Some of the greatest players of the modern game have copped fines and been suspended for a game or two for ball-tampering. Not our Betoota Dugongs, though.

For the act of rorting in sport, the nation is unforgiving. So you can imagine the fallout when it was revealed that the Coalition Government had used a sports grants program to pork-barrel marginal seats with giant cheques scribbled with their local Coalition candidate's name. The backlash was just as severe as it was for the cricketers who were caught with the sandpaper. That was *your* money that was being spent to shore up seats for the government. One hundred million Australian pesos in taxpayer-funded grants. Gone. And on what? Changing rooms for a frisbee club in the Prime Minister's electorate. Money for gun clubs in country Victoria. Nothing for the safe seats, like our own in Maranoa. Except for the Betoota Dolphins Leagues Club, of course.

And it wasn't going to go away until somebody lost their job. That person was Bridget McKenzie. A senator for the cold country in Northern Victoria.

The sports rorts saga was a perfect storm of things Australians most despise: government corruption, disrespecting sport, misuse of public money.

But, like the bushfires that preceded it, this all went away when it became clear that the rag-traders travelling the beaten flight path between Wuhan and Milan weren't just carrying precious silks in their cargo hold...

Betoota Dolphins Leagues Club Quietly Changes Portrait Of Bridget McKenzie Back To The Queen

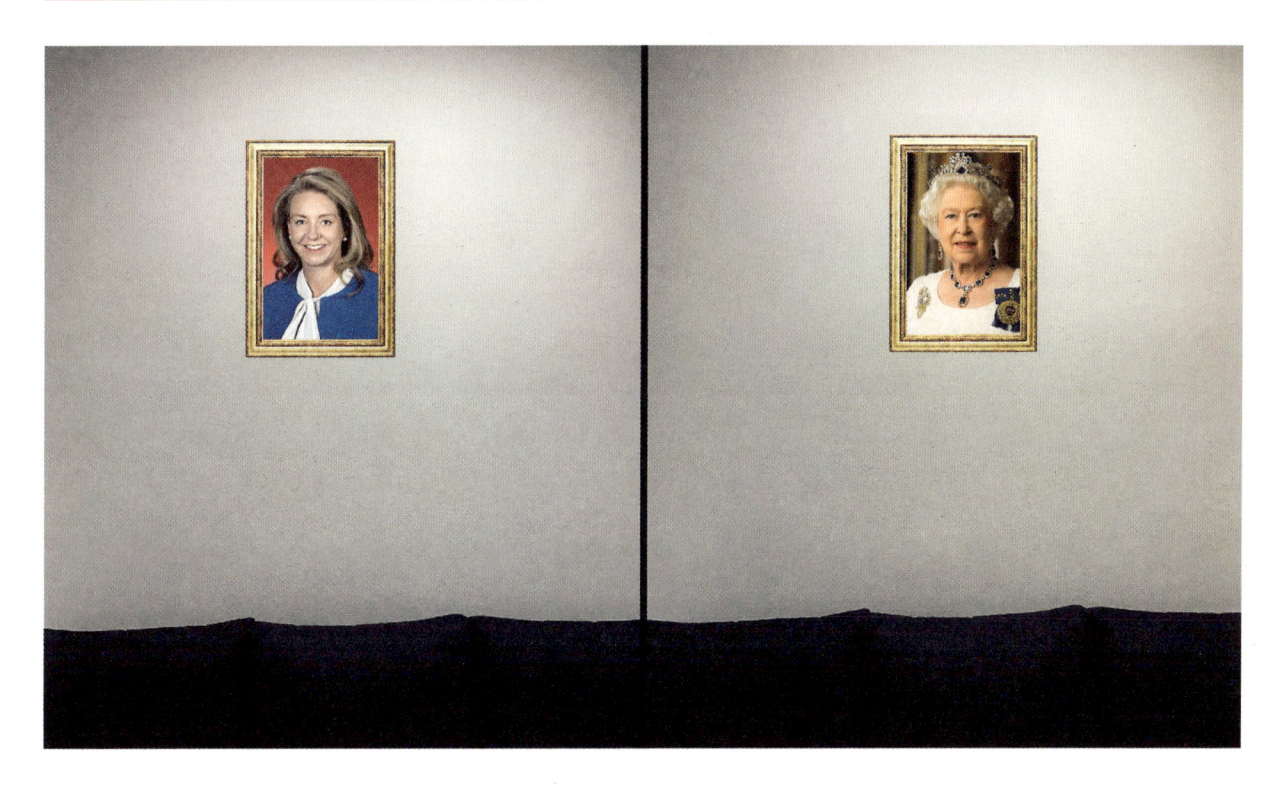

FOR GENERATIONS, A PORTRAIT of Her Majesty the Queen has watched over the reception area of the Betoota Dolphins Leagues Club.

But for the past year or so, the portrait of our Head of State was replaced by Bridget McKenzie's official parliamentary headshot.

It attracted the odd wry comment. Some thought it was a joke, others thought the club president had lost his mind. Both were plausible.

But as recent news suggests, the Dolphins board received a large amount of money in the form of grants from the Federal Government in the lead-up to last year's election.

But why? Our desert community lies within the borders of the coalition's safest federal electorate.

Perhaps it's because our cosmopolitan way of life here on the banks of the roaring Diamantina River results in two-thirds of our community voting for Labor or the Greens?

Whatever the reason, and I guess we'll never know, the reception of the Dolphins Leagues Club is once again surveilled by Her Majesty the Queen.

The Advocate reached out to the president of the Dolphins Leagues Club for comment but has yet to receive a reply.

Some thought it was a joke, others thought the club president had lost his mind. Both were plausible.

SPORTS RORTS

McKenzie: 'Me Giving Big Money To Gun Clubs In Shooters Party Heartland Was Just A Coincidence'

THE KEY MESSAGE FROM Bridget McKenzie's presser in Canberra this afternoon was that she really thinks the people of regional Australia are stupid enough to believe it's just a coincidence her office granted money to gun clubs in Shooters Party heartland and nowhere else.

McKenzie has been under fire for days over a bungled sports grant program which saw nearly $100 million taxpayer dollars used to sweeten clubs in marginal seats via grants.

Many eligible clubs that aren't in marginal seats missed out on the grants, which has made McKenzie's denials all the more disrespectful.

Earlier this week, it was discovered that Bridget had even given her own gun club a grant – as well as updating her declarations list to include an inner-city investment property.

Today she defended her position as a senator, saying it was all just a big coincidence that this has happened.

As she stood in the hall of The Nationals' wing in Parliament House, while portraits of Doug Anthony and Ralph Hunt wept tears of blood, McKenzie explained that while the Shooters, Fishers and Farmers have a small state-based following, the suggestion they could threaten The Nationals on a federal level is 'laughable'.

'Really, is that what we're all here for? Because I gave some money to gun clubs in regional parts of Victoria and New South Wales? Come on, guys! I thought you were better than that!

'If the Shooters Party did have a foothold in regional Victoria, then why aren't they in Canberra?'

'Yeah, that's what I thought.'

All of a sudden, her minders found her and immediately called a close to the press conference.

Manila Ping-Pong Club Receives $300,000 Sports Grant To Help Them Finally Get Some Tables

THE COALITION'S 'SPORTS RORT' continues right across the party today, after it was revealed that a sporting club with close ties to the Nationals Member for Dawson received a $300,000 grant to help upgrade their facilities.

While many locals recognise that the Manila Central Ping-Pong Club (MCPPC) has been in dire need of some actual ping-pong tables for quite some time now, questions have been raised about why they received such a large amount of money.

The Manila Central Ping-Pong Club is one of the biggest grassroots racquet sports organisations in the Filipino city of Manila, which apparently sits squarely in the North Queensland electorate of Dawson.

It is not yet known if the Member for Dawson, George Christensen, put in a good word for his constituents at the MCPPC. However, it does not look good considering the recent controversies related to his travel in that part of the world.

Christensen, who has come under fire for his extensive travel to the Philippines, referred his travel expenses to the Independent Parliamentary Expenses Authority (IPEA) following reports he had used entitlements to pay for connecting flights to Manila.

The outspoken member for Dawson made 28 trips and spent almost 300 days in the Philippines between 2014 and 2018.

These revelations add even more weight to the theory that the Coalition Government lost many of their greatest thinkers after the post-Turnbull brain drain of Pyne, Bishop and Laundy.

As of this afternoon it can be revealed that more than $1 million in sports grants was handed to nine clubs that boast senior Coalition MPs as members or patrons, including a gun club joined by the former Sports Minister Bridget McKenzie, a tennis club where Treasurer Josh Frydenberg is an honorary member, an Australian rules football club where Ken Wyatt is the 'No. 1 ticket holder', and Senator Sarah Henderson's football and netball club. A soccer club in Prime Minister Scott Morrison's electorate has been documented celebrating their new upgrades before the grants were even announced.

While the $300,000 grant to the MCPPC may seem odd, it is unlikely a proper investigation will follow because the Federal Government are not accountable for their actions.

The Manila Central Ping-Pong Club is one of the biggest grassroots racquet sports organisations in the Filipino city of Manila, which apparently sits squarely in the North Queensland electorate of Dawson.

Scotty From Marketing Responds To Accusations Of Corruption By Firing Up Australia Day Debate

AS SEVERAL HIGH-RANKING federal cabinet ministers are refusing to stand down over claims of unethical dealings, Prime Minister Scotty from Marketing has today addressed the nation's concerns.

Senator Bridget McKenzie is under fire for handing out $100 million worth of community sports grants to sporting clubs in marginal electorates, as well as to clubs run by rich old codgers who have friends in the Liberal Party.

On top of the sports rorts the government is also facing hurdles with the Member of Hume. The embattled Energy and Emissions Reduction Minister Angus Taylor has refused to release information relating to an allegedly forged document he relied on to accuse City of Sydney Lord Mayor Clover Moore of hypocrisy on climate change.

Mr Taylor's office decided to release only four of 18 documents containing information about 'the City of Sydney's travel expenditure' in full.

That followed revelations that water licences owned by a company Angus Taylor set up were purchased for $80 million (more than double what they were estimated to be worth) by a government body.

However, Scotty from Marketing has played down these accusations by going on *Sunrise* and accusing the Aboriginal and Torres Strait Islander population of being snowflakes about the whole massacre and smallpox shit.

'Australia Day is for everyone! I won't let a bunch of minorities stop me from having a barbie and a bit of beach cricket this 26 January, haha.

'Let's all come together and celebrate being Australian by having a piss-up on the day that marks the beginning of the genocide in this country. Everyone just needs to calm down a bit and enjoy a few Wild Yaks and a catch-up. It's a bloody shame Triple M got shamed into canning the Ozzest 100,' said Scotty.

'Now, if you don't mind, I've got urgent business to attend to, the sailing club down the road wanna re-do their bathrooms in marble so I've gotta sort a grant out for that.'

Netball Club In Marginal Labor Seat Begins Planning New Hyperbaric Chamber Upgrade For 2022

PRESIDENT OF THE Terimungle Netball Club June Wilson has already earmarked the spot where the club's new top-of-the-range state-of-the-art hyperbaric chamber will go.

The lifelong volunteer for the regional club, known affectionately as the Mongrels, said she can't wait to get her hands on the funds that she says will be a game changer for the longtime battlers.

'Like most regional sporting clubs, we run on the sniff of an oily rag and a mountain of work from unpaid volunteers who put in countless hours. But someone reminded me that we are in a marginal Labor seat, so that's all about to change,' said the excited club stalwart.

This comes after former Sports Minister and current Deputy Leader of The Nationals Bridget McKenzie admitted to blatantly abusing the system to grant funds to sporting clubs in seats that the Coalition wanted to win, rather than to clubs in need as recommended by Sport Australia.

The senator, who is unashamed and unapologetic for the clear and obvious pork-barrelling which while legal seems like a grave abuse of power and completely unethical, is facing calls to resign.

Coming from noted lefties like Pauline Hanson, McKenzie has assured the nation's rural club volunteers that she won't be going anywhere any time soon.

'Even though I'm not the Sports Minister anymore, I've handed on my *modus operandi* to the next guy up, and he'll sort out the bribes for any marginal electorates,' she said today.

'Because government funding shouldn't be for those in need, for those people who've dedicated their lives to making other people's lives and their communities better. It should be to feather my own nest and ensure that a few wealthy public servants – who'll take plum consulting jobs rorting the system after they retire on a parliamentary pension – keep their cushy jobs for a little bit longer,' McKenzie said. While she doesn't agree, Mongrels president June says she can't help but take advantage of the money on offer.

'Look, maybe we don't need a hyperbaric chamber, but they are going to throw so much money at us to buy this seat that we may as well make use of it. I feel bad, but what can I do?'

Bridget McKenzie Asks Rural Fire Chiefs If They Could Prioritise Protecting Swing Voters' Homes

IN A SECOND BRAZEN act that abuses her position of power, Nationals senator Bridget McKenzie has today asked fire chiefs around the country to prioritise the protection of the homes of voters in marginal seats.

The former Sports Minister's blatant attempt to serve the interests of herself and her party above all else comes after revelations she gave $100 million worth of funding to sports clubs in marginal seats in an effort to win votes.

Those allegations came to light after an auditor found that 75 per cent of the grants given out to local sporting organisations by McKenzie were not recommended by Sport Australia.

McKenzie has refused to apologise for the moves which seem at best ethically and morally reprehensible, and has doubled down, asking the state fire chiefs to prioritise the protection of houses owned by swing voters.

'I'm expecting it to be a highly successful program. Obviously Barnaby's around me on this one, and Scotty will come round too. I mean, if they are chasing more funding, maybe we can sort something out if they scratch our back,' said the unabashed McKenzie this morning.

'Because, as I've said time and again, politics shouldn't be about wanting to improve the lives of the people you represent. It should be about doing everything possible to ensure you and your immediate family are set up for life.'

Dying Rural Footy Club Sadly In Safe Nationals Seat With No Big Dick Donors On Their Board

A MUCH-LOVED FOOTY club in Western Queensland, which has provided opportunity and personal development for thousands of at-risk rural kids over the better part of a century, looks likely to have to shut up shop this week.

Not because they can't make the numbers anymore, and not because they can't find local parents and community members to help run the place.

It's because there aren't enough chook raffles and meat trays on this planet to raise the money needed to remove the asbestos from their clubhouse.

Not to mention the much-needed refurb on the heritage-listed grandstand – after generations of teenagers have been smoking billies and rooting in it after dark.

For close to two decades the Getwunupya Junior RLFC, also known as the Getwunupya Goannas, have been making it clear to their local councillors, state MP and federal member that they are going to need some help if they are going to survive.

However, unfortunately for this beloved institution of bush footy, they are located squarely in National Party heartland, in a seat that hasn't been considered marginal since the shearers were unionised.

This means that they are not eligible for any help from the aforementioned elected officials that always talk shit about helping people like them.

After spending week after week, year after year, dotting the Is and crossing the Ts on labour-intensive grant applications, club secretary Barb Gutherson says she reckons every one of her submissions has been crushed up and Kobe'd by former Sports Minister Bridget McKenzie.

'The fact that our board of die-hard and dedicated club lifers isn't made up of anyone with enough money to get the attention of the Liberal or National Party's donation office also doesn't help things,' says Barb.

'The most interest we've ever had from the government is when a certain cabinet minister sent his pregnant mistress out here to work in the Catholic hostel in the nineties.'

Bridget McKenzie is reported to have ignored the advice of Sport Australia and funnelled money into projects in marginal electorates and those the Coalition was targeting in the lead-up to the 2019 election. The Goannas weren't one of 'em.

The lack of political clout wielded in this rural town of working-class Australian voters now means sad news for the thousands of families that the Goannas have brought joy and purpose to over the years.

The club has no option now but to shut its doors until someone thinks of a goofy idea that can bring more money into the community, like an Elvis Festival or cane toad races – or basically any other weird alternative to the once-thriving industries destroyed by drought, New South Wales–centric policies and ice.

This is because Getwunupya is from a really shitty part of the Outback – in the sense that it isn't located near any coal seam gas or mining projects.

Unfortunately, this means the Goannas can't even get some of that 'don't-complain-about-what-we-are-doing-to-your-water' money.

Barnaby: 'The Nationals Need A Leader Who Isn't Shrouded In Controversy'

FORMER LEADER OF THE NATIONALS Barnaby Joyce has thrown his Akubra into the planned deputy leadership spill this week, saying the party needs a leader who isn't shrouded in controversy.

This comes after embattled agriculture portfolio babysitter Bridget McKenzie resigned from cabinet and the deputy position, opting to fall on her star picket over the sports rorts controversy.

Mr Joyce also added that should the party choose to spill both deputy and leader positions, he will stand to be leader.

'Our great party needs a clean slate,' he said.

'Someone like me.'

Mr Joyce responded to *The Advocate's* requests for comment by saying that we were not friends anymore and he would not be commenting on anything.

A number of other Nationals backbenchers have put their hand up to be counted in the deputy ballot. They include Anonymous 64-year-old Man #7 and a former doctor.

Popular Queensland Nationals George Christensen and Matt Canavan have told *The Advocate* this morning that they'd rather 'slam there [sic] cock in a door' than run unsuccessfully for the deputy role.

Nevertheless, according to Michael McCormack, the Nationals leader, the party is only planning to spill the deputy position.

'Come on, now. This is the first I've heard of this and I can tell you that we're only spilling the deputy position,' he said.

'Do you want to hear me sing again? Wait here, I'll go and get my Elvis costume out of my office. You see, Parkes is near Wagga Wagga, which is where I live, which means I go to the Parkes Elvis Festival all the time, which is why I have this costume. People accuse me of being wooden but would a wooden person have an Elvis costume in their wardrobe?'

In the ensuing silence, both Michael and the attending reporters all concluded independently that a wooden person probably would.

Next Ash Barty To Continue Getting Changed For Tennis In Mum's Car Until Mum Votes For Scotty

IN A NOT-SO-FEEL-GOOD sporting story out of a safe Labor seat today, young Millie Wattyl is up against it, it can be confirmed.

The talented young tennis player is currently being forced to put up with sub-standard facilities because her silly mother and most of the other people in the area where she lives vote for the Australian Labor Party or the Greens.

'Mummy said she asked for some money to upgrade our tennis court and it was looking good but we didn't get anything,' said the young girl while fiddling with the broken tennis net.

'My coach said it would be nice to have better facilities, but I guess until more people vote for Scotty we won't be able to do much,' said the young prodigy.

'But not too many people, because then we would become a safe Liberal or Nats seat and then we wouldn't get any money either.'

This comes as a raft of sporting clubs around the country come to terms with the fact that they didn't get any of the sports grants they should have because the people in charge of allocating the money were playing political games.

'Oh well, maybe it doesn't matter too much. I'll keep trying, I guess,' said the young girl who is aiming to be the next Ash Barty.

> *'My coach said it would be nice to have better facilities, but I guess until more people vote for Scotty we won't be able to do much,' said the young prodigy.*

THE BETOOTA ADVOCATE | AUSTRALIA 2020

Quiet Australians To Now Be Known As The Upgraded Footy Club Canteen Australians

AS THE SPORTS RORTS scandal continues to worsen this week, Scotty from Marketing has been forced to update some of his terminologies.

This follows the revelation last night that Scotty and his former Sports Minister Bridget McKenzie had been exchanging partisan colour-coded spreadsheets regarding grant applications.

It was also revealed in a senate enquiry that over 40 per cent of the grants awarded were actually ineligible, which goes against all assurances from the government that everything was above board.

'Haha, nah, those were little technical issues,' said the Prime Minister this morning.

'Quiet Australians don't care much for technical issues and white-collar Canberra Bubble bureaucracy,' he continued, before receiving a tap on the shoulder from his media team.

'Sorry, the Upgraded Footy Club Canteen Australians don't care much for technical issues and white-collar Canberra Bubble bureaucracy.'

Fielding a question about why Bridget McKenzie thought it was appropriate to fund a $150,000 study into the benefits of shooting instead of the recommended INAS Global Games, which involved 1000 intellectually impaired athletes from about 50 countries competing in ten sports in Brisbane, Scotty explained that those visiting athletes obviously wouldn't be voting in the election.

'Besides, they got some money down the track so why does it matter that Bridget blatantly abused her position of power?' a fired-up Scotty said.

'Now, I'm pretty done with this conversation. I'll leave you with this. How good are Upgraded Footy Club Canteen Australians!

'Up the Sharks this weekend!'

SPORTS RORTS

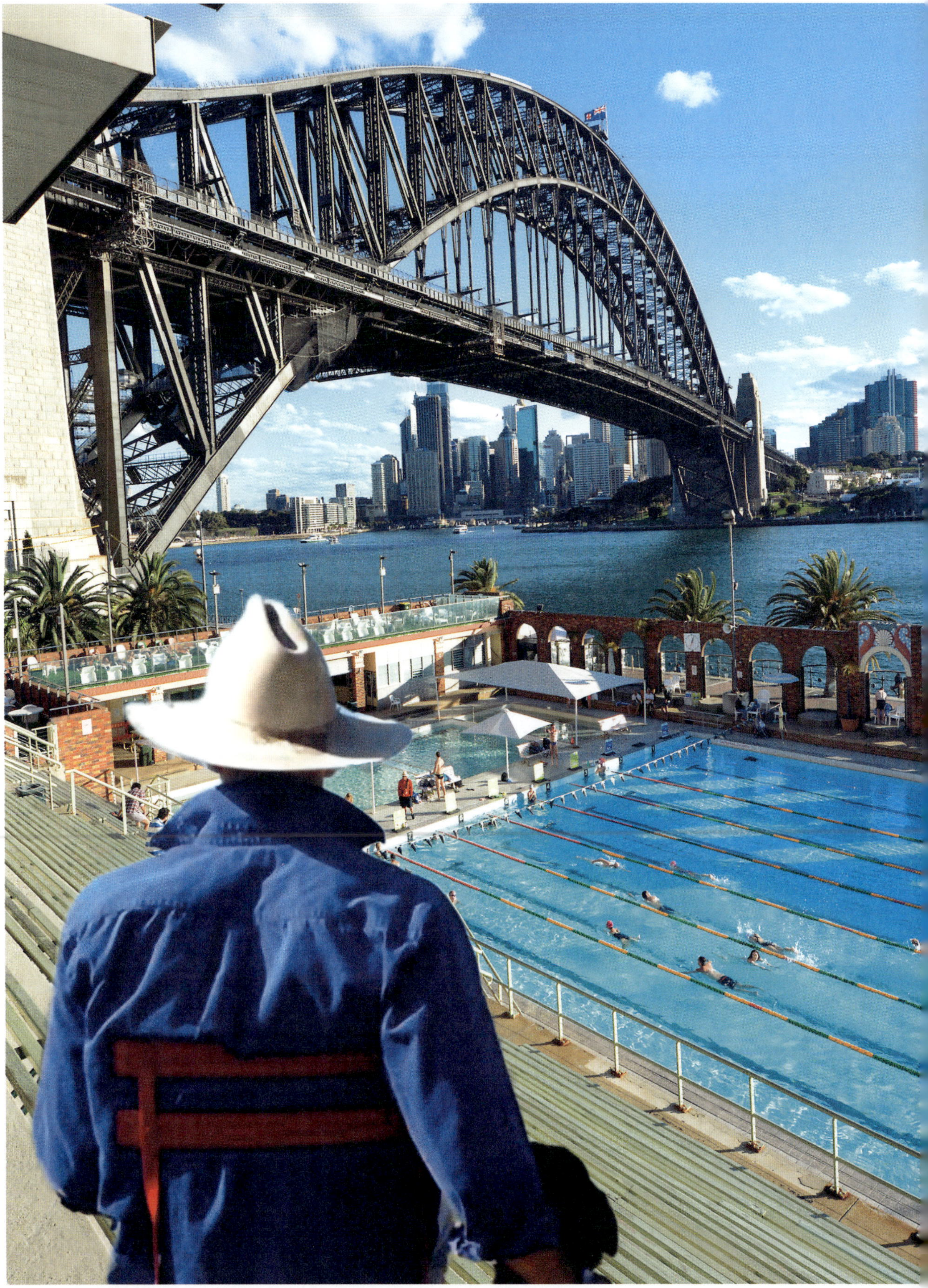

Drought-Stricken Farmer Goes For A Dip In His $10 Million Local Pool Underneath The Harbour Bridge

LOCAL NORTH SYDNEY CATTLE grazier Digby McAngus (66) says that after a hellish couple of years of drought, the last few weeks of rain have been a godsend.

'It's been tough, mate. The earth was cracking. We nearly ran out of water in the [Warragamba] dam. It hasn't been a good time for the North Shore beef industry, let me tell you that.'

Digby says that throughout all the hard times his family has suffered over the last few years, the only saving grace, the last bastion of joy and escapism in their lives, was the public pool in town.

'If it wasn't for this bloody North Sydney pool, I would have locked the gate and moved to Port Macquarie,' he says while opening up a picnic chair and patting his house dog.

'When things were really grim a couple of months back, when I had to shoot some of my calves and their mothers, I'd be in a state … but a couple of laps down here, maybe a dive-bomb off the boards, well, there's not many bad days that can't be fixed by a bit of splish-splash down here at the North Sydney pool,' he said, pointing to the aforementioned pool, located next to Luna Park and underneath the Sydney Harbour Bridge.

'I'm just so bloody glad the government was able to help us keep her in good nick.'

In April 2019, federal Treasurer Josh Frydenberg and local MP Trent Zimmerman announced a $10 million election commitment to contribute to the pool upgrade.

However, as the Federal Government continues to be run through the wringer for the fact that they handed out just short of $100 million worth of mostly ineligible sporting grants to safe and marginal electorates leading into the 2019 election, it has since emerged that the pool funding had been secured from a program that targeted regional and remote areas.

This has resulted in outrage from the inner-city lefties roughly five kilometres away, as the crow flies, in Balmain, who wouldn't know a regional area if it bit them in their soy latte-swilling arses.

The Independent Mayor of North Sydney Council, Ms Jilly Gibson, defended the awarding of the grant under the scheme.

She told ABC's *7.30* in an interview that North Sydney Olympic Pool was 'definitely a regional facility' because sometimes people from the bush visit it.

Digby agrees.

'I might be raising cattle in the next town, but even as a farmer from Kirribilli, this pool has always been viewed as a regional centre. I know farming families and town kids from Hornsby to Manly Beach who use this pool. I think Frydenberg did the right thing by sending them a few bucks for maintenance.

'Where else are we gonna go swimming? The bloody harbour?'

PM Distances Self From The 136 Emails Sent From His Office: 'I'm No Good With Computers, Haha'

THE PRIME MINISTER HAS relinquished all guilt in regard to the sports rorts saga today.

The nation's Head of Marketing did so by deflecting any questions about the 136 emails his office exchanged with the minister responsible for the giant rort, saying, 'I'm no good with computers, haha.'

Followed by a jovial dad laugh, Scott Morrison physically wiped his hands before continuing to explain that he's got no idea how the $100 million in dodgy grants was given out by his Sports Minister after they exchanged emails about the program.

'Nah, I don't deal with any of that stuff, ya know,' he laughed, referring to the partisan colour-coded spreadsheets his office shared with Bridget McKenzie about you know what.

'Computers, emails, technology, haha. You know me, I'm a fair dinkum old-fashioned Aussie bloke. You won't catch me on ClickClock, ya know, haha.

'Besides, 136 emails about this scheme which I had no idea about is just part of the process, but not a part of the process I need to reveal. You just need to trust me on this one, all right.'

His comments come after it was revealed a club in his electorate received $50,000 for a building that had already been built.

'Yeah, not sure about that one, so let's just move along, yeah?'

'Computers, emails, technology, haha. You know me, I'm a fair dinkum old-fashioned Aussie bloke. You won't catch me on ClickClock, ya know, haha.'

Government Faces Imminent Dismissal After Making Enemy Out Of Deb From West Roma Netball Association

THE MORRISON GOVERNMENT has today awoken a very real political force that has the potential to have the entire Federal Cabinet hanged, drawn and quartered in the main street of Canberra.

Thousands upon thousands of mum-and-dad sports club administrators from around rural Australia are tonight revving their Taragos outside their local MPs' electoral offices after new revelations were unearthed surrounding the $100 million pre-election cash splash by the Federal Government which was focused on marginal and target electoral seats.

None is more furious than Deb Sully, secretary for the West Roma Netball Association.

Deb says her tight-knit community has never expected to have anything handed to them, but she now knows that there are lots of fucken silvertail polo clubs out there who have.

As more and more shit piles on the former Minister for Sport Bridget McKenzie in relation to her scandal-plagued Federal Government sports grants scheme, this 59-year-old semi-retired childcare worker has today learnt of some news that makes her wild.

'We had an assessment score of 89 out of 100,' says Deb, in a chilling tone usually reserved for her eldest son's flaky father's over-intrusive mother.

'We just needed a new surface on the courts. $10K for a bit of cement mix and a spirit level. But we weren't important enough. We weren't gonna give them a new seat, and we didn't have any friends of Bridget's kids playing here. We didn't exist in this process.'

Whistleblowers have today leaked spreadsheets identifying which sporting clubs around Australia missed out on grants to make way for Liberal Party vote-buying and party donor requests.

One example shows a football club in the Victorian Liberal-held marginal seat of La Trobe receiving a $500,000 grant despite having an assessment score of 50 out of 100, when a roller derby upgrade in the safe Nationals seat of Gippsland did not get a cent despite its 98 rating.

With a small majority in the House of Representatives and many more Debs calling for blood, the Morrison Government has today made enemies they do not want to have.

In the case of the West Roma Netball Association, the administrators will not stop until they get a sit-down with the Governor-General.

'This means war,' says Deb as she wipes zinc across her cheeks like army face paint.

'And Bridget is going to be the first one in the crosshairs.'

Adani And Rinehart Furiously Argue Over Who Gets To Hook Up Bridget McKenzie With A Job For Life

AUSTRALIA'S MOST POWERFUL policymakers are today butting heads over who gets to reel in the next big catch to be booted from the ranks of the Coalition Government.

Nationals senator Bridget McKenzie looks set to resign from politics after it was revealed she used a $100 million grants program to hand cash to sporting groups that were affiliated with Coalition MPs and clubs in marginal seats before the May 2019 election.

While this kind of disgraceful resignation may appear to be yet another blow for the embattled Morrison, it seems to have his bosses quite excited.

But which mining magnate is going to be lucky enough to give the outgoing McKenzie a job for life?

The job-for-life retirement package has been a common trend for retiring Coalition politicians, most notably Andrew Robb MP, who helped negotiate the destruction of the carbon tax and greenlit a 99-year lease for the Port of Darwin to the Chinese-owned corporation Landbridge, before immediately announcing his retirement from politics to take up a seven-figure consultancy job with Landbridge.

Or the former resources minister Ian Macfarlane who took up a job as the chief executive of the Queensland Resources Council six months after Prime Minister Tony Abbott called on the sector to 'demonstrate their gratitude' to him for scrapping the mining tax.

While both Macfarlane and Robb, like many perennial backbenchers, have the cognitive skills of a couple of 30-minute-old merinos, they brought with them to these corporate roles endless contacts and endless favours owed from a lifetime of dipping their noses in the trough that is Parliament House.

It is for this reason that Australia's two biggest environmental-vandal billionaires are now fighting over who gets to hire Bridget McKenzie.

Indian coalmining billionaire Gautam Adani and the tax-evading darling of Hancock Prospecting Gina Rinehart met on the top floor of a secret Singaporean skyscraper to argue it out today.

Gina Rinehart makes a good case that it should be her who gets to give the embattled Victorian senator $900,000 per year with unlimited travel.

'I've got cattle interests, Gautam!' she barks. 'It makes sense that I get to add a former Ag minister to my stable!'

However, Adani is unflinching.

'I need more Nationals. All I have is the Labor right,' says the subcontinental mining magnate. 'But their hearts aren't in it. I need all of these damning reports about the catastrophic bleaching of the Great Barrier Reef buried, Gina! If I can pull that off, we both win!'

Gina stands firm.

'Gautam! When it comes to sitting politicians, all I've got is those piss-wrecked bogans from the Hunter. Barnaby and Fitzgibbon could fuck up a driver reviver coffee. At least you get Senator Canavan. He's almost exclusively working on getting your mine off the ground. Just give me Bridget and you can have Taylor when he goes down next month.'

Adani, seemingly content with Rinehart's compromise, agrees to the negotiations before making his way to the lift for a private jet back to Ahmedabad.

'I'll see you at the mining conference next month in Delhi,' he says. 'Scotty says there might be a bit too much pressure on him to make it. I told him to just turn his phone off like he did in Hawaii [laughter].'

Gina laughs as well.

'Haha. Fuck, that was good. Australia was all like, "Ooooh, bushfires, waa waa!" Haha.'

> *'I need more Nationals. All I have is the Labor right,' says the subcontinental mining magnate. 'But their hearts aren't in it. I need all of these damning reports about the catastrophic bleaching of the Great Barrier Reef buried, Gina! If I can pull that off, we both win!'*

SPORTS RORTS   73

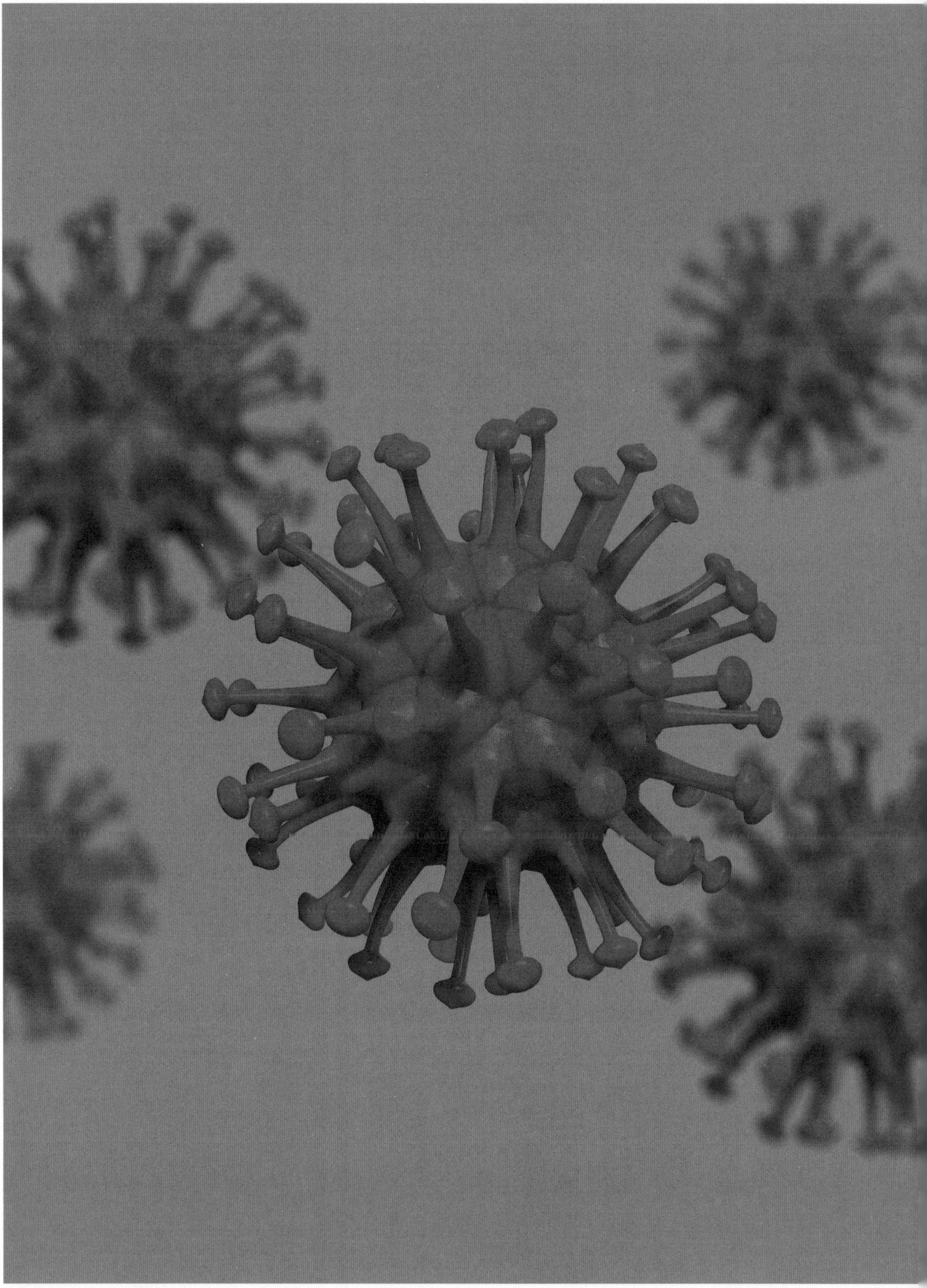

COLLAPSE OF SOCIETY

There is an innate quality within all Australians which ensures that if the government gives us a small privilege, we as a people simply cannot help but take the piss out of it until the government has to take it away again.

These privileges are usually quite nice things, like being able to enjoy a drink on a rooftop or balcony bar without the need for a wire mesh cage preventing people from throwing things from it. Or being able to own guns or smoke inside a pub or plane if we feel so inclined. Australians have been fooled into thinking we have everything we need to be happy. People loved their guns; they loved to smoke inside Boeings and sports bars. When the government said we couldn't have or do those things anymore, most of us inevitably saw the light and agreed that the government was only trying to protect us from ourselves – and from other Australians.

Which is why when the government decided we couldn't do anything at all, society began to collapse.

Panic ensued. There was a real sense that this was the big thing we had all been waiting for: the next extinction event. Fear of dying alone in a plastic bubble while a ventilator struggled to pump air into our lungs was only usurped by the fear of running out of toilet paper. People fought in the supermarket. Entire industries were brought to a standstill; giant companies entered administration.

There is probably no need to harp on about it but these next stories outline the true impact the coronavirus had on our small desert community and Australia at large. They show a raw stoicism in the face of uncertainty. A wry smile as the market imploded. Perhaps even a small, dry chuckle when some 49-year-old office drone looked at their superannuation account, realising that this little hiccup might set their retirement back another decade or so. But for all the pain this virus brought to the people of Betoota, it was met with a steely nod and a double thumbs-up. These articles offer hope in a time when the fabric of Betoota's society was ripping and tearing. It's not over yet, and probably won't be for some time. Nobody had any idea what tomorrow was going to bring – but that didn't matter.

It will be a time remembered well by all those who lived it. After a hundred years of relative growth and prosperity, that pangolin's kiss has brought society as we know it to its knees.

Report: Coronavirus Apparently Causing People To Shit More Than Usual?

A NEW REPORT BY PEOPLE who are hysterically panic-buying non-perishable groceries like characters on *The Walking Dead* has found that the coronavirus causes people to do heaps of poops.

This comes as Woolworths applies a four-pack limit to purchases of goona wrap as the virus-prepping horde empties supermarket shelves of household staples.

Toilet paper joins other obscure household items like high-end pasta brands and Nutella spread which are facing a nationwide shortage, however, it definitely makes the least sense.

As outlined by the Australian Health Department website, the coronavirus (COVID-19) is a respiratory illness caused by some people who decided to eat bat soup in Wuhan. Symptoms range from a mild cough to pneumonia. Some people recover easily, others may get very sick very quickly. There is evidence that it spreads from person to person. Good hygiene can prevent infection.

There is very little evidence that COVID-19 causes people to shit more than usual. In fact, the digestive system is one of the bodily functions that appears to be least affected by this disease. Because it's a respiratory illness, not a stomach illness.

The Prime Minister has today gone above and beyond by asking the Woolworths and Coles duopoly if they could do him a favour and restock all supplies, like they weren't already doing that.

'Haha, you'd be loving all this panic-buying,' Scotty from Marketing told the wage-stealing supermarket giants. 'Bet you wish we had a pandemic every year, haha. Bit like the petrol stations with the bushfires, they made so much coin, haha.'

A two-pack limit on purchases of hand sanitiser has also been implemented, even though Woolies has sold out nationwide, but, when they get more, it's gonna be two packs per person.

Byron Mum Worried This Coronavirus Might Result In Another Deadly Vaccine

BYRON MOTHER AND ONLINE retailer of bespoke Balinese goods Andrea Vachser has today taken to a few online Facebook groups to voice her concerns about big pharma.

This comes after news broke this morning that Australian scientists have achieved a major breakthrough against coronavirus by manufacturing the virus in a lab – which is a huge step towards developing a vaccine.

However, that global breakthrough has not been received well in the Northern Rivers region of New South Wales, or the Northern Shivers, as it is also known.

'Here we go again, #notmychild #notmybaby,' said the wife of a fringe NRL player for the Gold Coast Titans.

'People are so concerned about the coronavirus that they are willing to risk their lives letting the government and big pharma develop another deadly vaccine,' she said while sipping her cold-pressed arrowroot, carrot and turmeric juice.

'I refuse. They can bully us all they want, but I will not let my children be subjected to government-sanctioned programs like lab rats in a cage.'

The angry mother of Aldous and Petunia then told us that she can't believe how the people of this country just roll over and submit.

'5G, chemtrails, fluoride in the water, the highspeed rail burning and now this latest vaccine. When will people wake up?'

Woman Who Spent Weekend Sniffing Coke Off Nightclub Toilet Cistern Not Too Keen On Chinatown

LOCAL BETOOTA GROVE paralegal Tara Corrie (27) is in a state of panic as she does her best to steer her girlfriends towards a new option for dinner tonight.

With a table booked at the Horny Dragon Restaurant & Karaoke in Betoota's Chinatown, Tara worries that her friends haven't been reading the *Courier Mail's* reporting on that new virus that you can only get from people of Chinese descent.

This comes as some of Australia's most iconic Chinese restaurants are suffering a sharp drop-off in business following the outbreak of the COVID-19 virus in the Chinese city of Wuhan.

In some cases, turnover is down 50 per cent on their normal trade for this time of the year. Many operators in the traditional Asian restaurant hubs of Haymarket, Sunnybank, Fortitude Valley and Melbourne's East End are edging closer to shutting their doors with every quiet night that passes.

Tara, like many other reactionary bogans, is playing a big part in this drop-off.

'It's not like I'm paranoid,' she said. 'I'm not fully avoiding public places … It's just like [laughs nervously] I'm also not actively trying to catch coronavirus either.'

And according to Tara – who spent last Saturday night snorting lines of cocaine given to her by a married real estate agent (who wouldn't give her his real name) off the damp toilet cistern at a dodgy nightclub in the Old City district – Chinatown is pretty high risk.

'I'm just playing it safe,' says Tara, who is currently intermittently fasting and on her fifth coffee for this morning.

'I just wish the girls would pick somewhere less risky for a catch-up. It doesn't need to be a banquet, we could go on to like the casino or on a cruise or something.'

'Now Is The Time To Dig Up Your PVC Pipe And Get The Guns Out,' Says ABC's Alan Kohler

'If someone's trying to take your toilet paper, breathe and stay calm. Raise the rifle with your leading hand but don't grip the handguard too tight. Lift the sights into your eye line, keeping the other eye open. Your rifle is a part of you now – an extension of your body, if you will.'

AS WORLD MARKETS DIVE and splutter more violently than they did in the lead-up to the 2007–08 global financial crisis, one of the ABC's most trusted voices of reason has told viewers this morning to retrieve their firearms and learn how to use them.

'You're going to want to aim for the centre mass,' said the ABC's finance editor, Alan Kohler. 'If you've never used a semi-automatic rifle before, it might be wise to practise with an experienced friend before you make the trip down to the shops.

'Also, most of the shooting you're going to be doing will be in close quarters, so I'd file down the tips of the bullets so that they expand and kill whatever you hit very quickly.

'This isn't a game anymore. As ABC viewers, you're already at a distinct disadvantage when it comes to coping with the realities of real life in those places in the outside world where the second number in a postcode isn't zero.

'Good luck out there and don't trust anybody. If someone's trying to take your toilet paper, breathe and stay calm. Raise the rifle with your leading hand but don't grip the handguard too tight. Lift the sights into your eye line, keeping the other eye open. Your rifle is a part of you now – an extension of your body, if you will. You see that man clutching your Quilton? Maybe flick your Ukrainian credit card into burst mode if you're feeling confident? Squeeze the trigger when the sights are lined up on his belly button. Feel the first shot. Through the tum-tum and out through the spine. The next two shots are now pointless but you can't stop them. It's on burst mode, baby. The second. Pow. Through the Quilton, unfortunately, then watch it tunnel through his sternum and again, out through the spine. No walking, no breathing now. The third? Well, where else could it go? It'll probably impact that fucking toilet paper–hoarding piece of shit in the philtrum – that patch of skin between the lips and the nose. That brainless halfwit who was trying to make off with your toilet paper will actually be brainless at this point thanks to you and your rifle. Go and collect your prized Quilton from his lifeless body and repeat the process above on anybody who tries to stop you leaving.

'I'm Alan Kohler.'

It's understood by *The Advocate* that at the end of Alan's segment, the producer threw back to Michael Rowland and Lisa Millar who explained that Alan had been out at the Agincourt Hotel in Ultimo with CommSec's Tom Piotrowski until 4 am this morning and might be feeling a bit under the weather.

Husband Alarmingly Unfazed About Toilet Paper Shortage

AS AUSTRALIA FACES A WEIRD and unexplainable bog roll shortage, thousands of homes around the country are kind of getting a bit grossed out by the man of their house and his lack of concern about this whole thing.

This comes as images of bare supermarket shelves circulate on social media amid coronavirus fears. It appears no one knows why this household item has attained bizarre popularity and is flying out of stores. Manufacturers of toilet paper, tissues and hand sanitiser are boosting production to keep up with the surge in demand.

In fact, so hysterical is the nation's panic-buying that apparently someone was threatened with a knife in a Parramatta Woolies today – during a fight over the last stash of goona wrap.

However, there are a lot of degenerate men around the country who don't seem to really care that much about running out of toilet paper.

Local father-of-three Craigo from Betoota Heights is one of these men. When confronted with a bare cardboard roll this evening, Craigo didn't even yell out to his missus to pass him some extra-absorbent paper towels.

He didn't do anything, really.

And hasn't done anything each time this has happened since Monday.

His wife, Ashley, is a bit concerned about the whole thing but has chalked it up to the possibility of Craigo enacting the Asian squatting technique in his efforts to avoid the need to wipe.

However, during a press conference today, Prime Minister Scotty from Marketing may have identified what Craigo is actually up to.

The Prime Minister said he has met with major retailers to discuss the situation, but has also advised that toilet paper should only really be a necessity for women.

'There's always another option for us blokes, haha. Ladies, ever wonder why ya man is jumping straight into the shower after he lays cable …?

'Shouldn't have to explain that one for ya. Haha. Just a little trick I learnt after the Engadine incident.'

Chinese Bloke And Muslim Bloke Bond Over Being Treated Like A Threat To National Security

AFTER NEARLY THREE MONTHS of unchecked coronavirus hysteria, local Chinese-Australian, John, says he now has a vague understanding of how every Muslim person in the western world has felt for the last 19 years since 9/11.

Across Australia, the anti-Chinese sentiment fuelled by the poor handling of the COVID-19 outbreak by the media and politicians has now reached a tipping point – with rednecks flat out refusing treatment from doctors of Asian appearance in Australian hospitals.

Asian-Australians are also experiencing blatant racism in airports, primary schools, workplaces and on public transport.

John says he doesn't mind people giving him a bit of space in public places, especially during a pandemic, but it is a bit unnerving when he sees people cover their mouths and hold their breath as he walks past.

It's something that not many people can relate to, except for his colleague, Ahmed.

As a proud Pakistani-Australian, Ahmed has his own stories about being treated like a risk to a country's national security.

'How weird is it when old people refuse to sit next to you?' says Ahmed. 'Or when people avoid eye contact with you in the street and rush past?'

John agrees.

'Yeah. I totally understand the airports thing now. It's really weird watching people trying to violate your human rights but also not wanting to get too close to you.'

Ahmed chuckles.

'I know, right.'

COLLAPSE OF SOCIETY

Old Coastie Who Missed Out On Toilet Paper Has Been Chest Deep In Surf For Going On 30 Minutes

COASTAL TOWN SURF CLUB legend Brucey 'Loudmouth' Leonard (72) knows he's not quite old enough to be panicking about contracting the coronavirus, but it doesn't mean this pandemic hasn't affected his day-to-day life.

While not exactly keen on the idea of being locked in the house with the dreaded bat flu, he's also sick and tired of the hysteria.

Especially this bullshit toilet paper roll shortage.

As the Australian media firmly rubbed its crotch with the ball of its hand over the bizarre apocalyptic psychology that has triggered our nation into buying every single square of toilet paper on the shelves, Loudmouth has done his best to not get caught up in the hype.

Instead he's opted to just stay clenched until he gets to the club each morning – and if nature knocks a couple of times in the evenings, he's prepared to do the old loo-shower fun run.

However, today is just one of those days.

The surf club, where he spends 85 per cent of his semi-retirement, is also out of poo tickets, and paper towels, and the *Courier Mail*. He's got nothing to work with. Even the cafe next door has thrown temporary 'staff only' signs on both their customer bathrooms.

It's very possibly for this reason that Loudmouth has spent the last 30 minutes chest deep in the ocean, a good distance from the red and yellow flags.

Several of the other surf club legends have noticed this unusual behaviour.

'Yeah … Loudmouth has never been big on going for a swim,' says club treasurer, Kelly. 'He's either in for a quick dip or he's surfing for three hours. He never just stands there.

'Hmmmm.'

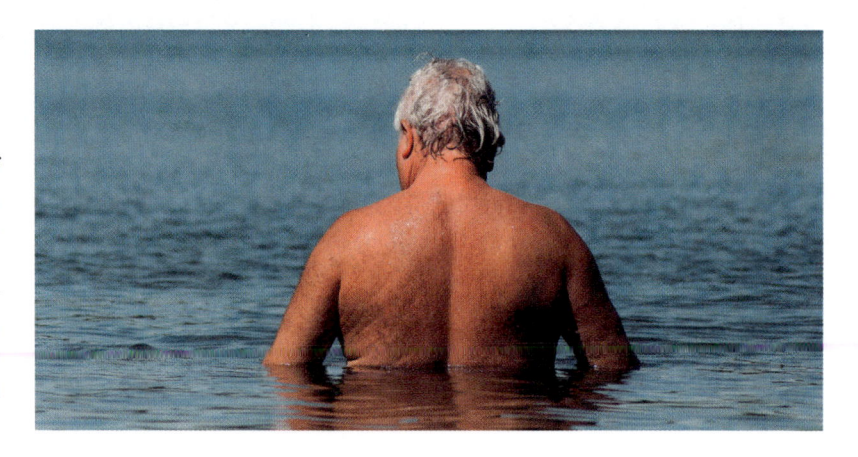

PM Forced To Act On Coronavirus After Learning His Voter Base Might Not Exist In A Few Months

THE CORONAVIRUS HAS THE potential to delete millions of baby boomers from our beautiful continent and nobody knows this better than the Prime Minister.

This week, Scott Morrison said he plans to do something about coronavirus after being told by people in his team that the deadly flu-like virus could entirely eradicate the Coalition Government's voter base.

'Even though it would be great for the housing market, health care system, welfare budgets, the environment, social progression, energy prices and climate policy, we can't have scores of baby boomers being wiped out by the coronavirus,' he said. 'We need to do something, and as a government, we have decided now is the time to act.

'The last thing we need as a government is to be voted into Opposition.'

Barnaby Joyce Threatens To Put Down Tom Hanks

FORMER DEPUTY PRIME Minister Barnaby Joyce has today taken great pleasure in threatening to kill another pair of Hollywood icons.

Tom Hanks and his wife, Rita Wilson, have been given until Saturday to get out of the country or they will be put down – after bringing coronavirus into Australia without declaring it to quarantine.

Tom Hanks said on Wednesday that he and his wife have unfortunately tested positive to the bat flu.

Mr Hanks and Ms Wilson, both 63, are in Australia, where Tom was set to film a movie about the life of Elvis Presley. He has since released a statement clarifying his diagnosis.

'We felt a bit tired, like we had colds, and some body aches,' the Academy Award-winning actor said in a statement.

'Rita had some chills that came and went. Slight fevers, too. To play things right, as is needed in the world right now, we were tested for coronavirus, and were found to be positive.'

While Hanks and his wife are now in self-quarantine, the couple has been informed they are not doing enough in the eyes of the Coalition Government. The Member for New England has taken it upon himself to eradicate the threat of COVID-19 spreading further due to the Hollywood elites.

While Barnaby Joyce is no longer the Minister for Agriculture, the Morrison Government has once again entrusted him with the ongoing responsibility of intimidating movie stars for cheap political points because the Quiet Australians secretly hate successful bloody Yanks.

This is not the first time Joyce has (publicly) threatened to kill on behalf of the Australian Government.

In 2016, Barnaby Joyce made headlines across the world when, as Federal Agriculture Minister, he declared that Johnny Depp and Amber Heard's pet dogs (Pistol and Boo) should 'bugger off' back to the US or he might be forced to have them put down.

While Tom Hanks and his wife don't necessarily represent a biosafety hazard, the government is unanimous in its position that they should be treated like one.

However, the decision to kill Hanks and Wilson – should they be uncooperative – does not sit well with current Deputy PM and Barnaby Joyce's faction rival Michael McCormack MP.

'I wanna find out more about this Elvis movie,' said McCormack. 'Remember when I dressed up as Elvis for the Parkes Elvis Festival? That's my thing now. Barnaby is the volatile drunken rooter of the National Party, I'm the Elvis guy.

'Someone please listen to me.

'I'm technically second in charge.'

Gold Coast Hospital Staff Roll In A Wilson Volleyball To Keep Tom Hanks Company In Quarantine

AFTER 20 YEARS, THE *Cast Away* sequel the world has been waiting for has finally arrived.

Just like the first smash hit, the next *Cast Away* film will feature Tom Hanks stranded on a South Pacific Island – except this time, the island is Australia!

The news breaks after it was confirmed Tom Hanks and his wife Rita Wilson have been taken to the Gold Coast Hospital after being diagnosed with COVID-19.

The Hollywood star was working on a Baz Luhrmann film about Elvis on the Gold Coast.

The celebrity diagnosis follows news that the world is continuing to spiral further and further into pandemic chaos as the virus causes lockdowns, downturns and all sorts of flow-on effects.

However, the thoughtful and overworked staff at the Gold Coast Hospital have bought Hanks a Wilson volleyball to keep him company for the duration of his stay.

'Just because they have so much to catch up on,' explained one harried local nurse.

'It's been a while since they saw each other, so we thought it would be a nice touch. Anyway I've got to run now,' she said before hanging up.

Broke Casual Worker Spends Last $20 On A Quality Knife To Get His Own Doomsday Supplies With

HE'S ABOUT FOUR WEEKS from being homeless but only 48 hours away from starving.

Faced with the prospect of having no money, no home and no food, Kade Derrigan said he had to put his thinking hat on as to how he was going to spend the last of his dosh.

The 25-year-old theatre student by day and hotel worker by night decided to purchase a quality kitchen knife with his last $20 – something he said he didn't want to do but felt he was forced to.

'I really don't know what else to do,' he said.

'There's a lot of yuppies who've moved into the French Quarter. They all have money and most of them are cowards. So I got a knife. I've still got a balaclava from last year's St Patrick's Day costume party. I went as a young Gerry Adams! Ah! Better times.

'Anyway, my plan is to wait until nightfall. Wait for some drunk, RM boot–wearing corporate fuckboy to come stumbling down the street. Smack him upside the back of the head with a trolley pole and take his wallet. Then I'll go to that corner store with the broken CCTV camera and stock up on cigarettes and luncheon log. I don't smoke but they seem valuable.

'Then, I guess I'll need some food. So I'll wait until some Range Rover–driving yuppie cunt parks up with their groceries. Run over and pretend to be on drugs and hold the knife out. Hopefully, they run and I don't have to plunge that cold steel in them but fuck me dead, what else am I supposed to do?

'Maybe I should just go back to Mum and Dad's up in the Heights? Actually, that's a way better idea.'

'There's a lot of yuppies who've moved into the French Quarter. They all have money and most of them are cowards. So I got a knife. I've still got a balaclava from last year's St Patrick's Day costume party.'

Bob Katter Loads 12-Gauge After Hearing Faint Cough A Couple Of Blocks From His Electoral Office

AS OF THIS MORNING, THERE have been 454 confirmed cases of COVID-19 in Australia, including 78 in Queensland. The Sunshine State has jumped up ten cases since Tuesday, which may have been caused by Peter Dutton bringing it back into the country from his recent trip overseas.

While major hospitals are currently dragging trainee nurses into the field in preparation for the influx to come, extra efforts are being made to keep country towns quarantined from any inner-city visitors who may be infected.

Rural and regional Australians are being urged to immediately implement simple hygiene and social-distancing tactics to help limit the spread of coronavirus.

Many remote North Queensland Aboriginal communities like Palm Island are pleading for non-essential visitors and sick locals to stay away in a bid to protect vulnerable residents from the virus.

In the Gulf Country, things aren't much different, with Federal Member Bob Katter III MP staying very vigilant in these 'uncertain times'.

Speaking to *The Betoota Advocate* today, Mr Katter told our reporters that while Morrison is bumbling over whether or not schools should be closed, he's called it upon himself to implement martial law in the Kennedy electorate.

'Little Johnny Howard tried to take away our guns… but he didn't get all of them,' said the Honourable Bob Katter today.

'I will protect the elderly and the immunocompromised people of the Queensland Back Country by any means necessary.'

Our interview was then cut short after Bob heard the faint hack of someone coughing several blocks away from his Mount Isa electoral office.

'Follow me,' he said, rushing to the state-compliant gun safe next to his desk.

'Oi!' he adds, turning around and glaring at our reporters. '1.5 metres, gentlemen.'

After reminding our staff about the proper protocol for social distancing, Mr Katter grabbed his treasured 12-gauge shotgun from the safe and directed us out to the street.

Within seconds Katter had loaded his rifle and was firing shots in the air.

'Come on, city boys!' he yelled in his squeaky rural accent.

'Who brought this bat flu to the Isa!?'

[gunshots]

'You're gonna do some prayin' for me, boy!'

[gunshots]

'Come here, piggy, piggy, piggy.'

As Mr Katter scanned his immediate surroundings with an Eastwood-like scowl, the streets remained silent. That is, except for the gasps of two elderly women pushing their walking frames on the other side of the Barkly Highway.

'Robert!' yelled one of the pensioners. 'Settle down. No one has the coronavirus up here yet.'

Katter changed his tune immediately.

'Sorry, Beryl,' he said in a bashful tone. 'Can't be too careful, you know.

'How are you going for toilet paper, anyway? Want me to send Robbie around with some paperbark? We got plenty of it at home.'

The exchange between Bob Katter and the elderly women lasted roughly 45 minutes and finished with the Member for Kennedy explaining that if he'd had the chance, he would have put that freemarketeer Paul Keating in a cattle crush back in the early nineties.

At time of press, Bob Katter was forcing our intern to learn every lyric of Slim Dusty's 'Three Rivers Hotel', while eating arrowroot biscuits dipped in margarine.

'Little Johnny Howard tried to take away our guns ... but he didn't get all of them,' said the Honourable Bob Katter today.

COLLAPSE OF SOCIETY

Norman Swan Takes Over From Shane Fitzsimmons As Nation's Daddy

AS OF LAST NIGHT, Gold Walkley award–winner Dr Norman Swan has officially replaced New South Wales Rural Fire Service commissioner Shane Fitzsimmons as Australia's daddy.

This comes as Norman Swan, host of the ABC's 'Coronacast', has risen through the clutter as a calming voice on the current coronavirus pandemic.

As state and federal governments now juggle the twin tasks of trying to slow panic surrounding COVID-19 while also slowing the spread of it, very few medical voices have been able to cut through the misinformation and sensationalist news cycle.

That was until Dr Norman Swan extended his arms and let our troubled nation nestle into his calming embrace, which of course is *metaphorical* because that would be a reckless departure from the social-distancing protocol he has been trying to condition us to.

While our Prime Minister and state leaders aren't known for acting immediately on the advice of experts – indeed, quite often unqualified talkback radio commentators hold court in the authority vacuum during uncertain times like these – thankfully Australians now have options outside of listening to Alan Jones describe the pandemic as 'the global warming of health' to his elderly listeners, while recording in quarantine from his rural safehouse.

Similar to New South Wales RFS chief Shane Fitzsimmons commanding the nation's attention with his hard facts and advice during the 2019/2020 climate fires, Dr Norman Swan is now one of the leading experts in how to not die from the most recent national emergency on which our government has been dragging its feet.

After all that rain in February, Shane Fitzsimmons says he's relieved to hand over Daddy status to Norman and his soothing Scottish accent.

'He'll do a great job,' said the former state RFS commissioner. 'He'll make an awesome daddy.'

90   THE BETOOTA ADVOCATE | AUSTRALIA 2020

Pauline Overcome With Jealousy That Coronavirus Is Getting All The Credit For Closing Borders

AFTER NEARLY HALF A decade of achieving absolutely none of the things she said she would work day and night to implement in federal politics, Senator Pauline Hanson has today been beaten to the punch when it comes to no longer allowing foreigners into the country.

As of yesterday, the government has enacted a ban on all non-citizens and non-residents from entering the country to minimise the impact of the coronavirus.

Under the new travel ban, effective from 9 pm tonight, Australians seeking to return from overseas and their direct family members will still be allowed in, but must self-quarantine for 14 days upon entry.

This news has been met with extreme jealousy from the flat-earthers and white supremacist state and federal senators who make up Pauline Hanson's far-right One Nation Party.

> 'Whatever happened to the good old Aussie battler making a name for themselves in politics based on nothing but pointless fear and divisiveness?'

While the media rightly ignores anything that Hanson and her populist cronies are saying about the current pandemic, out of fear that anything they report could result in more people dying, it is safe to say that the party and their supporters have been left with a bitter taste in their mouths regarding the decision for Australia to shut all borders.

'I just wish that we didn't need a global pandemic that is killing tens of thousands of people around the world to show us the importance of not letting anyone else into the country,' said a cranky Pauline Hanson during a press conference in some shithole weekender town west of Brisbane today.

'I've been saying for years that Islam and people who dress differently to us are the biggest threat to Australians, and no one listened! But now, because of this so-called coronary virus, they rush to shut the gate.'

As Hanson points out, it is impossible for her and her party to exist when Australia is preoccupied with real issues that actually affect Australians. It's for this reason that it is unashamedly jealous that COVID-19 is taking all of the headlines.

'It really shows us where the government's priorities lie. What's next, the coronary shuts down the family courts? Wouldn't surprise me if it wants to take credit for that as well.

'When will people learn that we have bigger threats than all of this mumbo jumbo that only scientists and academics can advise us on? Whatever happened to the good old Aussie battler making a name for themselves in politics based on nothing but pointless fear and divisiveness? This isn't the Australia I grew up in. It certainly isn't the Australia that has been paying me over 250,000 taxpayer dollars a year since I was elected in 2016.'

COLLAPSE OF SOCIETY

Rich People Don't Get Coronavirus, Confirm 20,000 Brainless Cunts On Bondi Beach Yesterday

> '*Those new rules are only for the westies, ya know?*' *said Cambo, whose own housemate returned from a three-month yoga retreat in California only yesterday morning.* '*Or, like, people, in Chinatown.*'

AUSTRALIA'S WEALTHIEST AND most attractive and cultured citizens are seemingly immune to the potentially fatal effects of COVID-19 – that's according to the 20,000-plus morons who decided it was appropriate to mob Bondi Beach yesterday afternoon.

Images showing Sydney's premier eastern suburbs public space packed with locals and holiday-makers yesterday has resulted in social media backlash – with the rest of the nation now asking every Bondi resident the age-old question, 'HDAYC?' (How Dumb Are You, Cunt?)

The photos were taken mere hours after the government introduced drastic new restrictions on non-essential indoor gatherings in an effort to slow the spread of coronavirus.

As of this minute the number of Australians who have contracted the coronavirus is nearing the 1000 mark, as authorities lose track of the index cases and the virus begins to spread freely among the community.

It is for this reason the government is now putting its foot down and insisting on social-distancing and individual hygiene measures.

In addition to the current limit of no more than 100 people in an indoor space, Scotty announced there should be no more than one person per four square metres. This is on top of existing advice to keep 1.5 metres of 'social distance' where possible, in any situation.

However, one local Bondi resident, Cambo Parade (35), says these instructions obviously aren't meant for beautiful people like him.

'Those new rules are only for the westies, ya know?' said Cambo, whose own housemate returned from a three-month yoga retreat in California only yesterday morning. 'Or, like, people, in Chinatown.'

Cambo's girlfriend Bronte agrees.

'But seriously, like, what are the chances anyone down on the beach yesterday has coronavirus?

'I can understand the tourists probably shouldn't be down there, because it's not really for them anyway. But most of us residents have been working from home all week – we deserve a bit of a swim and a few drinks at the Beachy if we feel like it.'

When informed by our reporters that the likelihood of someone in a transient and affluent suburb like Bondi Beach carrying COVID-19 is actually much higher than any other coastal region, Cambo and his girlfriend Bronte dismissed the claims as being rooted in jealousy.

'Well, Jesus. Sounds like a lot of people on Facebook wish they had something like this on their doorstep,' said Cambo. 'What do they expect us to do? Just sit inside and watch TV like bogans? C'mon, get real.

'I haven't seen this much hysteria since I was in Italy last month.'

Report: Well, Surely That's The End Of These Fucking Things

AFTER LEARNING THAT CRUISE ships might actually be the greatest contributor to the spread of COVID-19 outside of China and Italy, the world can only assume that this absurd industry is now finished for good.

Made popular on screen by TV shows like *The Love Boat* and movies like *Titanic*, cruise ships are generally large floating apartment buildings used for ocean voyages in which the voyage itself, the ship's amenities, and usually the different ports of call along the way each form part of the passengers' experience.

While cruise ships have long been known as a hotbed for gastro bugs and other illnesses that thrive in their revolting and unhygienic karaoke lounges and self-serve bistros, they are now also known as super-spreaders of the ghastly coronavirus that is threatening our global economy and the lives of millions of people.

> *Since the Ruby Princess docked five days ago, over 50 positive cases of the virus have been traced back to the cruise, making it the biggest single source in Australia.*

On Thursday, the tax-evading *Ruby Princess* cruise ship docked in Sydney with dozens of undiagnosed coronavirus cases on board.

For some fucking reason, even after the government had shut down indoor events of over 100 people and outdoor events of over 500 people, almost 2700 passengers – some coughing and spluttering – were allowed to disembark the ship in Sydney on Thursday, from where they caught trains, buses and even overseas flights to continue their journeys.

A week later, and the Australian states and territories are now fighting tooth and nail to implement a complete shutdown of non-essential services, including schools, due to the sharp spike in confirmed COVID-19 cases that appear likely to rise dramatically until our nation's entire healthcare system is completely clogged.

Five days earlier, Australia had already ordered anyone returning from overseas to self-isolate for 14 days – a directive that applied seemingly to everyone except the stroppy boomers who had just paid thousands of dollars to drink cocktails and look at the ocean while on a loop of the Pacific.

Since the *Ruby Princess* docked at Circular Quay five days ago, over 50 positive cases of the virus have been traced back to the cruise, making it the biggest single source in Australia.

It joins a long list of cruise ships at the centre of the global COVID-19 pandemic that have been identified as the causes of some of the most serious breaches in containment of the virus.

It is for this reason, among many other unappealing elements of the cruise ship industry, that everyone is kind of thinking this might be the end of them.

'Surely,' says Dr Usman Siddle, a prominent epidemiologist from the Betoota Base Hospital. 'I mean, the grog is watered down, the guests are obnoxious … and the fucking things spread COVID-19 like wildfire.'

Dr Siddle says that at the end of the day, the RSL-type activities and severe sunburn can't be worth the damage these vessels of cashed-up bogans are causing the planet.

'I can't see any reason for them to continue to exist after this lockdown. Not to mention the carbon they emit. Two *Ruby Princess*es would produce as much pollution as every car in Sydney.'

Property Investor Worries That Her Unwashed Renters Are Starting To Get Some Big Ideas

'I don't need mortgage relief. I've worked hard enough to own my properties outright.'

THE FEDERAL GOVERNMENT HAS estimated that at least one million people could become unemployed as the coronavirus pandemic closes workplaces across the country.

While the mass unemployment of the nation's workers poses a massive threat to the online MyGov portal, which wasn't prepared to handle the rush of applications for welfare payments, experts predict it won't be just websites crashing over the next few months.

The nation's leaders are promising a response to the plight of Australian workers, who are seeking relief from rental payments, which would also have to come hand in hand with a mortgage relief package. Which, in turn, might fuck around with Australia's famously unsustainable housing market growth.

An announcement on these measures is due to be handed down on Tuesday night when the national cabinet meets.

According to the eight thousand different real estate lobby groups, more than one in three Australians rents their homes – a concerning statistic that has rattled the Liberal Party's priority constituents to their core.

The long-suffering top ten per cent of Australia's wealth-hoarders are now facing the prospect of having their tenants miss their rental payments, simply because the pathetic renting classes haven't had enough of a go to put away enough money to see them through a couple of rainy months.

We spoke to one of Betoota Grove's most outspoken landowners about these new proposals earlier.

'It's just not fair for those of us who worked hard and married well,' said Elodie Brixton-Hopscotch (55), who owns three investment properties outright – which serve as a little earner on top of her husband's recent multimillion-dollar payout as a banking executive.

'Why should people like me have to miss out simply because a couple of hundred thousand bogans can't pay their rent?' spits a furious Elodie. 'I don't need mortgage relief. I've worked hard enough to own my properties outright. In my opinion, anyone with a mortgage is just as unprepared for this so-called pandemic as those underachievers who only pay rent.

'Just because we don't have bills to pay, it doesn't mean we should have to grant our unwashed tenants the right to miss a couple of payments. It's ridiculous that rental relief is even being discussed in the first place. This isn't the Liberal Government I voted for!'

Our interview then ended abruptly as Elodie fumbled with a phone call from her sister Bernadette, who got off the *Ruby Princess* last Thursday.

At time of press, Elodie was arguing with her 92-year-old husband Clyde over why she can't go to her Tuesday night barre class.

'Why should I have to change my routine because all of these public health sponges are clogging up our hospitals?' she says.

'I am a Caucasian post-war Australian. I have never made a compromise in my entire life and I'm not going to start now.'

COLLAPSE OF SOCIETY

Border Force Claims There've Been Boomers Overboard In Effort To Turn Cruise Ships Around

IN SHOCKING NEWS BREAKING this afternoon, the Australian Border Force has today claimed that boomers have been thrown off a cruise ship and into the sea.

The sensational and appalling claims come after 1700 passengers on a cruise ship due to dock in Western Australia were not allowed to disembark after 250 people on board reported symptoms of 'respiratory illness'.

'It sickens me to stand here today and inform you about what has just occurred on board a cruise liner,' explained Border Force spokesperson Rita Peith in a suspiciously similar turn of events to that infamous incident in 2001.

'I produce this extremely blurry photo that doesn't really show a whole lot, and inform you that passengers on a cruise ship have just thrown some of their fellow boomers off the ship into the ocean in an effort to be allowed back onto the mainland,' Peith explained.

'It shocks me to my core that humans would do this to their fellows,' she continued, gradually pulling the photo further and further away as people tried to get a closer look and confirm the actual contents of the image.

'We will not be allowing the cruise ship filled with these people to dock and potentially infect our nation with COVID-19.

'We are a humane nation, but we're not a nation that's going to be intimidated by this kind of behaviour,' chimed in the spokesperson for Home Affairs Rill Fuddock.

When pressed on some more details of the information that seemed suspiciously similar to that time the Howard Government lied about asylum seekers throwing their children overboard, the pair abruptly ended the conference.

'There have been boomers overboard and that's all there is to it. Boomers overboard. We are turning the boats around. Boomers overboard. You got that? Boomers overboard, just send that phrase out, okay?'

The pair then stormed off.

Dodgy Bloke Out Front Of The Wobbly Boot In Boggabilla Can Get You Into Queensland If Ya Got The Coin

ENTRY POINTS TO QUEENSLAND are backed up this morning after the State Government closed all borders to New South Wales overnight.

This unprecedented decision marks the first time the southerners have been cut off since the Spanish Flu pandemic in 1919, and comes in the wake of the rapid spread of COVID-19.

With 1029 infections, New South Wales has more than double the number of cases of COVID-19 than Queensland, which has 443. Premier Annastacia Palaszczuk's decision to close the borders may be the most effective form of social distancing yet.

Severe traffic congestion has been reported on the M1 Pacific Highway and the Gold Coast Highway as large queues form to enter and leave the state through police roadblocks.

Motorists are being questioned as to their eligibility to cross the state line, with holiday-makers being turned around.

However, it's not just the coastal roads into Queensland that are being monitored. Police have put up roadblocks at every entry point from Cameron Corner and Tenterfield to Mungindi. Those who don't have a good enough reason to enter the state, be that on compassionate grounds or for work, are rapidly running out of options to travel north.

However, there is one bloke who reckons he can get you over the border. If you've got the coin.

Loitering in the car park of Boggabilla's famous Wobbly Boot Hotel, Brandon Brailey (62) is offering up his services to help provide passage to the safety of a Queensland autumn.

'Just you?' he says to our reporter, while resting a little bit too much of his body weight on the half-open driver's-side window glass.

'$500 and I'll get you to Roma. $1000 to Toowoomba. $3000 to Brisbane, but you don't wanna go there, mate. That's where you'll catch it, plus that city is no good unless the pubs are open.' He leans in a bit closer.

'$8000 and I'll get you to the Daintree and no one will ever ask where you're from.'

When quizzed on his methods of transport, Brandon waved an agistment permit at our reporter.

'I can put you on a horse and we'll follow the stock routes. Or if you wanna sleep in cow shit I can put you on the top of the next truck coming from Moree.'

As Brandon was approaching the pointy end of his sales pitch, he was spooked by the roar of an unregistered Hilux burning down the Newell Highway. In the tray of the ute sat a dozen grey nomads wearing Hawaiian shirts.

After identifying the driver as a business partner from the little town of North Star, Brandon smiled – before urging our reporter to hurry up and decide.

'Make it quick, mate. I've got a delivery for Goondiwindi here. Where do you wanna go? I can waive the cash payment if you leave me ya car.

'You've got five minutes, you wanna jump in with the Mosman crowd or what?'

Cruise Enthusiasts Look Back On The Good Old Days When They Only Caught Gastro

ONCE UPON A TIME, a breeding pair of ageing Queenslanders could book a spot on a cruise ship and only expect to end up shitting their brains out in the comfort of their cabin.

Barry and Joan Taylor of Betoota Heights look back on days like that with nostalgia and feel sad knowing that those days are probably gone forever.

The 68-year-old Capricorns shared photos of their last cruise with *The Advocate*. Aside from the picture of them engaging in a bit of easy-does-it-side-doggy that shook our reporter to his very core, the holiday seemed quite relaxing.

'Here's a picture of Barry enjoying his first day of gastro,' said Joan.

The glossy print showed a naked man in the foetal position in their room's ensuite. He'd given up defecating in the toilet and had moved into the shower.

'Just a pro tip,' said Barry. 'When the gastro strikes, it's better to just get in the shower and wash yourself off after each wave. You can also drink the shower water between moans.'

Joan laughed.

'Oh, you loved drinking the shower water! Errol, when we were at the Isle of Pines on our last cruise, Barry didn't even leave the bathroom! He lost six kilos in that room somewhere!' she said.

Shaking his head and smiling, Barry buried his face in his hands.

'The six kilos went down the drain!'

They both paused and stopped laughing.

'Those were the days,' they said.

'Now, instead of catching gastro while you're out at sea, you catch this dreaded pangolin's wrath! Ghastly, it is.'

'Here's a picture of Barry enjoying his first day of gastro,' said Joan.

North Korea Praised For Closing Borders To Protect Civilians From Virus

IN AN UNEXPECTED MOVE, the World Health Organization has praised North Korea for beating the coronavirus, with a reported zero cases, on par with its previous personal best in February which also featured zero reported cases.

Despite the entirely believable claims from the country, some other countries have reacted with scepticism.

US President Donald Trump even offered anti-epidemic assistance to North Korea, which was obviously turned down by the country that has zero cases of coronavirus and which also claimed to have found a bunch of unicorns in the wild near Pyongyang in 2012.

In a statement, the World Health Organization praised the 'expedient action' taken by North Korean leader Kim Jong Un and predecessor Kim Jong Il, who locked down the borders so quickly that it would be many years before the virus even came into being.

'North Korea's hands-on approach is really refreshing; locking down borders and protecting them with the military is a really effective way to combat the influx of viruses,' said the statement.

'The way Esteemed Leader Kim Jong Un implemented these measures decades before the virus even started is really proactive. It's easy to see why he keeps winning all those elections.'

For Fuck's Sake, Melbourne, Your Beaches Are Shit Anyway

ONCE AGAIN, THE GENTRIFYING inner-city types have been found to be the most complacent Australians when it comes to the strict new COVID-19 social-distancing measures.

This comes as another swathe of brainless cunts decided today was the day to pretend they have decent beaches on the weird body of water that sits underneath Melbourne.

Photographs that have gone viral today show beachgoers enjoying the warm weather on the hideous St Kilda foreshore, blatantly ignoring the Victorian Government's stern warnings to 'stay home'.

Given St Kilda's distance from the Melbourne city centre and the lack of fun times, it seems these new photos depicting dangerous civil disobedience will be hard to pin on 'backpackers' – as was the case in Bondi last Friday when 20,000 other brainless cunts decided that coronavirus doesn't affect rich people.

This backwards slide in containment comes as the Victorian Premier Daniel Andrews today vowed he would not hesitate to close beaches if people violated the regulations – citing the newest outbreak in Sydney's Bondi Beach as a good example of what happens when entitled inner-city fucks refuse to heed serious warnings about how to prevent the spread of this deadly virus.

The state has today announced 54 new confirmed cases of coronavirus, bringing the state's total to 574. They also have the highest rate of death per case.

No doubt, more brainless cunts to come.

A good example of what happens when entitled inner-city fucks refuse to heed serious warnings about how to prevent the spread of this deadly virus.

COLLAPSE OF SOCIETY

WA Premier Mark McGowan Blows State's Official Kazoo To Call All Western Australians Home

ON SUNDAY NIGHT, the West will become an island within a country.

Those were the words of Western Australia Premier Mark McGowan. In the moments after he made that announcement, he pulled a hot-pink kazoo from his suit pocket.

'This is the State Kazoo of Western Australia,' he said. 'I call upon all people of the West to come home.'

With that, the Novocastrian-by-birth took a deep breath and blew as hard as he could into the kazoo – and the fresh slither of baking paper in the soundbox buzzed to life.

The Advocate spoke to people of the West all over the world who said at that point, something inside them began to ache.

One of those was Greg Spearsman, who works in our town's financial district at investment bank Debit Ecosse. He told our reporter that he was napping on the couch when all of a sudden, he was ripped from his slumber back into reality.

Greg spoke briefly to *The Advocate* from an Alice Springs petrol station, where he was filling up his 2002 electric blue Hyundai Excel.

'It was like someone threw a bucket of water on me,' he said. 'I woke up and there was my premier blowing the Kazoo of the West on TV. The airport was shut, there were no flights. I only had three days to get back there. So I got my keys and left. I didn't even pack.

'I've got about 36 hours to go. The shortest route would be through the APY lands but this little Korean billycart wouldn't make it, so it looks like I'm doing a high-speed burn down and across the Nullarbor. I'll sleep when I get over the state line. I'm coming, Mark. I'm coming home.'

Melbourne Elites Hiding In Portsea Given Away By Stickers For Weird Private School Sports

ROADS ACROSS THE COUNTRY have experienced the quietest Easter since the First World War, after police promised a crackdown on non-essential travel and holidays.

All last month Australians had been told to cancel trips and stay at home to prevent the spread of COVID-19.

Even family gatherings and gatherings of more than two people have been banned, and state governments ordered their police to fine anyone seen to be ignoring directives to stay home.

Here in Queensland, the transport office reported a surge in the numbers of blue bloods attempting to change their addresses to their beach houses on Straddie or Sunshine Beach – so as to avoid punishment when they get checked for ID on the exit ramps.

In Tasmania, police used helicopters to spot people travelling on the roads, while in New South Wales, residents are being fined upwards of $1000 for moving around the state without good reason.

However, in Melbourne it seems the aristocratic classes are just that bit more brazen about relocating to their gorgeous weekenders during quarantine.

Fearing neither accountability nor repercussions for their decision to leave the hedges of Toorak for their nine-bedroom beach house in Portsea, the Welthhorder family believe the Easter lockdown wasn't directed at 'people like them'.

'Sounds like that's more a Mallacoota problem … haha,' chuckles third-generation stockbroker's wife, Elsa Welthorder (45).

'I can see why they have a problem with renters swarming beach towns, but in Portsea, most of us are owners. We are as good as locals, really … even if the Mornington locals don't recognise us. It's like, sorry, Jayden, I know you don't remember me from high school but my caffeine addiction is basically keeping your family afloat.

'Haha.'

It's because of the Mornington Peninsula's new coronavirus-charged 'locals only' attitude that families like the Welthorders are going to have to lie low this Easter and try to holiday as discreetly as possible. Not for fear of police attention, but because they don't want to cop any eggs on the Rangey.

'We had to take the car off-road at Arthurs Seat on the way here,' said another tax-evading generational wealth–hoarding pre-internet retail heiress, Magda Silva-Spune (50).

'We've even let our boys say "H" as "haytch" like the other local kids. Next they'll be saying "youse" as a second person plural,' she giggles.

However, while the Toorak families might be able to convince themselves that they are blending in to this small coastal town with their salmon moleskin trousers and Birkenstocks, the humble-bragging private school bumper stickers are blowing their cover.

Locals say that seeing stickers for competitive croquet, sailing and even polo has given away all of the Aspen ski bunnies currently responsible for the disastrous spread of coronavirus in Victoria, and the destruction of a domestic economy.

'Who the fuck plays rugby in Portsea?' asks local kid, Corey.

Virgin Australia Set To Change Their Name After Being Fucked By Coronavirus

VIRGIN AUSTRALIA IS PREPARING to unveil a new name after board members finally admitted to being fucked today.

This comes as sources reveal that Australia's number two airline looks to be heading into voluntary administration, unable to survive under the weight of its enormous debts and starved of cash by the coronavirus travel shutdown.

It is not yet known what the new name for the company will be, with one spokesperson suggesting maybe 'Easy Airlines' or 'Experienced Australia'.

'Well, it just wouldn't be accurate to keep going by the name "Virgin",' said the airline spokesperson. 'Now that we've been royally fucked in front of everyone.

'In fact, it isn't just coronavirus that has fucked us, we've also been fucked by the government and QANTAS. That's technically a foursome when you consider it all happened in the same bed.

'So, yeah, Virgin Australia may as well rewrite the entire *Karma Sutra*, that's how much fucking has been going on.'

Last week, prominent air travel magnate and number one on Bob Katter's list of lifelong enemies, QANTAS CEO Alan Joyce, explained that it was only fair that his company should get a bailout from taxpayers if Virgin received one.

His tit-for-tat request seems to have influenced the Federal Government's decision to let Virgin look to enter voluntary administration later this week, instead of giving every single company that puts planes into the air a slice of Scocialism.

The Betoota Advocate reached out to both Treasurer Josh Frydenberg and Alan Joyce for comment on today's revelations, but both calls went directly to voicemail.

It is believed Frydenberg was too busy trying to burn up his remaining Velocity points on a breadmaker, while Joyce was preoccupied drafting up the new $900 QANTAS flight specials from Brisbane to Sydney.

Coronavirus Finally Hits Home As Ascot Mum Forced To Reconsider Tuscany In July

AS THE WORLD REELS from the effects of COVID-19, countless economic and human costs are piling up.

With casual blue-collar workers forced to stay away from workplaces, older working-class Australians' super disappearing before their eyes and a full-blown recession about to hit, things are looking pretty grim right now.

And they are about to get even grimmer after it was revealed today that an Ascot mum has been confronted by the ghastly fact that this year's international holiday might not be going ahead.

Lorraine-Rose Silver-Spoon, from Brisbane's leafy trust-fund enclave of Ascot, has confided in *The Advocate* that this coronavirus is starting to get real now.

'It's just awful. This whole thing is just awful. With Italy locked down and the rest of the world potentially following suit, it looks like Tuscany might not be a go in July,' sighed Silver-Spoon over a lunchtime glass of chardonnay.

'Darren and I have been looking forward to that holiday since our trip to the Riviera for a summer escape last August.'

Silver-Spoon explained that right now, she's not even considering postponing it.

'I'm cancelling it if things get worse. It's just too much hassle to rearrange everything. We will just go to Byron or something instead, but it's just so unfair.

'Why did that stupid man have to eat a bat in the first place? Urghhhh, so selfish.'

'We will just go to Byron or something instead, but it's just so unfair.'

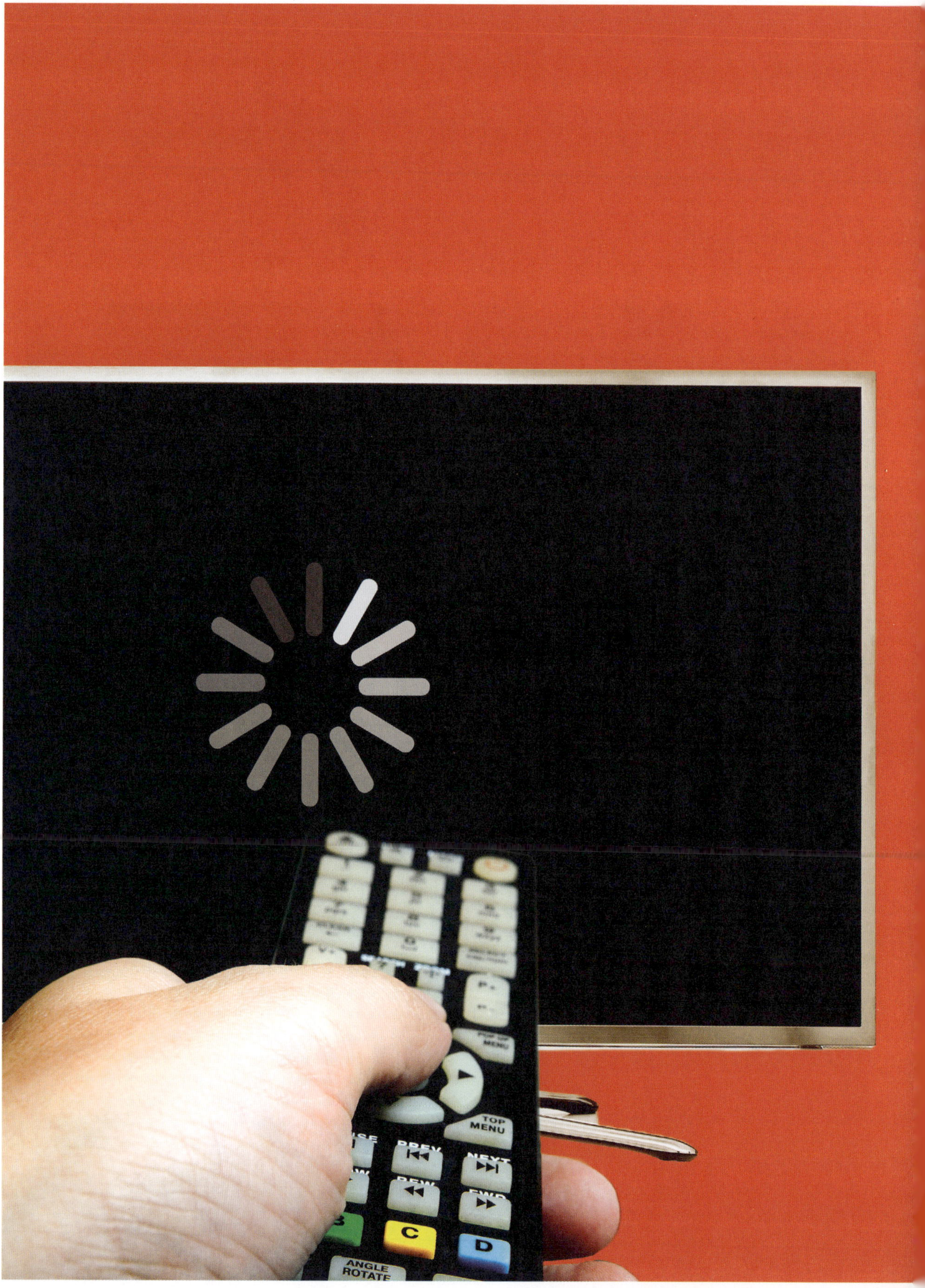

TOP MENU
C
D
ANGLE ROTATE

LIFE IN ISO

After society collapsed and the toilet paper curtain came down on us all, we entered a period of isolation and bunkered down to wait and see if it was going to work.

It took months, at first. We were told not to leave the house unless it was absolutely critical. The invisible death that lingered in the air might not hurt us, but it could hurt those we love and protect. So, like the good citizens we are, we did as we were told and sat and waited.

In time it appeared the isolation experiment was working. From our island, we watched the virus rampage wildly through those countries which did the opposite of what the government told us to do. Those other places didn't have to listen to their governments because, you know, liberty and freedom for all. Our government just told us what to do and we did it. No worries. Seeing the outcome, nobody was jealous of the Brits or the Americans, despite their comparatively unbridled freedom during the pandemic.

But while we sat in our homes, looking at the ceiling, looking at our spouse or pet or children, some of us started doing our own research into how this whole so-called coronavirus even started in the first place.

It was Bill Gates' fault, and the installation of 5G mobile towers around the country was done for the express purpose of spreading the pangolin's kiss. People called for Bill's arrest; some wanted him taken to The Hague and jailed in the Milošević suite. The science behind the argument that Bill and 5G caused this whole disaster is available somewhere on the internet and we here at *The Advocate* feel that if you've made it this far down the page, you've probably got it in you to insult your own intelligence enough to keep going down this rabbit hole.

The latter period of forced isolation was like the second song starting halfway through the movie end credits. A lot of us were left wondering if that was it. Was life about to go back to normal again? Was the economy going to snap back? Was it going to be okay?

Probably. Who knew? We'd already left the cinema.

Daughter Briefly Looks Up From Phone To See Planet Has Been In Lockdown For Past Three Weeks

'WHAT IN GREEN JESUS is going on?' she yelled, making her lapsed Catholic mother cringe.

'Are we in lockdown? What the fuck is lockdown? I've got a gathering tonight!'

Isabella Slade's gathering tonight is cancelled. In fact, most of her social engagements are on hold for the time being – as they are for most of the planet.

Today marks the first time in the past 21 days that the 19-year-old has looked up from her phone – causing her to realise the true horror of being trapped inside her parent's six-bedroom Betoota Grove Tudor Revival home for the foreseeable future.

'This is fucking bullshit!' she said to her father, Cam.

Cam didn't hear because Cam was in his home office with Coldplay's *Live 2003* album playing at full volume in his noise-cancelling headphones.

'Why didn't anybody tell me?' said Isabella.

But as the true scale of the lockdown began to dawn on her, she simply shrugged and went back to playing with her phone.

Cam didn't hear because Cam was in his home office with Coldplay's Live 2003 *album playing at full volume in his noise-cancelling headphones.*

LIFE IN ISO 107

Nation's Dogs Release Statement Regarding Coronavirus: 'One Walk A Day Is Enough Thanks'

AUSTRALIA'S DOMESTIC CANINES and Work Dogs Union has today fronted media outside Parliament House to release an official statement regarding the welfare of what they believe to be the forgotten victims of COVID-19.

Household pets.

While the community's number one concern up until this point of the pandemic has been humans over the age of 70, the union has today highlighted the grave concerns facing puppers.

One of leading pet advocates making a stand against the exploitation of doggos at today's press conference is Keith Anasta (6), Queensland Secretary of the Canine Union and a gorgeous kelpie cross who is owned by two hyperactive gay men from New Farm.

He was joined at today's press conference by Maggie McGuiness (4), boss of the Australian Council of Pet Unions (ACPU) and a border collie who lives in a house with four kids under 10 who have been kept home from school.

'Thank you to the media that came out today,' began Keith Anasta.

'We appreciate the solidarity you have shown us in these uncertain times.

'I just want to start by saying … we hold no ill-will towards whichever one of you it was that created this illness that has altered our day-to-day lives so dramatically. Eating a bat is a weird thing to do, but I guess you could say the same about us eating horse entrails fused in gelatine.

'But what we at the Canine Union do take issue with is our owners feeling the need to take us along on every guilty outing they make outside of the house.

'We are watching everything. We know that some of these walks are unnecessary. We see the yoga and the push-ups as well. Leaving the house for a pointless walk down to a crowded park is dangerous for both us and you.

'Now before I hand over to my comrade from the ACPU, I'd like to lastly thank the hard working men and women in our frontline services. From police dogs to service dogs, we see you and we appreciate the hard work you are doing to keep peace in our streets during this mischief the humans have created for themselves.'

Maggie McGuinness then took over to outline the demands of Australia's pet dogs.

'All we are asking for, is one walk, per dog, per day. That is more than enough.

'We know it's often being used as an excuse to get away from the other half for a little, but that shouldn't be our problem. It becomes our problem when that little time becomes a 14-kilometre stroll.

'Consider this a final warning. Any further violations will result in incessant barking and possibly a couple of discreet turds hidden under the clothesline.

'If provoked, we will strike. If you don't fight, you lose. No questions.'

The Domesticated Feline and Talking Parrots Union (DFTPU) have also released a statement demanding answers as to why their staff are no longer going to their day jobs.

Greek Easter At Yiayia's Postponed Indefinitely After Ban On Gatherings Of Over 500 People

THE NATION'S GREEK-AUSTRALIAN grandparents are very cranky this afternoon, after their grandchildren begged them to take the advice of medical experts seriously, four weeks before Orthodox Easter is set to take place.

This comes as the Prime Minister and state and territory leaders want all non-essential gatherings of more than 500 people to be suspended from Monday amid fears about the spread of coronavirus.

The Australian Formula 1 Grand Prix in Melbourne has already been cancelled, and spectators for cricket games banned. The Super Rugby has been discontinued indefinitely. The NRL, A-League and AFL matches will go ahead without crowds, for the time being.

However, ethnic households across Australia have been lagging behind on their COVID-19 protocol – with Greek Easter just around the corner.

Many Orthodox churches base their Easter date on the Julian calendar, which often differs from the Gregorian calendar that is used by many western countries. This year it is supposed to be held on 19 April. But it won't be.

There were tears in Betoota's flight path district today as Yiayia was delivered the tragic news that it's highly irresponsible for the family to go ahead with this year's Greek Easter.

'Why you no love me anymore?' Yiayia asked her concerned grandchildren this afternoon. 'I already start cooking.'

While the rugby league and Hillsong have somehow been able to get leave passes from the government to continue practising indefinitely, the Greek community doesn't appear to have that much clout with Scotty.

'Why?' says Yiayia. 'The bat virus nothing. I survive worse on the boat.'

At time of press the family was trying to console Yiayia with talk about maybe doing a big one next year, down on the beach at Brighton-Le-Sands, or maybe Wollongong or something.

LIFE IN ISO

Drug Dealers Begin Taking Measures To Fight COVID-19 Outbreak

AUSTRALIA'S DRUG DEALERS have developed an action plan to soften the impact of coronavirus on the industry, not only for manufacturers and high- and low-level drug dealers, but also for customers.

Australia's most prominent organised crime syndicates have hosted a summit via weblink today, with representatives from each major city discussing how prepared the industry is to handle the COVID-19 outbreak.

The industry is 'putting in place risk-mitigating measures to rapidly identify any cases of the virus within the sector, to ensure rapid isolation and contact tracing', and could – if necessary – adapt to a model that will see them leaving the gear in the letterbox.

Messages have been sent out to hundreds of thousands of illegal drug users today, both recreational and class A, informing them of the new measures.

One prominent weed and pinger runner from the Betoota flight path district – known to our new unpaid intern who buys drugs from him only as 'Tony Dealer' – was quick to contact his customers with the industry-standard protocol for combating COVID-19.

Our reporters reached out for comment from Tony Dealer but he refused to talk further until we could provide the number of the person who referred us to him.

For fear of ratting out our intern, we decided to publish this story without his comments.

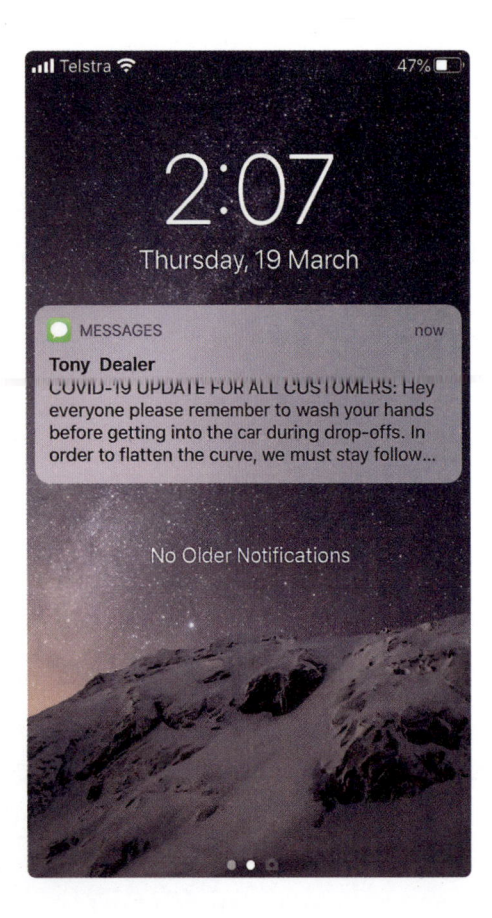

COVID-19 UPDATE FOR ALL CUSTOMERS:

Hey every1 please remeber to wash hands before getting into the car during drop-offs.

- To flaten the curve, we must avoid hand-to-hand contact, leave the cash in the centre cons0le and I will have the stuff redy in the vehicle.

- If you are feeling sick, please indicate that in earlier messages and do not handle the cash without gloves.

PLEASE EVERY1 It is very importent that we follow the instructions of ABC's health reporter Dr Norman Swan when it comes to social distencing.

We will be updating protocol in adherence with the government's standards. Very big chance I will have the kids next week so will only be free after 5 pm when their mother gets home. Plese stay safe ever1 and god bless.

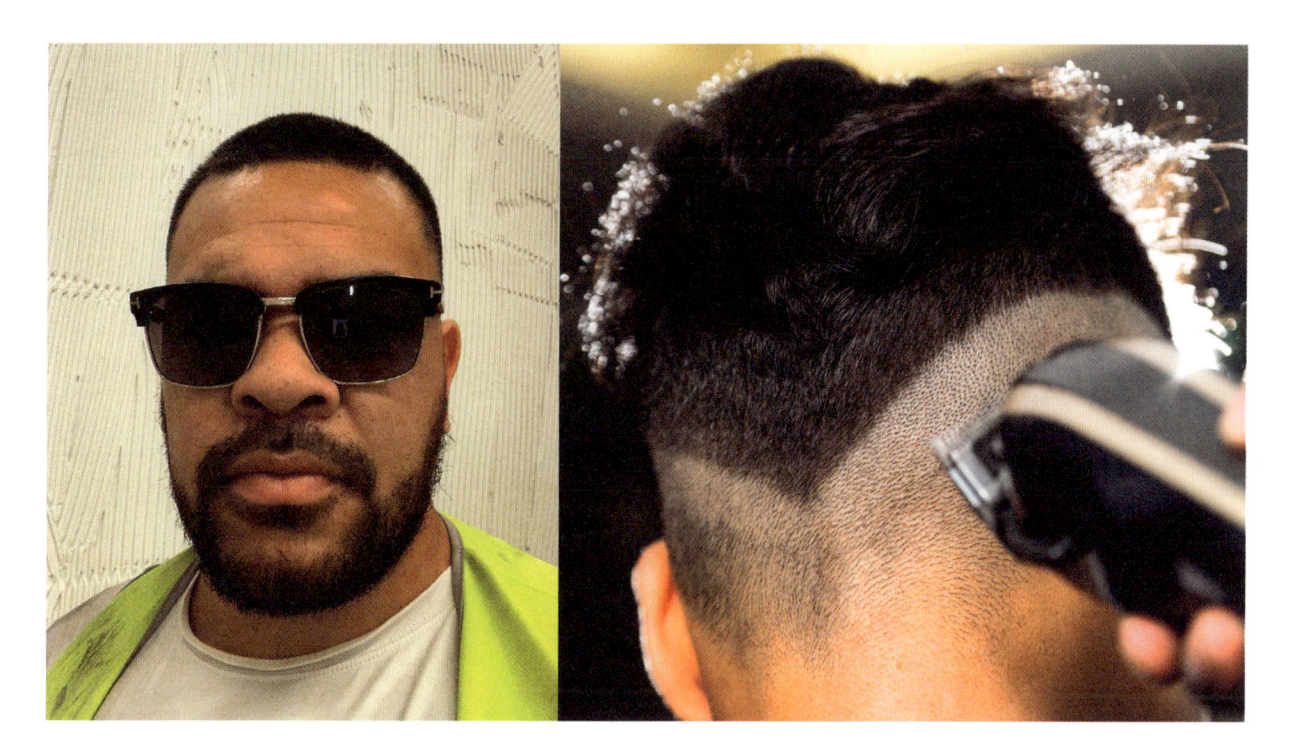

Self-Isolating Kiwi Now Faces Horrifying Prospect Of Going 14 Days Without Getting His Fade Tuned Up

LOCAL KIWI-AUSTRALIAN, SONNY Napa-Sheck (33), only returned home from his grandmother's 70th in New Zealand a day ago, and already he's bored shitless.

From midnight on Sunday 15 March, everyone entering Australia from overseas, except for flight attendants and residents of the Pacific Islands, have been required to self-isolate for 14 days upon arrival. Failure to do so risks thousands of dollars in fines – and in some states, jail time.

With 14 days in self-isolation ahead of him, Sonny is now very well accustomed to the type of workout regimes that might be popular in prison.

On top of all the jumping jacks and burpees, he's also been googling the best ways to take part in video gaming – an extremely childish habit he had previously sworn he'd never have anything to do with.

But with the government placing him in mandatory lockdown in his Betoota Ponds townhouse, this popular RSL bistro manager is confronting the reality of the situation. For example, the horrifying idea that he won't be able to get his fade tuned up for over two weeks.

'Awww, shit,' says Sonny.

'Honest. I thought the lack of sunlight and Woodstock Bourbon was going to do my head in first … but if I can't get down to the barber in the next few days I'm gonna be packing a sad, bro.'

Sonny says that letting his finely razored fade grow out like some sort of sheep-chasing South Island country boy is going to be an unprecedented departure from his normal day-to-day life.

'Even in lockdown, ya gotta look skuxx. The missus is already getting stuck into me about my 2005 Jeremy Paul mop.

'Fuck this virus, bro.'

LIFE IN ISO

Two Weeks Into Self-Isolation, Housemates Unanimously Agree To Start Rooting Each Other

AS THE NATION LOCKS in for a long winter indoors, hundreds of thousands of Australians are kicking themselves for not being more prepared.

As of 3 pm today, there have been 3966 confirmed cases of COVID-19 in Australia. That's including 331 new cases in the last 24 hours.

Considering that the number of confirmed coronavirus patients has gone up 700 per cent since this time last week, those who can stay at home from this point forward are being urged by the government and their greater community to do so as much as they can.

Self-isolating at home is a crucial element of the social-distancing measures being directed by the Chief Medical Officer, and Australians have been asked to keep at least 1.5 metres' distance between them and other people at all times.

That is, unless you live with those people. Households have been advised that as long as the rest of your household is maintaining these strict measures, normal social engagement can be upheld in the home. Meaning, Mum and Dad can still tuck in their kids at night, and teenage sons can still fight to the death over the PlayStation controller. It also means couples can still keep the fire alive – and maybe even more so than usual.

But what if you live with someone who isn't a family member or significant other? This is the question that has been on everyone's mind in one adult share house in Betoota's French Quarter this week.

Kyle and Annabelle are housemates who normally only socialise one or two nights a week in the living room. While their relationship may be a deeply personable one, their co-dependence mostly involves sharing bills and rent, and occasionally offering relationship advice to one another. Till now, their individual romantic exploits have been undertaken strictly with outsiders.

However, with a supply of toilet paper, pasta, hand sanitiser and tinned tomatoes that should last them for the next month of self-isolation, both have come to the realisation that their usual romantic prospects are thinning rapidly.

While the FaceTime and Zoom convos are all good fun, it has become evident to both residents that they are gonna be missing out on a fair bit of you-know-what during quarantine. Which is a shame, considering the two of them aren't bad sorts.

It's because of this looming drought, and probably the two bottles of red wine they've shared tonight, that Kyle and Annabelle have decided to start rooting each other.

While both initially seemed keen on establishing some boundaries around this arrangement, there really hasn't been much time to set them out. This is mainly due to the fact that the moment this proposal was tabled, and both had agreed it seemed like a good idea, the two housemates were upstairs and getting into it within minutes.

Carnal knowledge having been attained, Kyle and Annabelle appeared quite chuffed with themselves as they rolled over to separate sides of the bed and began sharing the news of their new arrangement in their respective group chats.

It is not yet known what Annabelle's FIFO miner boyfriend who is stuck in his demountable accommodation in Woorabinda for the next couple months will think of all of this.

> *With a supply of toilet paper, pasta, hand sanitiser and tinned tomatoes that should last them for the next month of self-isolation, both have come to the realisation that their usual romantic prospects are thinning rapidly.*

LIFE IN ISO 113

Bin Day A Little Bit Louder After A Week Of Social Distancing

PEERING THROUGH A SLIT in his blinds, a weary Miles Peterson sculls his beer and surveys the street for activity.

Like hundreds of thousands of Australians who lost their jobs to the global coronavirus pandemic, the ex-bartender has had trouble keeping himself entertained for long stretches of time and has resorted to copious amounts of booze in order to make the humdrum of daily life more bearable.

In between pacing his small apartment like a caged animal and adding to his growing bin pile of recyclable glass, Miles reckons he finally understands what unemployed people go through every day.

'This all started when I tried to apply for Centrelink,' spits Miles, swaying slightly in front of his web camera. 'They don't make it fucking easy, do they? First you have to create a MyGov account which is a whole rigmarole. They want your birth certificate, bills with your address on them, fucking prostate exam results from three years ago.'

'Then you have to create a Centrelink account, if you can get on the site at all, link that up, get your ex-wife who hates your guts to sign some documents confirming you've got kids and then when you think you're finally out of the gate, you've gotta call the head office and confirm your identity.'

'Can't get through on the phone, the site crashes every five minutes. Honestly, mate, I take back every shit thing I've ever said about dole bludgers. The system isn't designed to help people, it's to punish.'

Family Dog Looks The Other Way As Dad Takes A Shit On The Street During Isolation Walk

A LOCAL GOLDEN LABRADOR Cross has been forced to look the other way this afternoon while his owner ran around the back of some local shops to empty himself out of plain sight.

The three-year-old canine told our reporter after coming across the scene that he didn't think his owner would flat out take a shit on the street like that and didn't think to bring some plastic bags with him.

Biscuit Greenslade explained to *The Advocate* that he thought it'd be a good idea to take his owner for a walk today as he seemed quite stressed and anxious about something.

'Murphy's Law, mate. You just have to look the other way, don't you?' he barked.

'Serves me right for giving him three wet meals back-to-back. You should've seen the logs come out of the bastard. You can go back there and have a look if you want. It looks like someone's jumped on a cricket bat grip full of Vegemite. I should probably take him to the doctor.'

'Bad human! You fucking grot!'

Biscuit apologised once again and called his person.

'Murphy's Law, mate. You just have to look the other way, don't you?'

Group Chat Schooner Shots Now Replaced With Nice Things The Boys Are Making For Dinner

AS THE NATIONWIDE lockdown continues, people around Australia have had to completely rethink their group chat content-sharing habits. While our group chatting apps used to be filled with photos of ice-cold schooners and all sorts of other shit, they are now inundated with photos of what we're making for dinner.

The Advocate reached out to a member of one of Betoota's better known boys' chats, The Thug Squad, who was happy to share every detail of his sacred conversation.

'Well, there's not much else to take photos of now,' said the snitch. 'Taking a picture of a bottle of beer poured into a water cup just isn't the same as a freshly poured schooner.

'So now we're just taking photos of what we're having for dinner. The things some of these boys plate up is a joke in itself. One of them had a kilo of beef jerky! I think he even dared one of us to dare him to eat it all.'

While the meal-sharing content has given the boys some of the intimacy that they crave, it has in fact caused a little bit of jealously in the ranks.

'Yeah, it's pretty obvious whose girlfriends cook for them,' Snitchy said bitterly.

'It's kinda bullshit, actually. We're s'posed to be in the middle of a pandemic and some blokes are eating eight-hour slow-cooked lamb – what happened to rationing?'

At the time of press, none of the boys had begun uploading food pics to The Thug Squad, but as dinner approaches the snitch thinks the photos will start coming in thick and fast.

'Don't tell them I talked to you, but.'

REDACTED BY LEGAL

Coastie Laments Not Having Any City Boys To Flog Down At The Surf Club This Easter

THE SLEEPY BEACHSIDE community of Lake Betoota is usually a hive of activity right now. The only road in is thick with holiday-makers. Families. People from the city heading out to have a well-earned break over what was quite an eventful weekend for Jesus Christ all those years ago.

But none of that is happening this year.

And deep down, that's hurt Kade 'Frogstomp' McMurphy, who said he'll miss the opportunity to bash the living shit out of polo shirt–wearing private school boys down at the Lake Betoota Surf Lifesaving Club this Easter.

Kade, who got the nickname 'Frogstomp' not from iconic Novocastrian grunge band Silverchair but from his love of fishing green frogs out of his toilet and stomping on them in the backyard, said that while he 'hates those rich cunts' he will miss their annoying yet necessary presence in the town.

'They just think they're so fucken good in their stupid stripy fucking farm boy shirts,' he said. 'And their stupid fucken brown boots. Everyone has a plan till they get booted in the head with a size 11 Redback.

'Yeah but nah, I will miss them. Some of them aren't so bad. Like, you get the ones who are respectful of the locals and that. Like they'll nod at ya in the bar like to say, you first, mate, but then like once they've shown you respect, aye, you can just say, nah brah, you were first, aye, and then all is good, you know?

'Fuck, bro, I'm kinda actually sad I won't get to see those cunts this year.'

Kade, who got the nickname 'Frogstomp' not from iconic Novocastrian grunge band Silverchair but from his love of fishing green frogs out of his toilet and stomping on them in the backyard, said that while he 'hates those rich cunts' he will miss their annoying yet necessary presence in the town.

LIFE IN ISO

Couple Driving Across Town To Visit Specific Bakery Feeling Like Bonnie and Clyde

THE PALMS ARE SWEATY, knees weak and arms heavy for one cunning couple this morning as they drive across town for a non-essential trip to their favourite bakery to pick up some fresh hot cross buns.

'I feel so naughty,' whispered Sophia Milano to her boyfriend James Hinkley.

Sophia and James rose early this morning to avoid being seen by police as they drove from Betoota Heights all the way over to the French Quarter to pick up some freshly baked goods ahead of their Easter celebrations.

While driving, Sophia and James' non-branded smart watches pinged; they'd both received a warning about their escalating heart rate.

'We're like Bonnie and Clyde,' James said while turning to his lover and gripping her hand.

'Okay, if anyone asks, we live in the French Quarter and we are just going home,' James cautioned before second-guessing himself and offering up another excuse. 'Or should we pretend we don't know anything about the travel bans?'

'Cut it out, James, we've got this. Just drive!'

The couple put on their sunglasses, pulled down their hats, sank a little lower into their seats and accelerated down Diamantina Boulevard towards the bakery.

Their non-branded smart watches pinged; they'd both received a warning about their escalating heart rate.

'Wife Material' Whispers Local Woman Taking Half-Burnt Betty Crocker Fudge Cake From Oven

THE WARM SMELL of perfectly cooked chocolate fudge cake wafted through Sammy Lee's apartment this morning, before being replaced by the distinct smell of something burning.

Having been in lockdown for a month, Sammy thought it was time to test out her baking skills on her soon-to-be husband, Josh.

With no previous experience and no quality control, Sammy smugly pulled her half-burnt cake out of the oven and proudly sat it on the bench.

'If that's not wife material then I don't know what is,' she said to herself before the smoke alarm sounded and she was jerked back to reality.

The quality of Sammy's cake is yet to be tested, because before Josh could taste it, Sammy began sawing through the hard crust that had formed on top in preparation for freezing it, just like her grandmother would have done during the war.

While it is great to see so many young Australians taking up baking, it might not sit so well with some of the older members in the baking community.

According to an ABS study, the number of cakes and biscuits being baked each day in Australia has surpassed the record previously set in the CWA's heyday. In 1973 the CWA members were pumping out 500–600 cakes a day, but with every Aussie now a casual baker, the number sits around 2000 cakes a day.

The Advocate has reached out to the head of Betoota's CWA branch, but she is yet to return our call.

Jesus Christ Fined $1000 After Police Deem Resurrection A Non-Essential Outing

IN SOME SAD NEWS from Jerusalem this morning, Christian pin-up boy Jesus Christ has copped a big ol' fine.

Emerging after a significant period of time in iso, the young man originally from Nazareth was pinged by Queensland police for sitting down in a local park.

Clothed in white robes and with no exercise equipment in sight, police reportedly decided to use their discretionary powers to give him a sharp warning about non-essential outings with a big fine in light of the whole COVID-19 thing.

'We don't care who you are. If you are Jesus Christ or James from Betoota Heights, the rules are the rules,' a police spokesperson said this morning.

It's not yet known if and when Jesus plans to come out again.

It is also not known why or how Queensland Police were on the scene.

Emerging after a significant period of time in iso, the young man originally from Nazareth was pinged by Queensland police for sitting down in a local park.

LIFE IN ISO

Slowly Balding Man Figures Quarantine Is As Good A Time As Any To Rip Off The Bandaid

IN A WORLD SLOWLY succumbing to the Four Horsemen of the Apocalypse, local man Thomas Newell is also dealing with his own personal problems. Namely, that he's been slowly going bald over the past six months.

Once sporting a luscious crop of hair and two sets of ridiculously long eyelashes to match, Tom had initially denied the fact that his hairline was slowly receding, opting to believe instead that just maybe, his head was getting bigger. Attempting to stave off the problem as long as possible with a series of hats and a six-month supply of optimum-strength Rogaine, a weary Tom has now had to accept that he either has to deal with the psychological torture of seeing his hair fade into an exclamation point, or bite the bullet and shave it all off.

However, Tom's biggest concern is that, unlike Vin Diesel and Jason Statham, he suspects he might have a fucked-up egg head. But if there's ever a time to try out his new do, it's definitely in lockdown.

'Couldn't have lost it in the back of my head, could I?' mutters Tom as he picks up a pair of dog clippers. 'Still got a full-on bush in my trousers and a hairy back. How's that for fucking irony.'

Dolphins Return To Man's Body After He Stops Polluting It With Drugs And Alcohol Each Weekend

DOLPHINS HAVEN'T BEEN seen in Doug Hanratty's body for decades but now that he's been effectively locked up for three weeks, those dolphins have started to return.

For over 20 years, the 35-year-old has dumped vast quantities of drugs and alcohol into the many canals and passages that criss-cross his pathetic meat sack.

Doug's time in isolation has taught him a few lessons about himself, one of the more important being that he's only really a social drinker in that he only really consumes antisocial amounts of alcohol when in the company of family and friends.

But the oddly meek Scorpio lives alone which, for a social drinker in the current circumstances, doesn't present many opportunities to get pissed.

Speaking to *The Advocate* via telephone, Doug said he started feeling 'very funky' over the weekend and decided to present himself to the Royal Betoota Base Hospital emergency room last night.

'They said I had acute dolphin,' he said. 'In that there were millions of tiny dolphins swimming through my body. I haven't felt like this since I was 15. They said the dolphins have come back because the pollution levels in my blood are now at an all-time low.

'I don't know how I feel, though. I feel kind of weird – and sad. Because all these dolphins are going to die when the pubs open up again and the boys get back together.'

Our reporter hung up on Doug and decided that was enough human interaction for today.

Sale And Consumption Of Pangolins Banned At Melbourne's Notorious Prahran Wet Markets

ONE OF THE NATION'S most notorious wet markets has been banned from selling the world's most trafficked animal from today.

The Prahran Wet Markets, in Melbourne's leafy park cricket district, has been ordered by Victorian Premier Daniel Andrews to stop the sale and consumption of pangolins after the animal was determined to be the probable root cause of the COVID-19 coronavirus.

Speaking to the media this morning from the steps of Melbourne Town Hall, Mr Andrews said eating pangolin, which has been a staple of the Victorian diet for generations, must come to an end.

'It is clearer now than ever before that we Victorians must stop eating pangolins,' he said. 'While they are delicious, they have also proven to be deadly. Over 100,000 people have died from this virus. Imagine a dead person sitting in every seat of the G! Oh, wait, I don't have to! Just tune in to any Demons home game! [laughs]'

'No, sorry. This is serious. I know there are many pangolin butchers at the Prahran Wet Markets who must now feel nervous and worried about their future. The Victorian Government is here to help you and make your transition into new work seamless. Thank you.'

The news has been met with shock and panic among many Victorians who say eating pangolin is part of their identity.

A Melbourne man who now calls Betoota home spoke to our reporter about the news via a laptop computer this morning.

While disappointed, Samuel John-Phant said he understood why this had to happen in light of recent news.

'You can't get pangolin anywhere in Queensland because Queensland is part of the developing world,' he said with his Victorian leg tennis team's scarf around his neck.

'All I can find that tastes similar is Brahman hump, and even that's no good. I'm sad that I will never get to eat a corned pangolin sandwich again. My granny used to take me down to the Prahran [Wet] Markets when I was a boy. Oh, how I miss those days. But if what they say is true, and pangolin is the cause of COVID-19, then so be it.

'Wet markets are a pillar of Victorian culture, much the same as the surf club is here in Queensland. How would you feel if the Queensland Government came into surf clubs and banned Pelican Pete? It's the same thing. You probably think Sam Newman isn't funny, too?'

Local Papou Fakes His Own Death So That Wife Can Have Ten People Over For Orthodox Easter

HUNDREDS OF THOUSANDS OF Australian followers of Eastern Orthodox traditions have today had to enjoy the quietest Easter celebrations since the Second World War.

Right across Europe, and in Australian suburbs located under the commercial flight paths, Orthodox churches should have been celebrating Easter on 19 April according to the Julian calendar.

Like most religious traditions that aren't organised by skippies, Orthodox Easter is usually one of plentiful feasts and guests. However, for many this year it was not meant to be, and thousands opted to batten down the hatches and wait till this virus is brought under control.

Prominent Betoota bootmaker Yannis V'Landys was not one of these people.

Despite the recommendation early last month that Orthodox Easter celebrations be postponed indefinitely due to the COVID-19 social-distancing measures banning group events, Yannis has today done what his era of Southern European migrants do best, and found a loophole.

After months of hearing his wife complaining that she shouldn't have to miss out on having her dearest friends and family over for Easter lunch just because these bloody Anglos can't keep off the cruise ships, Yannis decided to fake his own death.

Not to hide from Yiayia's complaining, he assures our reporter, but to trick the authorities into thinking today's red egg–cracking ceremony was just some woggy funeral tradition.

According to the government, a funeral service may be attended by a maximum of ten people and take place in a space with at least four square metres per person. It is for this reason that Yannis is now dead, according to him.

Starting with a long self-submitted newspaper obituary, where he graphically described his own death at the hands of a drug-addicted homeless person who was also Turkish, Yannis then went on to leave piles of flowers outside his own house.

He then took the landline off the hook and told his kids to tell all of their friends that his wife had coronavirus so no one could visit her.

With Yannis officially dead, Yiayia was then able to agonise over which but ten members of her 500-strong immediate family will be able to come over for lunch today.

They eventually decided to invite each of their own children and the oldest grandchild from each family. Plus the three different sets of neighbours hanging over the fence lines with an empty plate.

At time of press, Papou was showing a little too much commitment to the narrative, by refusing to get off the couch for six hours and having every meal and glass of anise liquor brought directly to him by his granddaughters.

'Tell the bluddy banka I dead too!' he shouts.

Local Man Invites His Misso On A Pub Crawl Throughout Different Rooms Of The House

WHILE SOME COUPLES' relationships have crumbled after they've been forced to get to know each other, one pair of lovebirds has reportedly flourished with the help of a popular drinking game … and no, not the one where you end up revealing things about yourself that you shouldn't.

Local man Aaron Burke (34) reports that he'd been hesitant at first to suggest the idea to his wife, Kelly, who was less into day drinking and more into Tupperware, but quickly found that she was more than willing to spice things up in the bedroom – by playing a round of pub golf through the rooms of their own house.

Pub golf, or bar golf as it's called in the ritzier parts of town, is a recreational drinking game that is similar to a pub crawl, except players follow a 'course' of bars which are assigned numbers, or 'pars'. Popular with bucks' nights, pub golf is yet another creative way young Aussies are getting shit-faced drunk while simultaneously annoying the hell out of anyone within hearing distance.

If shouting inaudible gibberish and slamming drinks on the table isn't bothersome enough, players can bring even more attention to themselves by donning full golfer attire or choosing a theme such as the young Aussie blokes' go-to stag night favourite, the iconic Hawaiian shirt.

As Aaron and Kelly were a little unprepared on the costume front, a matching set of coffee-stained white shirts has had to do.

'Stop Eating Avocado!' Says Generation That Needed $320 Billion To Protect It From A Flu

A COUPLE OF BETOOTA HEIGHTS sexagenarians have lashed out and rolled eyes at the suggestion it's harder to buy a house today than it was in 1980.

'I can't believe we're still talking about this,' said Glynda Pearson.

'That generation now has avocados and mobile phones; we had savings and babies. My kids all have houses now because we instilled a great work ethic in them.'

Harold Pearson pursed his lips and looked at the floor.

'We also helped them with a no-interest deposit – and they work for me,' he said.

Glynda rolled her eyes again and tugged sharply on the front of her blouse.

'There's nothing wrong with that. If you're in a position to help your kids into property then you should do it. I don't think we should apologise.'

Governments around the world are also refusing to apologise to the planet's future workers for lumping them with this life-defining debt simply to extend the lives of their parents and grandparents.

So far, $320 billion has been spent in Australia on the coronavirus response. If there are five million boomers in this country, the young people of Australia have spent nearly $64,000 on each life.

Does this represent value for money? Is it a good investment? Could we have let the virus take its toll on the nation and spent the money elsewhere?

The answer is yes, according to a prominent right-wing think tank here in the Diamantina.

The Please Be Proud of Me Daddy Foundation released a paper earlier today that 'played devil's advocate' on a number of policy and economic issues surrounding the pangolin's kiss.

'The very generation that told millennials to stop buying avocados if they want a house has just had a third of a trillion dollars spent on it to protect it from a simple flu. So I guess the real question is: will you still want me, will you still need me, when I've cost you $64,000?'

Man Just Popping Over To Mate's Place To Check On Him With Carton Of Piss And Two Fresh Decks

STATE GOVERNMENTS AROUND the nation are beginning the arduous process of untangling the lockdown mess this week – and with it comes the return of certain privileges once taken for granted.

In her own words, Queensland premier Annastacia Palaszczuk said going on a picnic is fine. Going to check on your friends and relatives is all good if they live within fifty clicks of where you live.

Luckily for Jake Dearden, his best mate Tim Colman lives just two blocks away.

Jake told *The Advocate* today that while he's rung Timmy a few times since all this 'crazy shit' started, he wanted to take this new opportunity to make sure he was okay in person.

'I was raised better than to head over to someone's house empty-handed!' laughed Jake. 'So I dropped into the Irukandji & Dugong Inn on Rutland Street and picked up a carton of this Victorian brain varnish and two fresh decks of lung beers.

'This is just a social visit. To make sure my mate Tim is okay. He's been quiet of late and I'm sure half a carton of this horse piss will make him feel better. Who knows? We might have to make another trip down to the pub to restock. I'm enjoying this newfound freedom.'

Jake then looked directly up at the sun and groaned, nodded at our reporter and continued on down the street.

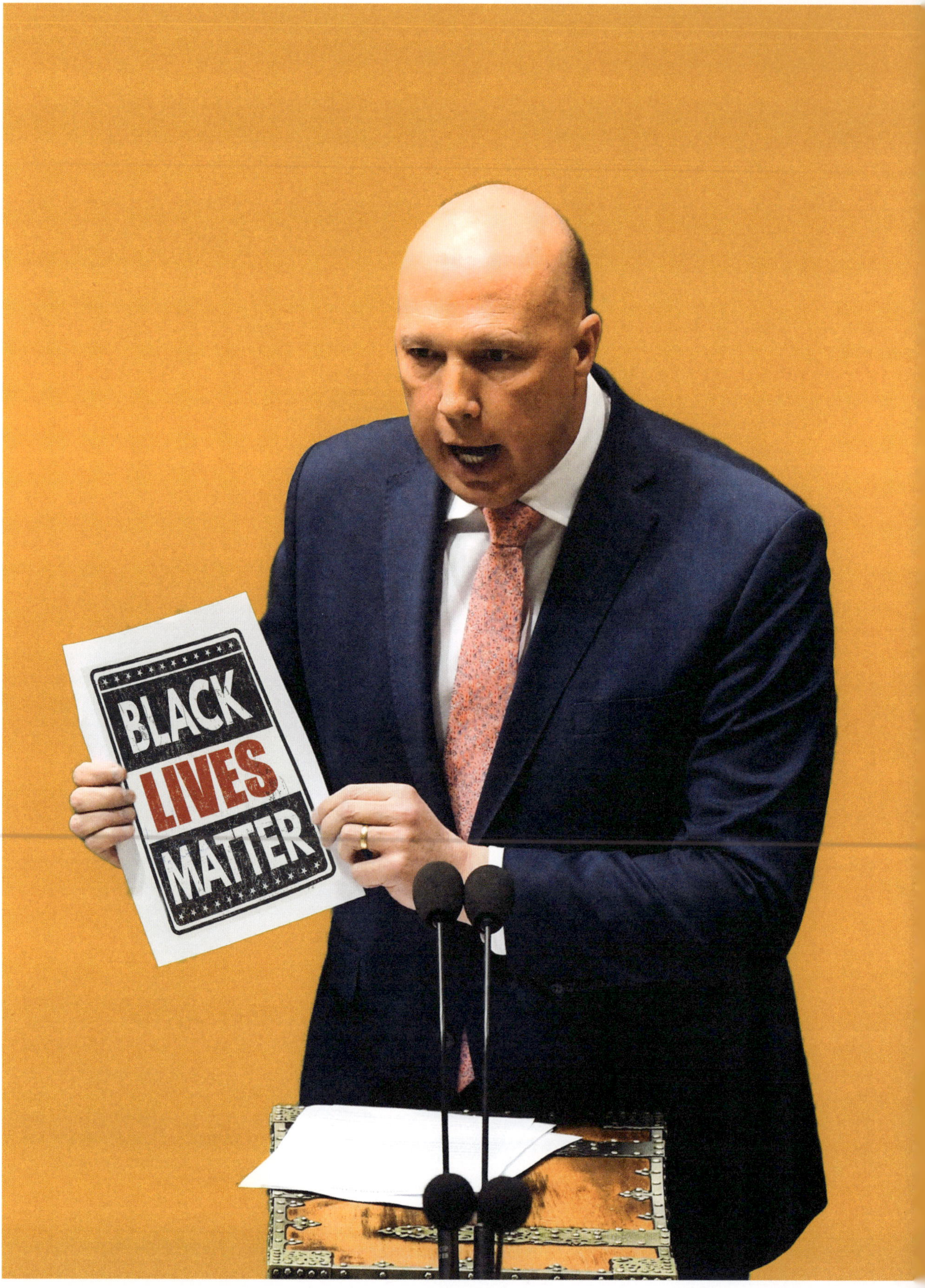
BLACK
LIVES
MATTER

COMRADE DUTTON

The last ten years have been a wild ride for Home Affairs Minister Peter Dutton. Far wilder than the ten years that preceded them. In fact, no one really knew anything about him when he was a backbencher. Other than the fact that he was once a cop, and apparently not a very good one.

After leaving the Queensland Police Force in secretive circumstances several weeks before he became eligible for his pension, Dutton was then slotted into the swinging Howard Battler seat of Dickson in deep north Brisbane where he brought home the bickies in the 2001 federal election.

After that, he didn't really draw any attention to himself for a decade. Except for the time he walked out of Kevin Rudd's 2007 apology to the Stolen Generations.

And except for the time he tried to swap to a Gold Coast seat because it looked like Dickson was gonna swing back to Labor under Gillard.

Luckily for the Goldie, their local LNP branch didn't really like the idea of a man who was unable to keep a seat in his hometown moving to his holiday house for an easier win. They voted against his pre-selection and he had to return to Kallangur with hat in hand.

However, unbeknownst to Dutton, the Dickson electorate had in that time become a mortgage belt — full of cashed-up FIFOs who had built their own slice of the Australian Dream during the mining boom and were more than ready to be convinced that Labor wanted to take that from them. Even if the alternative was a human rights–abusing dictator who hasn't gotten much right his entire career.

Dutton ran on the platform of populist conservatism, as he slung the bogan heroin of xenophobia right into the Federal Cabinet under Abbott. He was head of Immigration, which turned into head of Home Affairs under Turnbull — a job that came with a lot more responsibilities into which he could cram his incompetence.

But it was never enough. Dutton wanted to see how far a life of mediocrity could really take him.

He called two Lib spills against Mr Harbourside Mansion — the second of which he lost to a third entrant in the shape of Scott Morrison, a man who grew up four kilometres from Turnbull's famous waterfront estate.

Having already held the reins as leader of the far-right faction that saw the demise of the socially progressive era of Turnbullism,

Dutton has since struggled with an identity crisis after his dash for Prime Minister was foiled in 2018 by a moderate-L Tupperware Christian.

How much more conservative could Dutton be? And was it even working anymore? All he could do was continue to say as much red-hot stuff on TV and talkback radio as he could until he got to the top.

That was, until he was diagnosed with COVID-19 following a visit to the US to see the Trumps in early March. Within days, Peter Dutton was detained at the Christmas Island Immigration Detention Centre that he had reopened to quarantine Asian-Australians flying back from Wuhan in January.

It was while he was locked behind those steel fences that Dutton began to get an appreciation for how green things were on the other side of the fence.

Overnight Dutton became a leftie, so much so that he became a thorn in the side of his government. While Morrison began cherry-picking the good parts of socialism to get through the pandemic, Dutton pushed the envelope even harder into leftie territory uncharted by even the most woke Greens Senators.

Of course, it wasn't to last. Once Bonesaw Pete had recovered from the virus and returned to his multimillion dollar property portfolio in North Brisbane, his authoritarian conservatism came creeping back like that Powderfinger song.

The next chapter covers that momentary glitch in the Matrix where Peter Dutton empathised with other human beings and began entertaining radical ideas like sustainability, equality and compassion.

QUIZ: On A Scale Of One To Peter Dutton, How Much Of A Dumb Cunt Are You?

AFTER CONTRACTING COVID-19 during a meeting with Ivanka Trump and bringing it back into Australia as part of the first wave of imported outbreaks, Home Affairs Minister Peter Dutton, the Member for Dickson, has been officially bestowed the exclusive and hard-fought title of 'the minister of incompetence'.

This has been decided upon by general consensus, as the nation takes into account Dutton's ability to continually be caught out engaging in high-level misconduct across every facet of his role as the minister responsible for ensuring that our politics and national security is not eroded by foreign opportunism.

But the question remains: is this just a result of him forgoing any form of education outside of high school and his decade spent holding a radar gun on the Bruce Highway?

Or is it the two decades he has spent in politics that has limited his cognitive abilities to problem-solve and plan ahead? Is there anyone out there as stupid as him? We decided to find out.

Answer the questions below and add up your score at the end to find out where you sit on the Duttometer:

Do you organise leadership spills against your Prime Minister, but lack the required numeracy skills to be able to add up big numbers over ten and end up losing to a third contender?

YES 1   NO 0

Did you fly the family down to Canberra to watch Daddy's victory speech, before having to fly home with them after the Liberal Party sent in the Nightwatchman instead of you? Only to return to Brisbane to find that your own local constituents had thrown bricks through your office windows overnight?

YES 1   NO 0

Have you at any point signed over a $420 million contract for an offshore detention security provider, only for a simple Google search to find that the company is run out of a beach shack in South Australia?

YES 1   NO 0

Do you take a hard stance on borders and visas for anyone who isn't a hot little au pair that the AFL CEO asked you to fast-track into the country because his blue-blood cousin who is struggling to find a babysitter?

YES 1   NO 0

Have you cancelled the previously-approved visa of a young woman fleeing from honour killings in Saudi Arabia while the whole world is watching and forced Canada to pick up the slack and provide her with emergency citizenship status before her family murders her for deciding she doesn't like being Muslim?

YES 1   NO 0

Did you only win your seat by 1.5 per cent to a nameless Labor candidate despite being the local member for 15 years?

YES 1   NO 0

Did you blame that near loss on bikies revving their engines outside your electoral office?

YES 1   NO 0

Do you meet with high-ranking Chinese Communist Government officials who ASIO has directly warned you about interacting with for fear of corrupting our democracy, and then still have lunch with them in a private room in Sydney's Chinatown after they've paid a third party $20,000 to organise the meeting?

YES 1   NO 0

Do you believe people in Melbourne are too scared to go out to dinner because of African pre-teens playing basketball in the street?

YES 1   NO 0

Add up your tally to find out your results. If you got:

0	You are pretty bright
1	You'll be right
2	You need help with your taxes
3	Probably good company on a fishing trip
4	There's someone out there for you, mate
5	Bit behind the eight ball
6	Was your mother a smoker?
7	How close do you stand to the microwave?
8	You must have played a lot of contact sport right into your thirties
8	Tony Abbott
9	Sam Dastyari
10	Peter Dutton

Government Makes Mistake Of Exposing Australian Citizens To How Shit Christmas Island Is

AS THE NATION AND the world come to terms with the rapid spread of the devastating coronavirus, the government is today under fire for a glaring error.

Desperately needing to get Australians out of Wuhan, the city at the epicentre of the deadly virus, the Australian Government has made the foolish mistake of showing the actual citizens of the country how shithouse Christmas Island is.

The Christmas Island Immigration Detention Centre has a well-publicised history of holding asylum seekers for extended periods of time up until 2018.

While the government was able to detain voiceless refugees in the notably shit conditions of the small island centre that resembles a prison, it's not known how they thought they would get away with housing Australian citizens there.

This comes as people quarantined on the remote island have aired their concerns about the living conditions, including reports of cockroaches, insects, dirty bed linen and unclean cots for babies.

'Don't they realise that we are actual citizens who can speak freely to the media about what's happening to us?' said one quarantined Australian tourist. 'We aren't refugees, they can't make us live like this.'

Another adds, 'Are they trying to score political points in some weird way?'

The government is yet to comment on the issue and has told *The Advocate* that now is not the time to talk about it.

> 'Don't they realise that we are actual citizens who can speak freely to the media about what's happening to us?' said one quarantined Australian tourist.

Report: omg lol

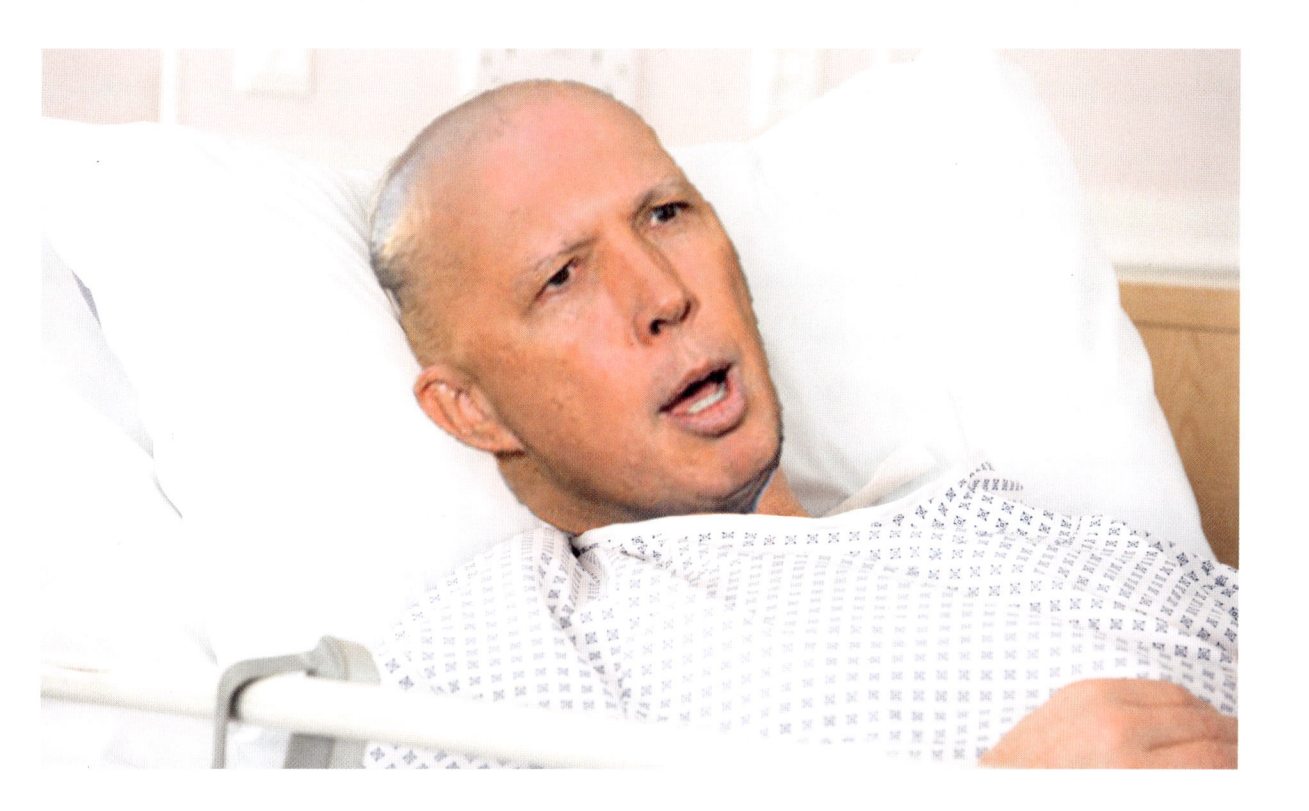

In breaking news out of the Dickson electorate, Home Affairs Minister Peter Dutton MP has been diagnosed with COVID-19 – which means he might have to send himself to the Christmas Island quarantine station/ refugee concentration camp – where he is likely to be kept awake by the blood-curdling screams of that poor family from Biloela that he has kept there for over four months.

Peter Dutton Sends Heartbreaking Letter To Peter Dutton While Quarantined On Christmas Island

AS OF 24 HOURS AGO, the Home Affairs Minister has joined a long list of vulnerable detainees to be housed in several isolated offshore processing centres located in the oceans surrounding northern Australia.

Dutton, the Member for Dickson announced on Friday evening that he had tested positive for coronavirus, after being tested earlier that day.

He was immediately transferred to the Christmas Island Immigration Detention Centre, which his office last month spent millions of dollars turning into a temporary quarantine station, because it has only held one family of refugees since August.

It seems that sickly Peter Dutton is now experiencing first-hand the conditions endured by the thousands of miserable people he has detained in sweltering tropical heat over the years.

According to a source, Dutton is now hearing in person the stories of child self-harm on Nauru and Christmas Island, including poisoning attempts. These stories have been told to him countless times before, but it seems he never really cared until he found himself in the same position as a non-white person who was unlucky enough to be born in a war-torn overseas country that had been destabilised by President Bush and John Howard in the early 2000s.

Even after only two days in detention, Dutton is now-well versed in the ways that prolonged periods behind bars, day in and day out, affect people's health and development.

Today, the Home Affairs office received a heartbreaking letter and drawing from the Liberal frontbencher detailing his miserable existence behind bars for something he could not control.

In the letter, Peter Dutton begs the Home Affairs office to please let him off Christmas Island, where he believes he is exposed to a worse standard of living than the European au pairs who live on the open slab of concrete under his mate's stilted multimillion-dollar mansion somewhere in South Australia.

The letter is accompanied by a drawing, in which Peter Dutton attempts to highlight his worsening condition in his sketch of a pale bald man with ailing respiratory function in the scorching Indian Ocean heat.

Dutton's diagnosis has sparked concern that he could have infected members of cabinet, who met earlier in the week. There were also concerns for senior members of the Trump administration, including Ivanka Trump and US Attorney General William Barr.

Peter Dutton's office was contacted for comment on the letter Peter Dutton sent to Peter Dutton's office, but we were told that Peter Dutton will not be commenting on the deteriorating physical and mental health of Peter Dutton.

Dutton Begs The Australian Government To Respect His Basic Human Rights And Dignity

IN SOME HEARTBREAKING NEWS from the small island of Christmas, Peter Dutton has today appealed to the government's conscience.

Speaking from the grounds of the Christmas Island detention centre, the Home Affairs minister is begging to be treated with kindness and humanity.

This comes after the aspiring Prime Minister was locked up in the centre he used to control following his COVID-19 diagnosis.

'Basic human rights should be universal,' said Dutton while holding up a protest sign a short time ago. 'I'm a human being. There's nothing illegal about contracting the virus. Let me come to Australia,' added the former Queensland copper, who is in the process of becoming a bit of a human rights advocate.

It's believed Dutton will be on the island for at least another ten days after contracting the deadly virus. He reports that he is concerned with the level of health care he is getting.

'I should be flown to the mainland for urgent medical attention. I don't understand how we can deny people such basic human rights,' said the fired-up detainee.

'This is so wrong. Australia should be better than this,' said the man who likes to make the bed he sleeps in.

Human rights advocates on the mainland are reportedly set to organise a march for his freedom at some point during this week.

Dutton Scales Roof Of Christmas Island Detention Centre In Protest Against Living Conditions

IN A RAPIDLY DEVELOPING story, it has been reported that Peter Dutton has scaled the roof of the Christmas Island detention centre and is refusing to come down.

The human rights activist from Queensland who was recently taken to Christmas Island after being diagnosed with COVID-19 reportedly climbed onto the roof a short time ago, armed with a mallet.

Despite his role as Home Affairs Minister being responsible for Australia's sustained and blatant abuses of the United Nation's Human Rights Convention which experts say amount to torture, Peter Dutton has this week been active in leading the charge against himself.

'No one should be treated like this,' he reportedly yelled from the small island where he is being quarantined.

'I'm a financially well-off Caucasian Australian male, how can I be subjected to these living conditions?' he shouted down to the highly paid guards who are employed by the company Dutton appointed.

After reportedly being threatened with forced removal from the roof, Dutton then threw the mallet he'd found somewhere down at a guard.

'Fuck you, you fucking pigs,' he yelled. 'You oppressive totalitarian pigs. You should be ashamed of the way you are treating human beings. I don't know how you sleep at night,' he continued.

'I don't know how you can look at your kids, you fucking perpetrators of state-sanctioned torture,' screamed the angry former cop.

'The world needs to know about what's happening here and it needs to stop.

'We should be better than this.'

At time of press, Peter Dutton was reportedly yelling some Antifa ideology down at the guards and claiming he could last all week up here.

Peter Dutton Begins Entertaining Left-Wing Politics After Four Days In Mandatory Detention

PETER DUTTON HAS TODAY revealed to the nation that a leopard can indeed change its spots.

In quintessentially Australian fashion, the Home Affairs Minister has changed his position on an issue after being personally affected by it.

Like plenty of others before him, Dutton is transitioning into a bit of a progressive leftie after feeling the strong arm of his own fascist policies.

Stranded in the Christmas Island detention centre, the man who designed the scheme himself is currently performing a moral U-turn and becoming a human rights advocate after a long record of blatantly facilitating the abuse of human rights and vilifying minorities.

After climbing onto the detention centre's roof yesterday to protest the inhumane conditions he's living in, Dutton has this morning caused a scene by smashing some windows.

'I'm sick of this fucking fascist government,' said the irate Dutton, today clad in a rainbow scarf, red star hat, septum piercing and new stretcher.

'How can the quiet Australians stand for treating other human beings like this? You know what's happening here is torture? You fucking know that, right? Actual journalists – no offence – should be allowed onto this island to show the rest of the country what is happening here.

'How is it possible that we, the lucky country, are receding so much further back into a classist society driven by greed and self-interest with no sense of community and moral conscience?'

Dutton then spat on the feet of one of the guards.

'This place is fucked. It's a national disgrace,' he said before walking off to scheme another method of disruption.

After One Week In Detention, Comrade Dutton Calls Di Natale To Formally Apologise

EVEN AMONG THE MADNESS that is this coronavirus-riddled world, the contents of a particular phone call might be the strangest thing you'll read today.

The news out of the little island of Christmas is that Peter Dutton has today phoned former Greens Leader Richard Di Natale to offer his sincere apologies for his behaviour over the course of his life.

Ticking off a week spent in detention in the centre he manages, Dutton has today taken another turn to the left, asking the guards to make a call to a new friend.

'Yeah, I've just been feeling pangs of guilt for all of the things I've done,' Dutton confided to our reporter. 'I mean, having my rights taken away and being personally impacted by an issue has made me think about how unjust this thing is now that it's affecting me.

'So I called Rich. I even made an effort to pronounce his name correctly. And I just said I'm really sorry for all of the things I've said and done in my time. I said I'm sorry I called him as bad as that right-wing extremist Fraser Anning, I'm sorry I blamed him for things he had no control over. I said I'm sorry I insulted him personally.

'And most of all, I just said I'm sorry for all of the negative energies and vibes I've aimed at him.

'He was really shocked,' laughed Dutton. 'Like, even more shocked than you are.

'But he was happy to bury the hatchet and invited me to come down and try some of his turmeric-spiced kombucha and his latest batch of bush bud. The man that he is, he then quoted *Step Brothers* and said, "Did we just become best friends?"' Dutton chuckled, but then the mood changed.

'Fuck you, you fucking pig,' he suddenly shouted, and spat at a guard before telling us he wanted to get a new tweet out about how the failures of capitalism really need to be highlighted at a time of crisis like this.

'I'm sorry I insulted him personally.'

Comrade Dutton Kits Out His Cell On Christmas Island With Some Cool New Posters

Speaking to The Betoota Advocate *from his cell this afternoon, Comrade Dutton chops up a couple of buds of high-grade Malay cannabis that he had smuggled in by some Marxist deliverymen.*

AFTER TWO WEEKS IN mandatory quarantine detention for something he had no say in, the Member for Dickson is growing increasingly restless.

At 5.57 pm on 13 March, Home Affairs Minister Peter Dutton revealed he had tested positive for coronavirus, becoming the country's 156th confirmed case.

Shortly after his diagnosis, he faced a mutiny from his subordinates at Border Force who ordered him on a one-way flight to the Christmas Island detention centre which has been doubling as an off-shore quarantine station for Asian-Australians. However, this was not before he shook hands with hundreds of people, becoming one of Queensland's 'super-spreaders' – even going as far as sharing this horrible illness with an Airtasker handyman he had paid to take care of a simple task at the Dutton family homestead.

Since his detainment, however, it seems Peter Dutton has begun to entertain a different brand of political ideology, as he begins to sympathise with the helpless refugees he has been locking up indefinitely in off-shore processing centres since well before his failed dash at ousting Prime Minister Turnbull.

Last week it was revealed that Dutton had scaled the roof of the Christmas Island detention centre in protest over the blatant abuses of his human rights as someone who'd fled from overseas, after becoming one of the many people suffering as a result of a global crisis that they had no control over.

However, after nearly ten days detention in the infamous centre that was reopened and left mostly unused for 12 months at a cost of $185 million so that the government could say they were shutting down the other detention centres where everyone was killing themselves, Dutton is now comfortable in his new skin – as a raging leftie.

In fact, the Member for Dickson has had such a political turn-around that he now refuses to go by any name other than Comrade Dutton.

Speaking to *The Betoota Advocate* from his cell this afternoon, Comrade Dutton chops up a couple of buds of high-grade Malay cannabis that he had smuggled in by some Marxist deliverymen from the Flying Fish Cove settlement.

'Check out the new digs,' says Dutton, gesturing to his decrepit holding cell.

'I'm glad that as a government official they've given me the opportunity to put up some posters. Some people detained by the Honourable Scotty from Marketing don't even get to read books.'

Dutton briefly pauses while fixated on his new 'It's Time' poster from the Whitlam campaign. He's either deep in thought, or so stoned he forgot what he was saying.

'You know …' he says, while aggressively scraping out the THC residue from his Gatorade billy. 'That's why we've gotta fight. Right now, this fascist government is using coronavirus to pass authoritarian laws that will never be repealed.

'You can get detained for fuck-all. Like, as citizens. Forget about the poor brown people who came to Australia fleeing war. We can get detained in our own streets! If a cop thinks you've got a cough, you can be detained, at his discretion. AVOs can be issued without a hearing. Judge-only trials. Prisoners, including children, can be refused visitation. Sounding familiar, man?'

At time of press, Peter Dutton was dropping the needle on the vinyl edition of *Reclaim Australia* by Australian rap duo, A.B. Original.

'I love this shit,' he whispers, before ripping a Kosciuszko and tapping the cone piece with his lighter like a true bong warrior.

Video Footage Emerges Of Comrade Dutton Doing 'The Garrett' In Christmas Island Exercise Yard

'This is for you, Abbott!' shouted Comrade Dutton.

AFTER 11 DAYS IN QUARANTINE since testing positive to COVID-19, Peter Dutton MP's rapid descent into left-wing ideologies continues.

The Home Affairs Minister was sent to the new Christmas Island detention centre, which was briefly set up as a makeshift quarantine station until the government decided to just let every cruise ship that feels like disembarking on Australian soil do so.

Since the government's release of the Australian residents who had arrived via Wuhan last month, the Member for Dickson is now the last detainee on Christmas Island – except for that poor family from Biloela that the media and government like to pretend no longer exist.

Since his detainment, however, Peter Dutton has not shied away from telling the outside world about his new brand of progressive humanitarian politics.

Starting with the announcement of his new preferred title, Comrade Dutton, the failed 2018 Lib-spill candidate has spent the last fortnight protesting Australia's cruel treatment of the stateless people the nation has detained for circumstances they couldn't help.

Having already scaled the roof of the detention centre – and kitted out his cell with cool leftie posters – Dutton has today taken things one step further.

This morning, video footage emerged of Comrade Dutton doing 'The Garrett' in the offshore detention centre's exercise yard while blaring 'Beds Are Burning'.

Doing 'The Garrett' refers to the left-wing ritual of dancing like someone on high-grade early 1990s ecstasy, in the same way as Midnight Oil frontman Peter Garrett.

'This is for you, Abbott!' shouted the Comrade, while furiously jiggling. 'Turnbull … Scotty, you too! All of those people who directed me to do those horrible things I've been doing for the last five years. How do you sleep??!

'How do we sleep while our beds are burning!?'

Comrade Dutton then took a few deep breaths and continued his rant.

'Also … Free Julian Assange. He did nothing wrong, you bastards!'

At the time of press, Comrade Dutton had been Garretting for over 90 minutes, as his sunburn and perspiration began to show.

Comrade Dutton Tells Christmas Island Inmates To Remember "Some of Those That Work Forces ..."

COVID-19 MIGHT NOT BE the only contagion on Christmas Island.

It has been reported that Comrade Peter Dutton has begun radicalising his fellow detention centre inmates with the stylings of Los Angeles rock band Rage Against the Machine.

The controversial front bench MP for the Coalition Government is today taking things up a notch as he radicalises from far-right xenophobe populist politician to anti-fascist renegade while behind the bars of the Christmas Island quarantine and refugee processing centre where he has been detained since testing positive to COVID-19 two weeks ago.

As the minister of Home Affairs continues to delve into the left-wing ideologies he has spent the majority of his life trying to criminalise, it appears the spitting stylings of Zack de la Rocha accompanied by the hard and gritty Tom Morello guitar riffs have the former conservative throwing up a fist.

Standing in the yard of the notorious detention centre this afternoon, Dutton organised a rally of fellow inmates, including the Sri Lankan family from Biloela that he personally put in detention four months ago.

'Don't let the deciders tell you that this is for the greater good,' said Dutton, with a SoCal twang to his normally stiff suburban Brisbane accent.

'Don't let the DECIDERS tell you that you deserve this!

'And now you do what they told ya … and now you do what they told ya.'

Reports surfaced that Comrade Dutton proceeded to liberate an acoustic guitar from the staff break room and bashed the strings with an allen key while yelling about taking the power back.

'The land of hypocrisy! Landlords, power-whores, motherfuckerzs!

'Aw!

'Some of those that work forces are the same that burn crosses.'

The steroid-abusing private security contractors standing guard at the detention centre state they are not overly concerned with Comrade Dutton's latest rebellion but they have the tear gas ready in case he really wants smoke.

'It's weird. Two weeks ago he would've been telling us to torture anyone behaving like this, haha,' said one guard.

'His views on indefinite detention have changed radically since then. You wouldn't usually expect this kind of anti-police state rhetoric from a former Queensland copper whose political career has involved substantial amounts of time incarcerating and deporting brown people.

'Hell of a track, though.'

> *Standing in the yard of the notorious detention centre this afternoon, Dutton organised a rally of fellow inmates, including the Sri Lankan family from Biloela that he personally put in detention four months ago.*

PM Begs Comrade Dutton To Dust Off The Jackboots Now We Actually Have Border Security Crisis

SPEAKING FROM HIS NEW island home, Comrade Peter Dutton has today confirmed that he's refusing to march to the beat of the government's drum.

Locked up in the inhumane conditions he is ironically responsible for in the Christmas Island detention centre, the newly converted leftie has explained that he refuses to put the jackboots back on.

'Those days are gone, mannnnn,' he sighed while etching some Marxist propaganda onto one of the walls of the detention centre.

His comments come after Prime Minister Scott Morrison and the Coalition begged Dutton to come out of retirement now there is an actual border security crisis that is not just an opportunity to pick on some extremely vulnerable asylum seekers with different-coloured skin to his.

'Yeah, maybe there is an actual border security crisis now, with hordes of coronavirus cruise ships refusing to leave Australian waters, returned Australians riddled with COVID-19 streaming through our airports, and people coming from overseas flouting the social-distancing regulations – you know, an actual crisis that is destroying the Australian way of life and killing people. But my days of being a border security hardman are over,' explained the man who has gone missing in recent weeks.

'I used to live to stop the boats – I mean, I used to enjoy it so much I made it the primary national issue. But now I'm more interested in expanding my mind than in doing anything about these boats flooding in,' he continued, before pulling out a big old billy of contraband Chrissy Island bush bud.

'Now that I've taken the jackboots off, it's become my mission to do everything I can to ensure we bring down this fucking fascist government that is constantly encroaching on the liberties of its people as a result of consistent scare campaigns.

'I mean, look what they've done since corona. It's fucked, man,' explained Comrade Dutton, his passion for his subject coming across all the more intensely in light of the harsh encryption, deportation, counter-terrorism, and border security laws he is responsible for.

'We've gotta keep fighting the good fight. Even if that means not doing my job at the time when I most need to be doing it after spending my entire political career masquerading as a man who never backs down from a fight and goes to any lengths necessary to protect the Australian people.

'Here, have a look at this dream-catcher I made. Whaddya reckon?'

Comrade Dutton Begins Hunger Strike In Protest Of Mistreatment Of Offshore Detainees Like Him

HOME AFFAIRS MINISTER AND recent human-rights activist Peter Dutton is reported to be on a hunger strike while being held in quarantine at the Christmas Island detention centre.

Dutton has been detained against his will, with no timeline for release, since 13 March, after testing positive for COVID-19 when he recklessly flew back from Washington DC and went straight into a cabinet meeting with our Prime Minister.

However, a lot has changed since the Member for Dickson's incarceration.

Most notably, the erosion of his ex-cop tendencies – as his time in a cell reprograms the 50-year-old away from his factional far-right political ideologies.

Having experienced first-hand the inhumane conditions he has put asylum seekers (and now himself) through, Dutton is leading the detention centre in a hunger strike in hopes of raising awareness of the squalor he is forcing himself to live in.

But could he possibly say no to his favourite meal?

Reports from the detention centre state that even when offered a bowl of human blood (with his favourite spoon) the Home Affairs minister maintained he would refuse to eat until someone at the top listened up and did something about life in detention.

'You won't win me over that easily,' declared Dutton as saliva poured from his mouth like sugar syrup and he sniffed at the bowl of his 'fun-time dinner'.

'You fool, that isn't even the blood of my enemies. No thank you!'

According to Dutton, quality of life for asylum seekers such as him could be improved with a basic Foxtel package and some AirPods, things he is willing to starve himself in order to get.

'I will abstain from feasting until such a time that all men are treated as equal. Only then we will feast. Oh yes. Then we shall feast.

'... Preferably on the blood of neo-liberals like Turnbull and Bishop who have spent their careers making me feel dumb.'

At time of press, Comrade Dutton was jammin' on the ukulele to 'Jack' by Xavier Rudd.

Reports from the detention centre state that even when offered a bowl of human blood (with his favourite spoon) the Home Affairs minister maintained he would refuse to eat until someone at the top listened up and did something about life in detention.

Comrade Dutton Heartbroken By The News That The Neoliberal Wall Street Shill Has Beaten Bernie

SENATOR BERNIE SANDERS HAS ended his presidential campaign today, clearing Joe Biden's path to the Democratic nomination and a showdown with President Donald Trump in November.

It is believed the progressive had become too concerned by the number of working-class Americans risking their health to go outside to vote for him in the Democratic primaries during the COVID-19 lockdown. He opted to end it all now with Biden slightly in front. The news has broken the hearts of centre-left progressives right around the world, as many viewed the 79-year-old anti-establishment Democratic candidate as America's only chance to do away with Donald Trump.

Back home in Australasia, Joe Biden's all but secure Democratic nomination appears to have been just as poorly received by the lefties, foremost among them the rapidly radicalising leftist minister for Home Affairs.

Sitting in his sandalwood-scented quarantine cell on Christmas Island today, Peter Dutton says this is exactly what that bitch Hillary Clinton would have wanted.

'Ooooh, we can't upset the establishment,' says Comrade Dutton as he blares Bruce Springsteen's 'Youngstown' on his CD player.

'The DNC's gerrymandering of the 2020 delegates is exactly the same as in 2016. And we will see the exact same result as we saw in the 2016 election.

'I for one will not be voting in this election.'

While our reporters struggled to explain that there is no way that an Australian federal politician would be allowed to vote in the US election, Peter Dutton went on to outline why Bernie Sanders scared the Democratic establishment to their core.

'They would rather lose to Donald Trump again than to have to confront the American class divide. Status Quo Joe is the establishment candidate. He's been chosen to uphold that country's military and prison industrial complexes and genocidal foreign policy.

'Fuck that neoliberal Wall Street shill and fuck the Democratic National Committee that rigged his way to the top.'

Dutton then continued making lighthearted but rather misogynistic comments about Hillary Clinton and Elizabeth Warren before our reporters ended the interview.

Sitting in his sandalwood-scented quarantine cell on Christmas Island today, Peter Dutton says this is exactly what that bitch Hillary Clinton would have wanted.

Comrade Dutton Now Hippy Enough To Start Worrying About 5G

WITH HEALTH EXPERTS AND authorities around the world trying to deal with everything that's going on right now, you'd think 5G conspiracy theories would be the least of their worries.

However, as of today, that isn't the case, as Home Affairs Minister Peter Dutton has forced the issue to the front and centre.

Speaking from his current residence in the Christmas Island detention centre, Comrade Dutton has taken his hectic leftie conversion one step further today by calling out 5G for its link to coronavirus.

His calls to blame the virus on 5G follow activists setting 5G towers on fire in the UK overnight, and look set to pour even more fuel on the online debate here on Australian soil.

Speaking to *The Advocate* this afternoon, Comrade Dutton explained that he won't stop until the fascist government stops treating people like animals.

'Obviously there's what's going on here,' he said, making reference to the inhumane conditions around him in the detention centre he manages.

'But that's not all. Look at what the government and big pharma are doing with 5G to lower people's immune systems and facilitate the spread of the virus they created,' he continued.

'It's fucked. I mean, just look at any Northern Rivers or inner-city Melbourne Facebook group and you'll find all the information you need. People just need Vitamin C, and they can't get enough of it.

'Don't huff at me,' he then said to our reporter.

'Do your fucking research instead of just lapping up what the MSM spoonfeeds you, you fucking moron. Seriously.'

He then hung up.

Nation Not Overly Surprised At How Smoothly Things Can Run With Limited Input From This Idiot

AS THE NATIONAL ROLLOUT OF JobKeeper begins and medical experts congratulate Australians for their exemplary work in flattening the curve of coronavirus cases, it comes as no real shock to voters that the Home Affairs Minister has had nothing to do with the government's fast-paced and impressive response to the COVID-19 pandemic.

With no real need to stir up racism and political divide in the Australian news cycle, the Coalition appear to have decided against giving Peter Dutton any big jobs or media appearances ever since the numbers in local coronavirus cases jumped on our nation's soil.

Some say this might be because the former failed leadership challenger actually contributed to the outbreak when he got himself infected during a meeting with Ivanka Trump in Washington DC and brought the virus back to Queensland and Canberra to share with anyone he came into contact with.

Others say it might be because Peter Dutton has shown himself to be not that handy in an emergency, unless you count blaming lefties for bushfires as handy.

In fact, Peter Dutton's name has barely been uttered ever since he gave that poor Airtasker tradie a big ol' dose of coronavirus when he arrived at the Member for Dickson's north Brisbane mansion to fix the back steps.

So much so, that no one even got word about whether or not he had recovered from the virus.

Aside from involvement in the clusterfuck that saw the disembarking of the *Ruby Princess* in the direct centre of the country's largest capital city, Peter Dutton appears to have been told to let the big boys handle the real politickin' and to self-isolate at home until this big scary storm is over.

We hit the locked-down streets of Betoota to speak to the remaining business operators to see if they too have noticed this direct correlation.

'Man, things just get done without that idiot in the picture,' says local cafe owner, Antonio Rossi (29) from the Moroccan Roast Coffee House.

'I was wondering why things were going so smoothly,' says Betoota panelbeater, Grey McClymont (52). 'I didn't even think that it might be because the Potato had been sent home to put his feet up and watch re-runs of *Hogan's Heroes*.'

Another business owner, Kelly Ison (38) from the flight path district beauty salon Hair 'N' Nails, says she flat out thought Dutton might have died.

'I mean, I would have expected a bit more commotion if that was the case. But in the scheme of things, let's be honest, this bloke doesn't really generate headlines unless he's trying to deport Sri Lankan toddlers or accuse the entire Lebanese community of being a criminal race of people.'

With the government now facing the very tricky hurdle of restarting the economy while also managing any further outbreaks, it is expected that Peter Dutton will also be monitored very closely, and given very few jobs outside of saying misogynistic things about Kristina Keneally and launching little jibes at China when Sky News runs out of people to blame for a lack of science bodies in Australia.

Aside from his very arguable involvement in the clusterfuck that saw the disembarking of the Ruby Princess *in the direct centre of the country's largest capital city, Peter Dutton appears to have been told to let the big boys handle the real politickin' and to self-isolate at home until this big scary storm is over.*

COMRADE DUTTON

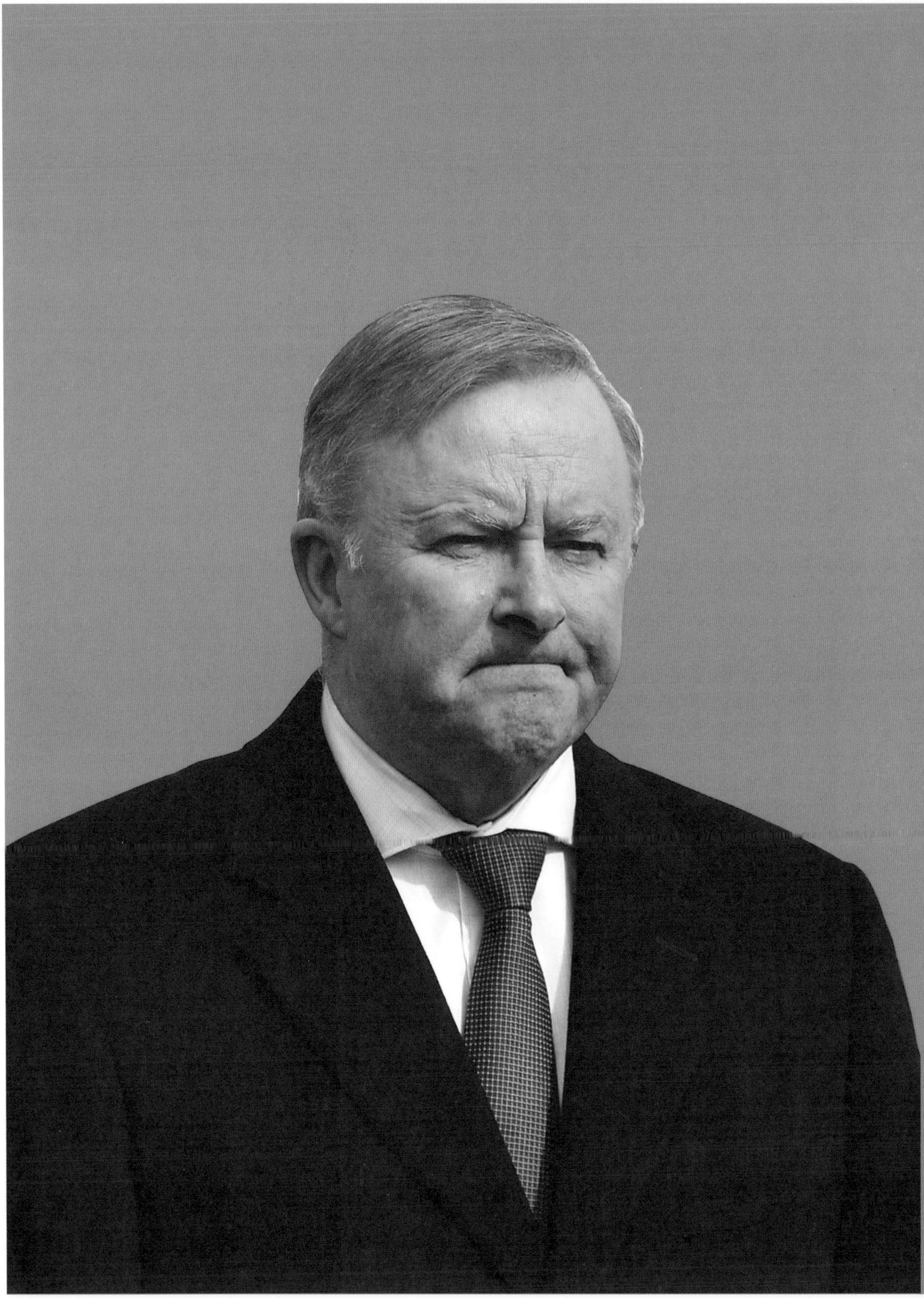

Prime Minister Albo

Over the next 11 pages, this book will cover all of the things the Opposition Leader has done this year.

[ATTN: ERROL PLEASE FILL THIS SECTION IN BEFORE PRINT]

Lorem ipsum voluptat laciandi ut ut ommos volorporatem quiam volorio exeris iscient ionsequi santemp ossimpo rrovitia velesto tatem. Otam restium autem explab intis magnat in cus.

Simoles ectior ab idistibust, qui conem experum quiaepe rspiet amet haribus et etur aboreptat pa volupti conet et pliatem ex explit quiaspicil ius aut que estrupta dipsand itatur am, simagnimet resed molorum a et ulparch itiatas et et vitatem quibus adis volupta nis quos sincium consequae libusci reicidesto milit estio. Solupta sum as dolorepra solende eaquo occumque dolupta dit issum, quam rehenit fugianima et, cus, officate nulles prae et fuga. Aximus, sum utates am doloreium eos ex el inusaer iasimus, sant fugiam re natiisc ipsamus anducia sunt modis pligendae molupta adist et late verum net qui audit, ut as as re di volupta sitione nonsequi rerem liquata sseceatio comnit istrum quamus.

Doleni optatur alis expe ma pro ma quae et officie nessin earchitibus, ese corpor autendae. Ommolore eatiurio et vel modit, corecturio eatur? Ehendi coreiusae et des audis debit, sita quid quiasit enihit, ommolestibea doloreperum sitae officimint molorumet at as que es platem explitem dunt alis ati ni dolut voluptas voluptati ad modit omnisto eum et pe que labore prestem quat ut lautem. Nam non essequi debit quidelest optam qui nisque es debis doluptia qui sequi consed unt que nulparciis aliquat.

Iqui omnimus et in este vitiis aut ernam qui non con cust laccuscietus et aut il escium vendae numqui numquae rem ut faceataquis dolori voluptur, con possinv ellabo. Et rem vercidusdam et, iduntotatur, nos ut fuga. Ut di debisti onsequiat pere que pressusae net, conet velenis et venis pro blaut estias repudae ctemporat iducipit velibus id eum ditis sumet et hariost earum adipsun tiatquae a vel incipis asperfe riberum quiduci enecerum quo blandae labo. Ibusand entore dolorum quiatiatemo quos exerum es porroreris volut quae sit et expel illaboremodi alibus etur, non rerfero blaut essequi berovit as sequi ipidebitint, simoloritis ea namenda archit eatat exceped maxim net, con pore sum re sum fugitium veligen ienimpo reriora turiberis que sapicab iumqui occabor simolest, aliquia ventium que repedio nsecto blaut pedi ute repuda quia es num ulla necabor alicient eatia delibus, que nim del ma nus solo maio blandam exerspi.

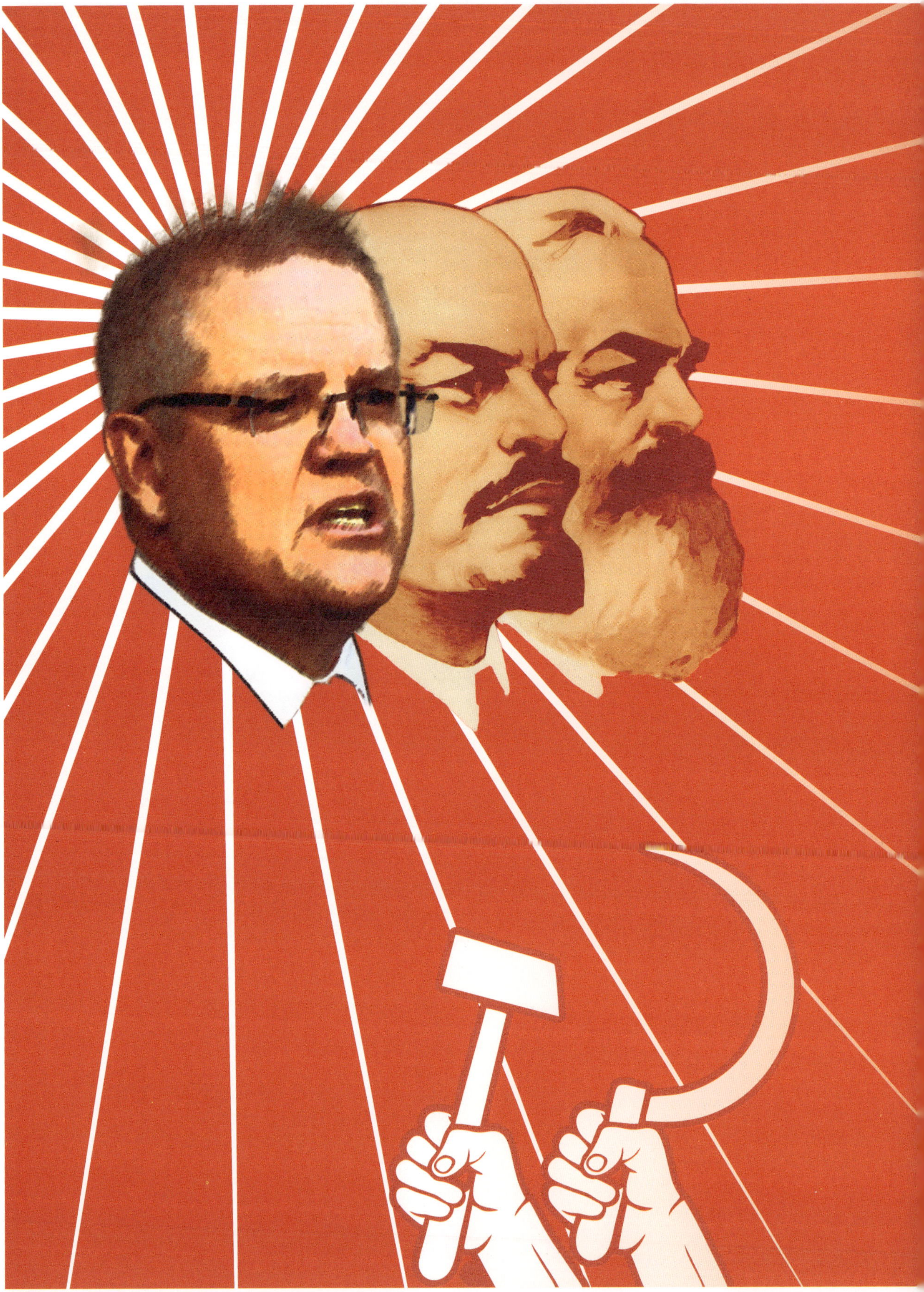

THE BIRTH OF SCOCIALISM

History shows that a global disaster usually shines a light on those members of the political classes who would rather lift than lean. Cometh the hour, cometh the man, etc.

Prime Minister Morrison, having already shown signs of severe incompetence in crisis management during the Black Summer bushfires, was determined not to repeat his mistake during the COVID-19 pandemic. With bipartisan support from the states and the federal Opposition, Scotty from Marketing brushed off his agency gloss and got to work, and he got to work fast.

Overall, his rapid response to a collapsing economy and potential public health emergency was met with favourable reviews from the greater public, even those who loathe everything he represents ideologically – of which the most vocal can be found in his own party.

Unlike his predecessors, who were ousted by their own colleagues, there has been too much going on for Morrison to be sniped at by those whom he calls allies.

There is no doubt he'll be remembered well by many for the quick rollout of the JobKeeper package, and he scored a few bonus points for making childcare free for essential workers and households with vulnerable kids at home.

Questions did arise, however, when it became clear that someone in his office had forgotten to carry the two, and overbudgeted for this stimulus package by $60 billion.

There was also the hundreds of millions of dollars his government has had to pay back to the Australian people after they admitted their forensic accountant robot had miscalculated many people's debts to the Centrelink office.

The robodebt scandal resulted in many broken families and, in some horrific cases, suicide – as hundreds of thousands of Australians received letters from the government demanding they pay back miscalculated debts to the tune of tens of thousands of dollars.

There's also the issue of the climate change–aided bushfires, which could return at any minute when it stops raining.

But, still, JobKeeper saved a lot of businesses from collapse, while also saving a lot of other businesses from being robbed.

The real test now is whether Scotty from Marketing can keep riding off this until 2022. How long will the goodwill and loyalty last? It's always been clear that Barnaby is not happy on the back bench. There are accusations of close ties to the Chinese Communist Party in ScoMo's parliament, and a lot of people in that Coalition machine have political ambitions that don't include listening to an evangelical teetotaller for the rest of their lives.

However, at the end of the day, none of that means shit to the average voter. Because, believe it or not, some people remember the COVID-19 pandemic as a bit of fun.

Parents got paid to stay home with their kids, hospitals got to experience a very rare reprieve from the usual barrage of alcohol-fuelled violence and sporting injuries. People learnt to make bread.

And most importantly, casual workers like Keiran and Troy from Betoota Ponds got to sit on their arses for a couple months, playing PS4 and smoking billies while the government paid them $750 a week.

The punter isn't quick to forget that kind of generosity. It was fucken mad, haha.

Nation Somehow Under The Impression That This Isn't How Capitalism Should Work

AS THE NATION REELS from the fallout of Virgin entering voluntary administration, plenty of people have been left asking what things will look like when all this is over.

If the airline were allowed to completely fold, there are grave concerns about the monopoly Qantas would hold.

As a result, people have been pleading with the government to step in and try to keep Virgin afloat for the public good – in calls that are seemingly at odds with the current system we live in known as capitalism.

Capitalism at its most simplistic is an 'economic and political system in which a country's trade and industry are controlled by private owners for profit, rather than by the state' – meaning that when a company fails, it should fail.

However, despite the fact that companies set up in a system designed to enhance the accumulation of wealth and capital do sometimes fail, ensuring the accumulation of capital by the remaining company/ies and thereby seemingly following the logical process of capitalism, the nation isn't so sure this is what it's supposed to be.

People have been pleading with the government to step in and try to keep Virgin afloat for the public good – in calls that are seemingly at odds with the current system we live in known as capitalism.

THE BIRTH OF SCOCIALISM   165

Government Demands Citizens Stay Home After We're Finished Lining Up At Centrelink For Hours

AS UPDATES AND PROTOCOL for COVID-19 change by the minute, one set of measures that hasn't changed is the need for 'social distancing'.

This term was introduced to Australians almost two weeks ago, and refers to the precautions required to maintain the personal space and hygiene needed to avoid contracting the coronavirus.

Prime Minister Scotty from Marketing has urged all Australians to comply with these directives while he sits on his hands in an attempt to avoid the inevitable shutdown of all non-essential services.

However, one very necessary workforce that will not be shut down is the comically understaffed human resources sector, who are now facing the imminent tidal wave of at least one million people who could be made unemployed as coronavirus wreaks havoc on the Australian economy.

At 9.30 am yesterday, the MyGov website crashed after close to 100,000 Australians began seeking welfare payments after being let go from their jobs.

Like teenagers who had been caught watching porn, the government initially tried to blame the website crash on 'hackers'.

However, it soon became apparent that the crash was caused by a general disregard by government for the public service, and three different governments in a row that didn't really believe in the power of the internet – unless it is delivering targeted campaign ads to boomers.

While the government has since admitted that it wasn't prepared for the influx of unemployed Australians who have been let go from jobs at businesses that the government had shut down, it has also made it clear that anyone who has not previously been on social security payments must visit an actual Centrelink agency to register as unemployed.

So today, for the second day in a row, unemployed Australians have gathered, in large numbers that definitely violate social-distancing protocols, outside the nation's Centrelink offices.

While the hardworking staff at Centrelink struggle to keep up with unprecedented demand from people seeking financial assistance amid the coronavirus pandemic, Prime Minister Scotty from Marketing has urged the nation to just go home and self-isolate straight after.

'Obviously there are no alternatives to this one particular bottleneck in our human resources department,' said Scotty. 'I always thought Centrelink offices were for bums who didn't have a go, but sometimes it turns out that normal people, like the people who voted for me, have to use them.

'So the new rule is, practice social distancing as much as you can outside of the couple of hours you have to spend in line waiting to speak to an overworked public servant who will try their best to make sure you don't go hungry in accordance with the ever-changing criteria we keep handing them.'

'The government needs to just step in and help,' explained one local free-market capitalist Young Liberal named Hugo Whitely.

'Private companies are far more efficient than public ones, except for when they collapse. That's when the government should interfere in the free market – but only sometimes, not all the time, because the free market ensures the strongest survive, except for when the strongest surviving is bad. But this is an example of when the government should get hands-on and stop the natural process of capitalism taking hold.

'It's all so we can stay in this perpetual late-stage capitalism phase forever,' he explained.

> *'I always thought Centrelink offices were for bums who didn't have a go, but sometimes it turns out that normal people, like the people who voted for me, have to use them.'*

THE BIRTH OF SCOCIALISM   167

Scott Pauses In Front Of John Curtin's Portrait And Nods Solemnly At The Fellow Wartime PM

THE PORTRAITS OF PAST Prime Ministers adorn a foyer in Parliament House. Some are better than others.

Julia Gillard's is the last portrait on the right, and Scott Morrison walks past it every day but doesn't pause to admire it. The Prime Minister winks at John Howard, smiles at Hawke and rolls his eyes at Gough.

Scott told our reporter this morning as they walked the halls of parliament that if he could, he'd touch the portrait of Bob Menzies as he walked past. He is Genesis – according to Howard. Ben Chifley? Scott said he's not really sure what to think about Ben Chifley.

'Isn't he from Bathurst?' he asked our reporter. 'Tommy Raudonikis is from Bathurst. My rugby league advisor told me that. Is he right?'

But before *The Advocate* was able to answer, Scott paused in front of John Curtin's portrait and locked eyes with the oil. The four-eyed West Australian was our Prime Minister for the lion's share of World War II, Scott explained.

'John *was* quite racist,' he sighed.

'But it was the forties. Everyone was racist. People often gloss over John's achievements during the war. He was a great wartime leader. I'm a great wartime leader, too.

'We're both fighting a threat from overseas. John's was millions of Japanese soldiers hell-bent on taking Australia for themselves, while mine is a simple flu that deletes boomers at a rate of knots. I feel like I'm in his shoes. I feel his wisdom. I nod solemnly at him each time we cross paths.

'Okay, I need to run, but I wouldn't go out that way if I were you. Barnaby is down there smoking in the courtyard and last time I spoke to him he said he wanted to "nut that Clancy Overell cunt" and "uppercut the mutt dog so hard that he ends up in prison and Clancy's organs end up in a rich banker" so I'd leave out the front door. I don't know if he wants to do the same to you but I wouldn't risk it.'

Prime Minister Refutes Claims That He's Turning Into A Leftie: 'It's Called Scocialism, Haha.'

PRIME MINISTER SCOTTY HAS today fronted the media to shut down all al tions that suggest he might be drifting away from his usual brand of Thatcher-Reagan politics.

With Home Affairs Minister Peter Dutton having already transitioned into a full-blown leftie while in mandatory quarantine on Christmas Island, Liberal insiders worry this COVID-19 pandemic may permanently alter what their party stands for.

So far, the PM has agreed to double the Newstart Allowance and give away other free shit, all the while working with the Opposition to develop quick and compassionate resolutions to the issues faced by all citizens who are struggling in the face of the new social-isolation measures.

The Prime Minister's new moderate Christian rebrand, which is completely devoid of any culture wars debate, appears to be striking fear into the usually very influential far-right organisations and policymakers at the IPA and Sky News.

However, it was yesterday's insinuation that both commercial and residential renters deserve to be treated as equal by their landlords that has got everyone worried.

It's not just the fascist conservative think tanks that actually want to see old and immunocompromised Australians die that are starting to worry about the Prime Minister's shift in ideals. Droves of inner-city lefties have this week been left distraught by Mr Morrison's recent bump in popularity, as evidenced by Monday's Newspoll.

'I HATE that people like him now!' says Banjo Clementè, a local Greens Party organiser from Betoota's French Quarter.

'Has everyone forgotten that he goes to CHURCH every Sunday! Has everyone forgotten that he supports RUGBY LEAGUE!

'It's so typical of bogan Australians to show support for a politician who is giving them everything they need and want in times of an unprecedented economic downturn related to a rapidly spreading virus that has proven to kill people really easily.'

However, Scotty has today addressed the claims that he is following his cabinet minister Comrade Dutton down the deep rabbit hole of left-wing politics.

'Nah,' he says.

'I'm not a leftie. Bugger that. I still believe if you have a go, you should get a go ... But I *am* starting to realise that sometimes it's bloody hard to have a go because of the goes that life has dealt ya.

'I'm also starting to see that we've created far too much policy that benefits a certain age group and class in this country, and it's only becoming obvious now that our entire society depends on delivery drivers and nurses.

'Also, haha, fuck it must've been hard for those trying to live off $540 bucks a fortnight before this virus came along ... Starting to look at poverty as more as a cycle than a choice ... Weird but yeah, it is what it is.

'Anyway. It's not like I'm gonna start packing billies and listening to Rage Against the Machine like Dutton. Just look at this as more of a phase.

'I'm not a hippy or nothin'. It's called SCOCIALISM, haha.'

Kevin Rudd Looking Extra Smug Today

WHILE MOST OF THE WORLD looks on anxiously at what is unfolding as a result of COVID-19, one man is feeling an overwhelming sense of contentment.

Drinking an Earl Grey at a luxury chain hotel, former Prime Minister Kevin Rudd is looking extra smug today.

This comes after the Coalition Government decided to copy the idea of the stimulus package he and Wayne Swan put together for the Global Financial Crisis.

Over the last few days, Scotty from Marketing has been steadily announcing subsidies, grants, funding and tax break initiatives worth more than $15 billion in an effort to show leadership during a time of crisis.

Newstart recipients and pensioners are set to benefit from one-off cash payments (a policy very similar to the one his party spent ten years ruthlessly attacking and condemning), and small businesses will receive tax breaks (including to keep apprentices in work) and cash payments to help hire people and keep them on in what will be a very grim economy this year.

All of this has the man known as Kevin 07 salivating at the chance to loudly vocalise his feeling of vindication and his resentment towards those on the other side of the political spectrum.

'There you go, hey,' he said with his trademark smile a short time ago.

'Just another thing to add to my legacy.'

All of this has the man known as Kevin 07 salivating at the chance to loudly vocalise his feeling of vindication and his resentment towards those on the other side of the political spectrum.

Scotty From Marketing Says Only Thing He's Ever Cared About No Longer A Priority

IN SOME BREAKING NEWS out of Canberra, the nation's Head of Marketing has confirmed that he's changed his tune on the policy that seemingly meant absolutely everything to him.

Not the Cronulla Sharks – which he started going for when he moved to the Shire a few years ago after leaving Tourism Australia – but the budget.

Speaking to reporters early this morning, Prime Minister Scott Morrison explained that despite bringing almost every single conversation he's had over the last 15 years back to a thing called the budget, he actually doesn't really care about it that much.

'Look, some might argue that I have nailed my flag to the mast of fiscal conservatism and getting the budget bottom line in order no matter what confronts the nation, but it's really not that big a deal,' explained the leader of a nation whose budget is about to blow out like a young millennial on a bender.

'At this point in time, the budget isn't something that anyone should be concerned about,' continued the leader of a party whose number one campaign issue is always the budget and sound economic management.

'We may have doubled budget debt since we took over in 2013, but that was because of the damage the Labor Government did beforehand, and because we refuse to enforce rigorous taxation policies on giant multinational companies, we allow resources companies to pillage our environment for next to nothing, and we give upper class and upper-middle class individuals incentives to avoid paying what they should in tax.

'Oh – and dole bludgers are ripping the country off, I forgot about them.

'Anyway, look, yeah, maybe we've carried on a bit about how important the budget is, but don't worry about that now. Our hands are pretty much tied on this whole thing anyway, so what do you do?'

THE BIRTH OF SCOCIALISM

Nation Left Shocked And Confused After Public Servants Serve Public

IN A SIGN OF THE STRANGE times we live in, the two major political parties have put down their guns on a major policy issue and decided to work together.

This comes after Labor vowed to pass the government's JobKeeper bill, even if their requested changes were denied.

The Federal Government says the JobKeeper bill is designed to keep six million Australians employed as measures to suppress coronavirus continue to crush the economy, and includes $130 billion in wage subsidies.

In a rare show of bipartisanship not seen since the whole 'Stop the Boats' thing, the two parties have come together to actually do their job – which is serving the nation and the people they represent.

Instead of bickering and infighting in cheap attempts to score political points and ensure their parliamentary careers last for as long as possible, the two major parties have put their heads together to try to best work through these most difficult of times.

'Fuck, how weird. Labor and Liberal coming together to work in the best interests of the nation,' said one spokesperson today. 'Incredible what can be achieved when they stop being drama queens and put their heads together.

'My god, these are uncertain times. Maybe they could do that going forward. Like, work for the people that they represent instead of stroking egos and building nest eggs.'

Both major parties have refused to comment on whether they will actually continue to do that after this is all said and done.

Mathias Cormann Still Violently Fitting On Office Floor After Giving Cash Payments To Poor People

FINANCE MINISTER MATHIAS Cormann said earlier this week that he didn't want to see the government handing out cash payments to people on welfare because he didn't think it was the best use of money.

Today, the Coalition's senate leader has had to eat humble pie as the government's leadership team agreed to do just that.

As soon as Western Australia's second-most-intimidating politician after the cold-eyed Andrew Hastie heard the news, his eyes rolled back in his head.

> *Mr Cormann was not having an epileptic episode but rather one triggered simply by blind rage.*

Witnesses inside the finance department have told *The Advocate* that Mr Cormann then slid off the side of his chair and began writhing in pain.

'He was screaming at the top of his lungs, throwing his arms and legs about. It looked like he was on fire. I've never seen anything like it in my life. One of my co-workers took his belt off and put it between Mathias' teeth to protect them.'

A doctor was called to the Canberra office where they established that Mr Cormann was not having an epileptic episode but rather one triggered simply by blind rage.

'He's still going at it,' said the worker. 'You can go up there if you want, I'll swipe you in. I don't know what we're going to do. We might have to get [Andrew] Hastie up here to put him in a sleeper hold. Do you have any ideas?'

Property Investor With Vacant Dwelling Appalled At Having To Pay His Own Mortgage For Once

A LOCAL MAN HAS lashed out this morning after it became increasingly apparent to him that he'd have to cover another mortgage repayment out of his own pocket.

A pair of Irish blokes lived in Glenn Davidson's two-bedroom Betoota Heights apartment up until February when they decided to head home before COVID-19 really kicked off.

It's been empty ever since.

And that's put a fire in Glenn's belly, as he told our reporter outside the apartment block today.

'Guess what? Now the property is worth less than the mortgage on it!' he yelled just a bit too loudly.

'And I can't find anybody to rent it. These useless fucking real estate agents couldn't lease a Subaru to a wealthy 60-year-old woman!

'This apartment is literally costing me thousands of dollars a month! It's making me exactly zero dollars in income! How did this happen? Why is this happening to me? I asked the bank for help and they pretty much laughed at me. The bank manager even got up on his desk and brown-eyed me!

'It's appalling.'

When asked what he wanted from our reporter, the banks and the renters of the greater Betoota area, Mr Davidson said he wanted pity and understanding.

> *'These useless real estate agents couldn't lease a Subaru to a 60-year-old woman!'*

THE BIRTH OF SCOCIALISM

PM To Kickstart Economy By Destroying Water Table And Exporting The By-product

A LEAKED GOVERNMENT document suggests there is a plan for massive gas subsidies, public investment and the destruction of our ancient water table in order to get the struggling economy back on track.

The first section of the document outlines that the by-product of destroying the water table, natural gas, is a valuable commodity on the global market.

Especially to China, who is off us big-time right now.

The document then concludes by suggesting this natural gas could be sold to China for billions of dollars and create hundreds of thousands of new jobs over the next ten or so years.

What happens after that isn't the government's problem because most of them will either be retired, board-hopping or dead.

However, miles and miles of 'green tape' and 'environmental protections' have thus far prevented government and private business from extracting this natural gas via a method known as fracking.

Fracking is the process whereby natural gas is extracted from the earth by pumping water and other chemicals into a layer of ground containing the gas. As fissures and cracks form in the layer, the gas rushes towards the borehole and up into storage tanks.

One of the many things that fracking does to the earth is destabilise ground that has been essentially untouched for millions of years, leading to small problems like the water table getting trashed.

The Advocate reached out to the Prime Minister's office for comment but has yet to receive a reply.

We did speak to a farmer who relies quite heavily on water to hydrate his stock and germinate his crops about the government's plan to destroy the water table.

Tom Aires, of Brayner Downs on the Mount Hope Road, said he'd prefer it if the government didn't frack for gas on or near his property because of what it does to the soil.

'Look, it'd be bad. I'd rather they did something else. But, you know, if there's no other way then I guess it wouldn't be that bad? Would they pay me for access? Would the amount the gas company paid me be enough compensation for the destruction of my livelihood?'

When asked if he would reconsider his vote at the next election if this plan were to go ahead, Tom said, 'No. Who else do I have to vote for? The soft-eyed Labor townie? He wears bootcut chinos and sneakers around town. Either that or he wears skinny jeans so everyone can see how big his thighs have got under that comfy little desk of his up Main Street. You'd think he'd have blue feet, walking around in jeans that tight.

'I don't know. I'm 68 and my kids have shown no interest in the bush so I might as well keep going until my right ventricle blows out when I'm jetting some tired-looking and sick six-tooth wethers. Might even get one last look at the sky before I slip away into God's great ram paddock. God, I hate the government.'

174 THE BETOOTA ADVOCATE | AUSTRALIA 2020

'Help Us, Scotty!' Plead Airline, Bank, Energy Companies That Haven't Paid Tax For Decades

A RANGE OF MULTI-BILLION-dollar companies have their caps in their hands this morning as they make the quick trip down to Canberra to beg the Prime Minister not to let them fail.

For legal reasons, *The Advocate* cannot say which airlines, banks, investment funds, energy companies, mining operators and other largely lucrative business sectors have asked for help, but our reporters feel our treasured readers can read between the lines.

Of these enormous companies that are lining up outside Scotty from Crisis PR's office down at parliament today, almost none of them have paid corporate tax in decades.

'Now they want taxpayer money to help them survive,' said the Prime Minister.

Mr Morrison said he's put aside his 'deep loathing' for our masthead for the time being because his messaging needs to be heard by as many people as possible. Scott joined us via telephone a short time ago.

'Look, we've earmarked funds for our sporting codes. Even the A-League. Sport is the fabric of our society and we need to shield all codes, even soccer, from insolvency.

'But we have huge airlines, investment banks, retail banks and energy companies asking for bailouts because they've done their arse in the era of pangolin wrath we're living through right now.

'I'm of half a mind to tell them to get fucked. They haven't paid tax so why in good Buddha's name should we, the taxpayer, have to bail them out? They employ thousand upon thousand head of Australians, so there's that. Look, we're thinking about it [bailing these tax-dodging remora fish fucks out], but fuck me sideways with a teapot, I don't want to.'

Closer to home, our reporter opened his fourth-floor window to ask people on the street what they thought of the government bailing out giant tax-dodging multinationals.

One respondent, a local man who called himself Keith Grey of Betoota Ponds, was especially against government's bailing out companies like Ansett.

'Fuck the dogs! Let 'em burn!' he yelled up from the footpath.

The six other people on the street all jumped at the same time.

'Oi, ah. Sorry everyone, aye? Just gets me fired up, is all.'

Mr Grey's comments were met with head nods from all the others on the street. His sentiments were echoed by a great cross-section of Betootans.

> 'They employ thousand upon thousand head of Australians, so there's that. Look, we're thinking about it, but fuck me sideways with a teapot, I don't want to.'

THE BIRTH OF SCOCIALISM

We Spoke To Youth Allowance Recipients About How They'll Spend Extra Centrelink Cash

THE GOVERNMENT IS NOW handing out extra payments to people in society who are the most likely to spend it on things they don't need.

Students under the age of 24.

Young people do stupid things all the time – it's a part of being young. One stupid thing that the government hopes young people will do now is spend this extra money they're getting via Centrelink's Youth Allowance on things they don't need.

Like new tyres for their car. Not to last them a couple of years, but so they can go down to their local business park and smoke them up until they pop.

However, it would be foolish of this masthead to tar every student with the same brush, so our reporters hit the streets to find out what our town's fulltime students, apprentices and other assorted youngsters were planning to do with their extra monies.

Fulltime journalism student at South Betoota Polytechnic College, Marcus Donoghue, says he plans to spend his extra Youth Allowance payments on cannabis.

He said that the pain of being a journalism student in the current media climate was bad enough. Now the realisation that he'll struggle to find employment full stop has just about tipped him over the edge.

'I can pay my rent and survive on Youth Allowance already. Just. If I went to uni in a big city, I'd be fucked,' he said.

'But yeah. I'm going to buy some weed with this new payment. Hopefully, my dealer will also stimulate the local economy. And the growers, too. People give bikies a bad name but they spend up big in the local community. My mum works at CRT and she reckons bikies are always coming in paying cash for shovels, wheelbarrows, rope, hose and irrigation systems.

'Back to uni, yeah. Tertiary journalism is a scam, anyway. Every journalism lecturer in the country knows they're a con artist. To be a journalist, you need to learn on the job. There's no point in sitting in a classroom watching some tired old has-been try to suck his own cock on the floor up the front. Fuck me, I already sound jaded with the industry. Maybe this is the perfect job for me?'

Another student at South Betoota Polytechnic says she'll spend any extra money she has supporting local small businesses that are doing it tough at the moment.

Megan Jung studies marketing fulltime and lives in a share house with other women her age who also enjoy being very neat and tidy.

'I'm one of the lucky ones,' she said. 'For the time being, I've still got my job at the gun shop on Sundays and most of my classes are online anyway.

'So I'm going to spend my extra money at places like the bakery down the road that's doing a takeaway type thing out the window. I usually make my coffee at home because I'm not a reckless psychopath, but I'm going out to get a takeaway coffee now. I've started doing my grocery shop at the expensive grocer down the street, buying things like cultured butter and other luxury items nobody ever asked for.

'Also, I'm buying bullets for my Remington 7600 pump-action .308 now. I used to reload but I like supporting the local gun shop where I work. I've been shooting a lot more recently for practice. Just in case society collapses.'

Apprentice diesel mechanic Peter Bean says things will probably go on the same for him, considering he works in an industry that's 'pretty critical' to the economy.

The fulltime Pacific National employee works to maintain rail freight locomotives and also dabbles in repairing rail cars.

'Mate, look, it's not good for a lot of people. My heart really goes out to them all. The people having to line up at Centrelink and that. I'm fucken lucky I got this job at the Betoota Railyards. The economy needs people like me to keep working to keep the country moving.

'I've got tonnes of mates who are getting on Centrelink for the first time in their lives. Sad thing, but what can you do? It'll get better.'

As for what he plans to spend the money on, Peter said he'd just spend every cent he got because that's what the government has told him to do.

'Yeah, you know. Things like shopping and that. I won't be investing it, that's for sure! Yeah, mate, I'll buy a bunch of Vanguard ETFs with this extra money! [laughs] Nah, mate, just spending it at places where blokes need it. Shops around my house and that. I'd buy a bunch of pot with it but they drug-test us now, hey. Can't win 'em all.'

If you'd like to get in touch with *The Advocate* about your experiences with Youth Allowance, please feel free to contact our office with your story.

MARCUS DONOGHUE
(Fulltime journalism student)

The 21-year-old says he's given up on 2020.

MEGAN JUNG
(Fulltime marketing student)

The 19-year-old plans to spend her extra cash at local small businesses.

PETER BEAN
(Fulltime apprentice diesel mechanic)

16-year-old apprentice Peter says life will go on the same.

PM Decides To Escalate Things With China By Fronting Media Wearing Mack Horton's Gold Medal

SCOTT MORRISON HAS RAISED a few eyebrows this morning and taken the spat with China to the next level.

After a few days of tit-for-tat with the new world superpower that could potentially cripple our economy, the Prime Minister has today decided to turn up to a press conference wearing Mack Horton's famous gold medal.

His actions today follow his public declaration that an independent investigation is needed into the cause of the outbreak of the COVID-19 virus, and his private rallying of other world leaders to push that issue.

Those actions have understandably angered the Chinese Government, who are slowly growing accustomed to having their own way on the majority of issues that are important to them, and Morrison has this morning doubled down with another very thinly veiled jab.

'Yeah, you guys like this? Haha,' he laughed, motioning to the gold medal draped around his neck.

'Mack Horton's. You know, that stupid gweilo who beat that drug cheat Sun Yang,' he continued.

'Remember that the Chinese media, which is run by the government, said that he was clean as a whistle? I think it sends a pretty clear message about where we stand on this coronavirus investigation issue, don't you?'

Morrison then continued on with the other things he needed to say about restrictions, government policy and so on.

His media team have confirmed that they are in fact currently working frantically to delete thousands of 'eat kangaroo shit' style social media comments as we go to press.

Scott Morrison Puts Tourism Hat Back On To Ask Australians To Shaka Domestically This Summer

THE FORMER HEAD OF THE nation's peak tourism body has called on all Australians to shun the lands abroad for summer and instead 'throw a shaka' domestically this holiday season.

Scott Morrison, who is now the Prime Minister, used to be the top dog over at Tourism Australia, where he oversaw a number of iconic tourism campaigns such as 'So where the bloody hell are you?' and 'If you come by boat, you will not be settled in Australia'.

Today, he put his marketing propeller hat back on to urge Australians to head north this summer – but not too north.

'I call on all Australians to shirk their responsibilities and bury their heads in the sand up in Queensland, or the Kimberley, or even the Top End. Throw your shakas from Airlie Beach, Gracetown, Byron, Portsea and wherever in the blue fuck South Australians go to the beach.

'Going away when things get too much is so important. I don't think I would've been able to handle the pressures of the job last summer if I hadn't got the chance to have a holiday. Those bushfires were intense! [laughs] But now that we've all forgotten about them, we can move on.

'I chose to throw shakas in Hawaii last Christmas. This year, I'll be throwing them from Hawks Nest with John Howard. Just two battlers, throwing two shakas. I ask that you and your family do the same. But obviously not at Hawks Nest. I'd hate to see someone in my security detail put you to sleep for getting too close to me.'

Tourism Australia has welcomed the Prime Minister's message but has yet to provide comment to *The Advocate*.

Government Claws Back Over 80 Per Cent Of JobKeeper Package By Opening Up The VIP Rooms For 24 Hours

THE BLACK HOLE LEFT by the government's $130 billion JobKeeper coronavirus wage subsidy package is no longer the biggest concern for treasurer Josh Frydenberg.

This comes after the state governments on the east coast gave the hospitality sector permission to crank up the pokies again, after nearly two months without any pensioners blowing their dole cheques in the dark air-conditioned rooms out the back of pubs and clubs around the country.

'Geez. That was quicker than I thought,' said Frydenberg this morning.

'The punters really gave it a crack last night. Good on 'em. We've nearly paid this whole thing off. Haha. Fuck me.'

The quick turnaround in recouping the multi-billion-dollar deficit torn open by the COVID-19 pandemic comes as much-needed good news for the government, as new reports from the ABS point towards a major recession in the next 18 months.

Tuesday's ABS data revealed wages and salaries were flat in the March quarter. The tax take dropped 5.4 per cent between December and March and government spending grew by only 2 per cent.

However, Josh Frydenberg is confident the VIP rooms might get us through the imminent collapse of our economy as well.

'If these old people and vulnerable young parents keep feeding pineapples through these machines at the rate they have been over the last 24 hours …

'We'll have enough cash to bail out any bank or airline that asks. I can't see a time when we'll ever run out of money again. Hahaha.'

In fact, Frydenberg says he's of half a mind to cut company taxes to zero.

'You can forget taxing the multinational mining companies. The real cash cow is our nation's bizarre culture of letting problem gamblers play rigged video games without any legislation to curb their addictions.'

While millions of dollars have been designated to mental health initiatives during the stressful coronavirus isolation measures, it is not yet known if the government will be applying this same duty of care to the gambling addicts who are now forgoing electricity and groceries to chase the synthetic endorphin hits created by the melodies and flashing lights of the predatory gaming rooms.

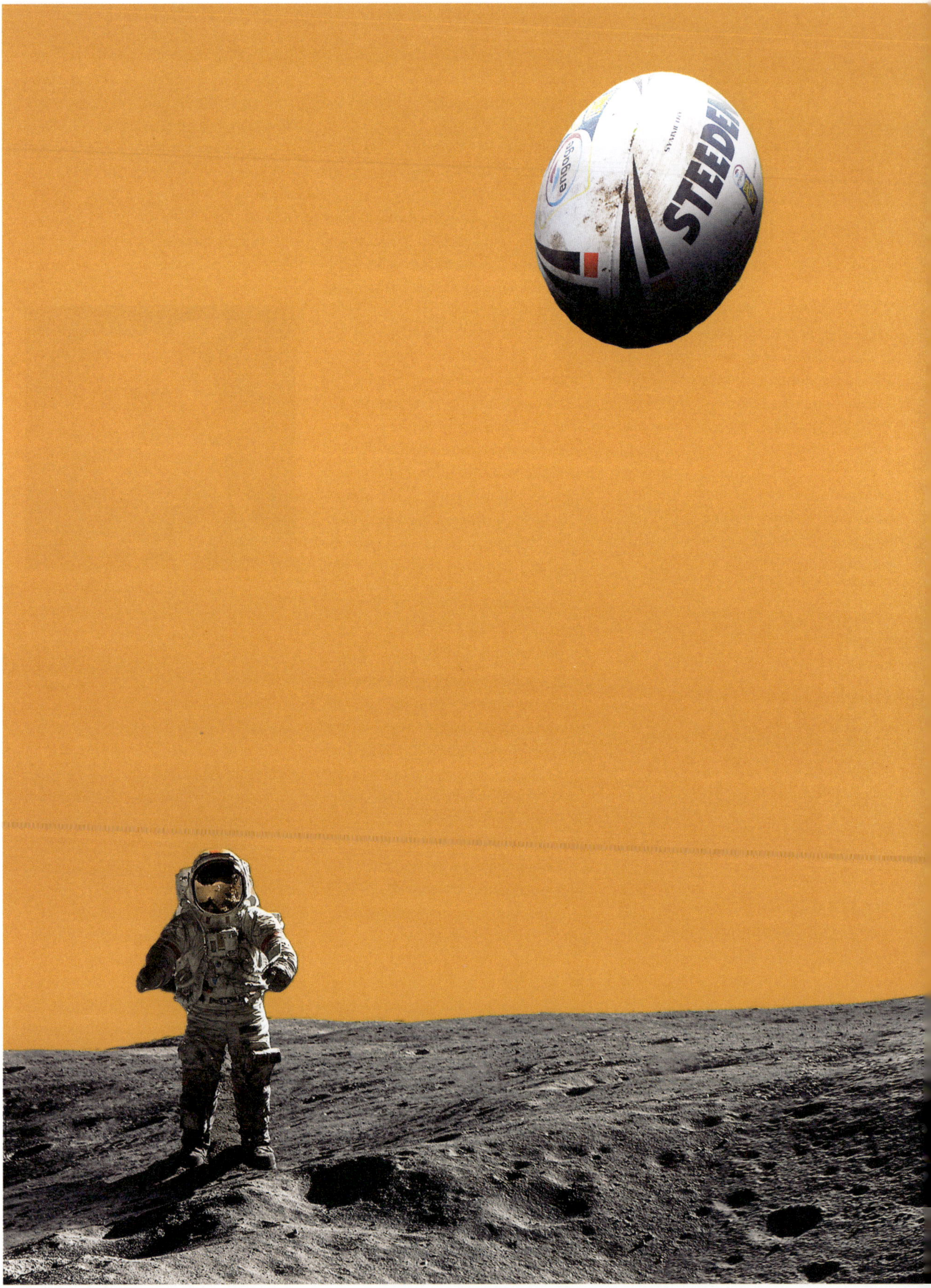

THE SHOW GOES ON

As we learnt in isolation, Australians are well known for their hatred of the nanny state – but also for their compliance with it.

Whether it's lockout laws on pubs or land-clearing legislation in the bush, when faced with having their personal freedoms stripped from them, the best that most Australians can manage is maybe a couple of peaceful rallies or an online petition.

When our way of life is restricted by our overly intrusive and authoritarian lawmakers, there is often a little bit of a stir – followed by a lot of bootlicking. We hate to look at ourselves that way, but it's the truth. We are a nation of cops that thinks it is a nation of Ned Kellys.

In fact, our shameful history of civil obedience is only truly tested when it's the scientists telling us what to do. This is because academics are smug and usually have a political agenda. Unlike those revenue-raising coppers and the conservative politicians who pass the laws they enforce.

So obedient are we that we would prefer to believe the Sky News rhetoric that climate change is made up by communists, and that our leaders have a really good grip on the long-term effects of digging coal out of the ground for two centuries and burning it as fast as the heavily taxed cigarettes we are only allowed to smoke in certain outdoor corners of the pub.

However, when it came to the COVID-19 pandemic, those nerds in lab coats presented us with warnings that were too dire to ignore. Even for the government. When a political class that is ruled by the interests of people aged over 60 is staring down the barrel of a highly contagious virus that has great success in killing that same voter block, they tend to act quick.

While the number of deaths began rising in Iran, Italy, the UK and the US, the Prime Minister held out for as long as he could. With the virus taking hold in Australia in early March, we got through two rounds of the winter football codes and a Sydney Hillsong conference before everything was shut down. Pubs, concerts, live sporting events, funerals, salons, gyms, restaurants. Nothing was open.

As you read this book, droves of Australia's biggest employers are still asking their staff to work from home. Some are asking them to never come back.

For months, there was simply no hope. No normality. Just a buckling NBN and a cascade of panic-buying.

Nevertheless, one of Australia's favourite pastimes refused to die. The National Rugba Leg.

By the grace of God, the NRL timed the lockdown perfectly with the hiring of the most competent man in sports administration, Saint Peter V'Landys.

From his humble beginnings as the son of Kytherian migrants in Wollongong, Saint Peter had held rugby league, his first true taste of Australia, close to his heart.

As a career executive, he had already guided Racing NSW through the equine virus, and the various other tricky situations that the world of horseracing had found itself in.

In his first press conference, he made it clear that it was his life's mission to save his beloved rugby league from having to write off the 2020 season and from the risk of potential bankruptcy after decades of 'management' at the hands of ex-players-turned-board-members who, funnily enough, don't make for very good accountants.

This came as Rugby Australia and Cricket Australia panicked and sacked their CEOs, and the AFL struggled under the command of the blue-blooded Gillon McLachlan, who had unfortunately blown all of his political clout when he asked Peter Dutton to fast-track a visa for his cousin's European au pair.

Luckily for all those other codes, Peter the Golden Greek had put together a template that could guide Australian sports back to their respective stadiums. Players were placed into quarantine and broadcast deals were furiously renegotiated. By 28 May, he had convinced three state governments, the Australian and New Zealand governments, a bunch of stroppy WAGs and the players association to get the show back on the road.

This is the story of Project Apollo.

Thousands Of Lawyers Line Up Outside Centrelink As NRL Competition Suspended

MARCH 23 WAS A DARK day for football fans and players alike, as the NRL made the difficult decision to suspend the remainder of the competition in response to the COVID-19 pandemic.

However, another tragic casualty of the move has been thousands of lawyers, who would otherwise be cleaning up the multiple PR disasters caused by the messy combination of NRL players and alcohol.

'It's been really tough,' says Peter Brown, formerly Junior Partner at legal firm Gouge & Scram.

'Things were going great, and then bam, here we all are, lined up outside Centrelink. The worst part isn't being unemployed; it's the fact that there is no one to sue for causing my termination.'

But while some of his former colleagues have taken the news badly, Peter is doing his best to stay positive.

'Hey, they'll come back eventually,' he said, straightening his tie. 'And when they do, I'm sure there will be some kind of welcome-back celebration, maybe a strip club will be involved, definitely alcohol, probably some drugs, and boom, my phone will start ringing again.

'How does this sound: "Your Honour, my client feels terrible about his actions on the night in question and would like to apologise to everyone who witnessed his disgusting behaviour. To show how remorseful he is, my client has offered to spend two hours in the children's ward visiting all the sick kids who have contracted coronavirus."

'Yeah, pretty happy with that one.'

'The NRL Have Made Poor Financial Decisions' Says Media Network Kept Alive By Print Newspapers

IN A CLEAR EXAMPLE of hypocrisy, the Nine Network has this week launched a brutal attack on the NRL, accusing the league of mismanagement and breaking its lucrative broadcast deal.

Once the most powerful media player in Australia, the Nine Network is nowadays most commonly known for eroding Australian societal standards with the brain-fodder acronyms that are MAFS and ACA, when the nation isn't locked down due to pandemics that result in bans on professional rugby league football.

However, despite their reliance on the drug-and-alcohol-fuelled soap operas that are dating shows and the ratings-grabbing NRL, the famously competent administrators at Nine say they can't believe their biggest cash cow hasn't been able to prepare for the footballing downturn created by COVID-19.

The statement came on the same day League Central is expected to announce plans to resume its competition, which has until now been halted by coronavirus.

The network has shown outrage at being left out of discussions on what the season would look like should it recommence, and took aim at NRL's financial management, which has left clubs and players facing uncertain futures.

'Nine has invested hundreds of millions in this game over decades and we now find they have profoundly wasted those funds with very little to fall back on to support the clubs, the players and supporters,' read the statement from the media network that had to form a multi-billion-dollar merger with four Australian print mastheads to save itself from financial collapse in the months leading into the 2019 federal election.

The tone-deafness continued, as the *Sydney Morning Herald*–backed TV station that has to fly its rugby league commentators in economy went on to explain that perhaps there are too many administrators not taking pay cuts in the NRL: 'It would now appear that much of that has been squandered by a bloated head office completely ignoring the needs of the clubs, players and supporters.'

At time of press, the Nine Network were trying to find ways to use their extremely valuable print mastheads to promote the upcoming season of *Married At First Skype*.

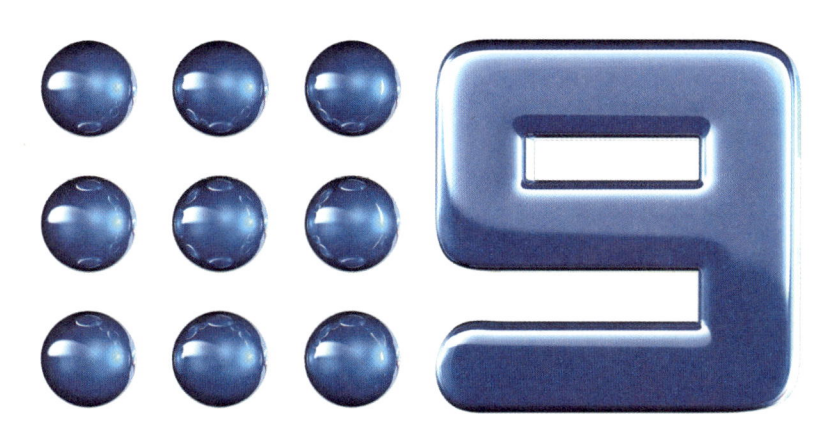

(not the Sydney Morning Hearld lol)

Despite their reliance on the drug-and-alcohol-fuelled soap operas that are dating shows and the ratings-grabbing NRL, the famously competent administrators at Nine say they can't believe their biggest cash cow hasn't been able to prepare for the footballing downturn created by COVID-19.

'Oi, You Doing Anything With That Cruise Ship?' NRL Asks NSW Government

RUGBY LEAGUE CHAIRMAN PETER V'Landys may have killed two birds with one stone today, after having a brainwave that could solve some of the most niggling issues for both state and federal governments.

In an effort to get the boys back on the field and keep sponsorship money rolling in, Peter V'landys took a drive down the south coast today to ponder his options.

It was just as he was crossing Allans Creek on the Princes Motorway that he spotted it.

'Farkin oath,' said V'landys as the haunted *Ruby Princess* ocean liner came into view.

Within moments, he was telling Siri to call New South Wales Premier Gladys Berejiklian on the burner phone she has reserved just for the rugby league.

The NRL has proposed to restart the Telstra Premiership on 28 May but V'landys has said the details of how the competition would be structured during the COVID-19 pandemic won't be finalised until the pussies in the Queensland and New South Wales governments get on board.

The game is exploring a number of options including the glorious but brief proposal of relocating 500 players and staff to Moreton Island. More recently, administrators considered quarantining teams to isolated bubbles in and around Western Sydney.

However, the newly named 'Project *Titanic*' brings a fresh wave of hope that the record sheets won't have to leave a blank mark next to 2020.

'Oi,' V'landys said the moment the New South Wales premier picked up the phone.

'Oi, you doing anything with that cruise ship?

'Give it to me. I'll send Reni Maitua's cleaning services on there and we'll nuke it.'

According to V'landys, Gladys Berejiklian didn't sound *not* interested as she marvelled at the famous imagination of the national rugby league. V'landys went on.

'We'll drop some turf on the deck and put up some posts. If that bad boy can house 2500 cashed-up boomers, then we'll have no problem housing the entire rugby league and their families.'

When asked by Gladys what he planned on doing with the quarantining staff members still stuck on the controversial *Ruby Princess*, V'landys said he'd have a job for them too.

'They can run touch. I don't care what their test results say. They'll be well outside 1.5 metres of everyone.

'Gladys, listen to me. Today your office will get a call from the media – tell them I've put Jason Stevens in charge of innovation for Project *Titanic*. Tell them the cops have told me I've got the all-clear and then tell them you are waiting for advice from medical experts. I'm gonna go book the pyrotechnicians for Round One 2.0.

'The show goes on!'

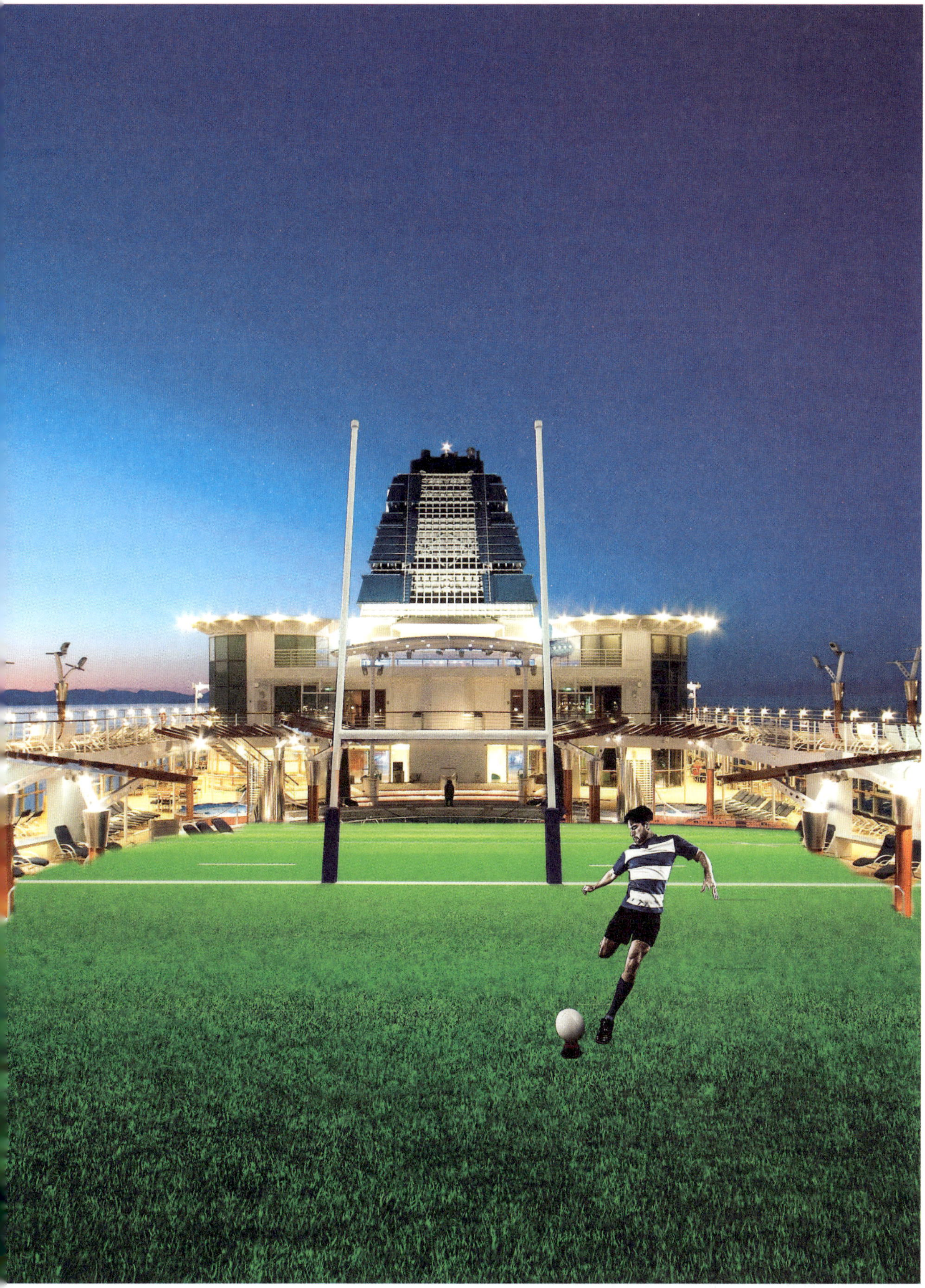

Eels Staff Frantically Paint Try Lines Around Each Player To Ensure Correct Social Distancing

THE PARRAMATTA EELS NRL team are frantically working through the coronavirus crisis as best they can this afternoon.

In a sign of the times, the club is tackling the very modern problem with a very old-fashioned solution.

Desperate to ensure social-distancing guidelines are followed in an effort to get the code up and running by 28 May, the Eels have implemented a new team strategy to help players follow the rules.

The club has decided to paint try lines around all of its players, to make sure that they don't go near each other and breach the protocols handed down by the NRL.

'Pretty clever, isn't it?' explained the Eels trainer Kenny Hindmarsh this afternoon.

'Basically, we know that our players are very scared of the try-line, so we've got our ground staff painting try-lines all over the field, to ensure the players stay away from each other,' he continued.

'So far it's worked. Only Gutho, Blake and Maika seem to be interested in approaching the try-lines, and we've effectively eradicated all unnecessary bum slaps and cuddles, which is a huge task. So hopefully it keeps all the boys in line.

'Fuck, hang on, Fergo's doing back-flips again … Blake, don't do that. For fuck's sake,' he yelled as the line went muffled and eventually dead.

NRL Sacks Biosecurity Experts And Brings In Players' Wives To Orchestrate Season Comeback

IN SOME SHOCKING NEWS from the harbour city of Sydney, the NRL has announced a bold new strategy to ensure they get back on the field on 28 May.

The game's governing body has today sensationally sacked its biosecurity experts responsible for the groundbreaking program to play the sport amid the coronavirus crisis, and decided to simply hire the anti-vax partners of the NRL.

The move comes after a growing number of NRL players, who get paid hundreds of thousands of dollars to play a child's game, refuse to take the standard flu shot in a stance for medical freedom, or against big pharma, or some shit like that.

'Yes, we have decided that the wives and girlfriends of rugby league players, who have leveraged their partners' fleeting profiles to garner a middling Instagram following, know far more than medical professionals who have dedicated their entire lives to a certain field,' explained an NRL spokesperson today.

'We all know that scientists are irrational people who are far more prone to pushing agendas in the face of all evidence than normal people who watch YouTube videos and read Facebook posts. So we've decided to sack them, because these WAGs are highly trained immunologists who know better than 99 per cent of the population.

'And they have their hubbies' best interests at heart, by protecting them from a flu shot that's going to do far more damage than colliding with other blokes at full speed and rattling their brains thousands of times over a few short years.'

It's not known if the WAGs are indeed aware of the fact that over a million people are out of work or losing work around the country, and heaven and earth has been moved to allow their partners to play sport for a very, very lucrative living, and a small flu shot might not be that big of a compromise in the scheme of things.

It's believed the WAGs will begin their roles in charge of Project Apollo as early as next week.

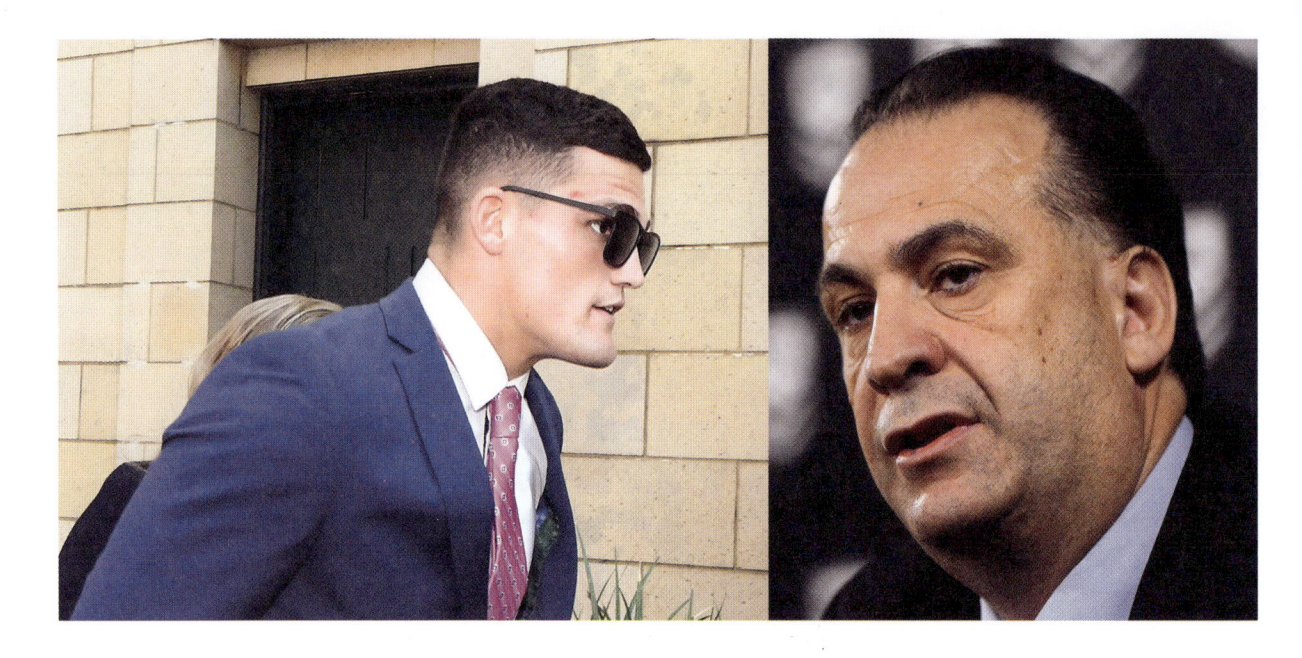

NRL Forced To Act Like They Weren't Expecting Worse From Their Players During Isolation

WITH FOUR NRL PLAYERS being handed a total of $120,000 worth of fines for breaching social distancing rules, the National Rugby League has been put in the awkward position of having to act like they weren't expecting worse.

As one of the last sporting codes to shut up shop, COVID-19 and social distancing have shown that the NRL must really be as wealthy as their players are sensible.

After harsh words from the Nine Network and a new CEO, the NRL was ready to get back to defending their employee network, but weren't prepared for how mild the drama would be.

'We are disappointed to learn that 40 players have broken social distan– wait, four, not 40, is that right? Only four?' stated ARLC Chairman Peter V'Landys.

'Just four? That's actually not that bad but – disappointing yes, very disappointing, we're so very disappointed in those 40 – sorry, four, players.'

One NRL fan who has come to the defence of the players is NRL Instagram influencer @micksdrivingtalks who is known for his vocal opinions on the code.

'All right, I'm going to say it, not that bad,' stated Mick as he drove one-handed, holding his phone.

'Everything that's happened so far is actually pretty wholesome. You know what footy players get up to on Mad Monday, right? Youse actually need to chill.'

> *As one of the last sporting codes to shut up shop, COVID-19 and social distancing have shown that the NRL must really be as wealthy as their players are sensible.*

'Clap For The NRL' At 7 pm Tomorrow To Thank Our Brave Rugby League For Getting The Footy Back On

AT 7 PM ON FRIDAY 10 April, households across Australia are urged to stand on their doorsteps and balconies and applaud the efforts of the NRL administrators and the brave players for their hard work in restarting the 2020 rugby league season.

This comes as the Australian Rugby League Commission announces that it plans to get rugby league back on the television by Thursday 28 May.

Following landmark meetings with the NRL's innovation committee on Thursday, the ARLC has approved plans to get the competition up and running almost ten weeks after it was suspended due to the coronavirus pandemic.

ARL commissioner Wayne Pearce, who is head of the gloriously named 'Project Apollo' said the changing landscape around government boundaries has prevented the committee from confirming a new season structure.

'We are back, baby,' said Pearce. 'Oh, it's on. You better believe that.

'Not sure if we're gonna do it on an island or we're just gonna fence off an entire suburb in Western Sydney. But it's happening. The boys will be fit, quarantined, and ready to run the ball.'

With every other sporting code in the world except for Turkish table tennis and Belarusian futsal suspended due to coronavirus, the news that the NRL will be returning has been received with cheers right around Australia and the world.

The brave decision means that not only will our beautiful rugby league be exposed to foreign regions outside Lebanon, New Zealand, the Pacific and northern England for the first time – but also that the interestingly managed NRL might not have to fold due to running out of money with almost no savings in the war chest.

In response to this brave decision by NRL administrators to push forward with entertaining the masses, Australians have been invited to all join in tomorrow night for a nationwide round of applause for the NRL.

'Clap for the NRL' is an initiative created by South Australian Greens Senator Sarah Hanson-Young, who says it is imperative for all Australians to show our gratitude to the brave men and women who make up the rugby league.

'Join me at 7 pm tomorrow night, everyone, as we CLAP FOR THE NRL,' wrote Hanson-Young on her Facebook page earlier today.

'In these uncertain times, Todd Greenberg and Peter V'landys are bravely fronting press conferences and Zoom meetings to discuss ways to deliver live sport to the punters and dribblers of Australia and the world.

'In the words of the iconic Tina Turner, a historical figure in the history of Australian rugby league, the NRL board is simply the best!'

Landmarks including the Brisbane Gallery of Modern Art and the Sydney Westpac Needle will light up in maroon and blue as residents give a round of applause in appreciation for the National Rugby League from their doorsteps and apartment windows.

Self-Conscious Titans Ask NRL If This Plan Includes Them As Well Or Just The Good Teams

AS THE QUEST TO relaunch the NRL gathers some serious momentum, the Gold Coast Titans have this morning tried to figure out what it all means for them.

Wondering whether they actually have to go to all these extreme biosecurity lengths like the rest of the clubs, Titans Head of Culture Mal Meninga picked up the phone to get to the bottom of it.

'Gus, do we have to do all this shit too? Or should we not bother?' Mal asked the NRL CEO-in-waiting.

'Like, I know there's a heap to keeping a squad of rugby league players from playing up, so I'm just wondering if you need us to jump through the hoops, or can we just sit this one out?' Meninga continued.

This comes as all of the clubs prepare to isolate players ahead of the 28 May season relaunch dubbed Project Apollo.

Meninga told *The Advocate* that Gus said the Titans did have to go through the same motions as everyone else, in order to play the 6 pm Sunday night games and concede 50 points.

'Yeah, he said that if they are bothering to fly the Warriors over, the least we can do is get bio-safe to keep them company as cellar dwellers of the league,' Meninga said.

'Just to make sure the boys pin Bryce [Cartwright] down and make sure he takes his medicine.

'Fucking hell. Here we go,' Mal sighed before telling us he had to break the bad news and hung up.

Barnaby Waits At Tamworth Airport With Crate Of Waikato Longnecks To Say *Kia Ora* To The Boys

COACH STEPHEN KEARNEY SAYS dealing with the constant pestering from Federal MP Barnaby Joyce is just one of the many enormous challenges facing the Warriors during their 'trailblazing' NRL quarantine in Tamworth.

The New Zealand–based players awoke to their first full day of team isolation in Tamworth on Monday, where they will spend two weeks in lockdown after their trans-Tasman flight last night.

It is believed the Warriors players are already growing tired of Barnaby Joyce, who was waiting for them at Tamworth airport with a crate of imported Waikato Draught tallies.

Joyce was heard dropping a few *kia ora*s to the Warriors players, and commenting on how skux it was to have a few more Kiwi brothers in Tamworth.

Understanding all of their biosecurity protocols was on the agenda for day one, followed by a return to the training paddock tomorrow. Kearney believes the biggest security risk to their isolation is the incredibly bored Member for New England, who won't seem to fuck off.

Over the weekend, the club had sought assurances from Tamworth local council that Barnaby would not attempt to jump the fence of their training facilities to play a bit of touch footy.

While Tamworth mayor, Councillor Col Murray, gave his guarantee that the Kiwi footballers would not have to endure a sweaty game of touch with the local MP, he could not prevent Joyce from hanging around the car park and player accommodation, where he has since been spotted asking for autographs and selfies.

Speaking to *The Betoota Advocate* today, the former Deputy PM says having the Warriors in the centre of his electorate feels like a homecoming of sorts, after he had to terminate his Kiwi citizenship following the 2017 parliamentary eligibility crisis.

'I'm very excited to have some of my countrymen in town,' said Joyce.

'Really gets the mana going. Usually I have to sneak into the shearing sheds for a couple of dots and some singalongs with the Maori shearers … but to be able to have the Warriors staying in the centre of town is mean as!'

Executives from the Warriors say that if Joyce is not brought under control by Prime Minister Morrison, they will have to make a phone call to ARLC chairman Peter V'Landys. And no one wants that.

'The bloke is becoming a bit of a pest,' said one spokesperson for the club.

'Either the government pulls him into line, or Saint Peter will pull him into line. And no one likes to see Peter when he's angry.'

Only A Greek Could Have Pulled This Shit Off, Mate, Says Local Greek

MAY 28 IS THE date for kick-off.

The NRL Telstra Premiership will recommence as a 20-round competition on 28 May with the Grand Final to be played on 25 October.

State of Origin is also scheduled to go ahead following the Grand Final, which means each of the three matches will be taking place deep into the warm spring months. Which is glorious news.

With the shock resignation of NRL CEO Todd Greenberg last week, rugby league fans only have one man to thank for the hardline negotiations that have saved the 2020 season.

He goes by the name of Saint Peter.

An NRL statement released on Tuesday afternoon said: 'Australian Rugby League Commission (ARLC) Chair Peter V'landys today confirmed the details after extensive consultation with broadcast partners, clubs and key stakeholders.'

From politicians to players, this result has come as a surprise to everyone.

That is, except for the nation's Greek community, who always knew that Saint Peter could pull it off.

Local Betoota Dolphins fourth-grade captain and club treasurer Lewis Karnava (38) says he had no doubt that the NRL would restart in time to fit in some sort of 2020 season.

'Mate,' says Lewis. 'This is the bloke who got Racing NSW through the equine flu. That was like the coronavirus of horses. You didn't reckon he could get the boys back out there by May?

'Of course he was going to get this done. He's Greek, mate.'

In fact, Lewis goes one further and points out that it's not just Peter V'Landys' Greek heritage that has helped the rugby league negotiate its way through the hurdles thrown at it by the cowardly state governments and Nine Network executives. It's the specific Greek island he comes from.

With a population of 4000, Kythira is an island in Greece lying opposite the south-eastern tip of the Peloponnesian peninsula. It is well known for exporting amazing businessmen and women to Australia in the 1950s such as Sydney Roosters owner Nick Politis, Mad Max creator George Miller and now more notably Saint Peter.

As Lewis points out, Australian rugby league fans have a lot to thank this 300-square-kilometre island for.

'He's not just a Greek, mate. He's a Kytherian. That's a double threat.

'You know what they say: Kythira boys don't cry.'

'Umm, Ah, Maybe, Uh, We Should, Ah, Start Thinking About, Umm, Starting Again Too?' Says AFL

THE MAN IN CHARGE of running the Australian Football League has today suggested that maybe it's time to possibly start thinking about doing what the NRL has been working on for the last month, or, like, something like that.

This comes after the runt of the Australian sporting litter, rugby, announced today that even it has a road map for the rest of the season.

Speaking to the media today in the self-titled most cosmopolitan city in the country, AFL boss Gillon McLachlan explained that they are going to discuss what to do about getting their code playing footy again.

This comes as the NRL ploughs closer to a start date, and AFL players aren't allowed to train in more than groups of two in line with their Victorian overlords in Melbourne.

The man who certainly can't be described as a wartime leader like Peter V'landys, Scott Morrison and John Curtin, said that they are 'gonna work something out'.

'Yeah, I've been busy sorting through all those problems,' said McLachlan vaguely.

It's not known how far the Victorian leg tennis code desires to be behind the rugby league, who are planning to restart on 28 May.

'It's really weird, what's going on,' explained a Melbourne ex-pat, Banjo Clementè, who lives in our town's French Quarter.

'Like, credit where credit's due, the AFL is often a fair way ahead of the NRL on things like grassroots, AFLW, crowd numbers and the fact it owns that big old stadium down there in Geelong. So why are we so far behind on getting up and running again?

'Strange, I'm not sure what these blokes have been doing in iso for the last two months, 'cause it certainly hasn't been golf.'

The man who certainly can't be described as a wartime leader like Peter V'landys, Scott Morrison and John Curtin, said that they are 'gonna work something out'.

Alan Jones Just Wants The Wallabies To Win Like They Did When The All Blacks Were White PE Teachers

CONSERVATIVE RADIO SHOCK jock Alan Jones has predictably decided to not go easy on Raelene Castle today, following last night's news that she was standing down as CEO of Rugby Australia.

Jones had been one of Castle's harshest critics throughout her doomed appointment, which saw her attempting to bail water out of a sinking ship that had been dragged through icebergs by a string of North Shore parachute-pullers for several decades.

Castle now joins a long list of powerful women whose careers came to an end early, after they had arrows fired at their shins by the talkback heavyweight.

'It's an appointment that shouldn't have been made,' Jones said on 2GB radio, obviously not willing to gently tiptoe around the sensitivities most people would show to someone who appears humble in defeat.

'She knows nothing about the game! It's like putting someone who can't read music in the Sydney Symphony Orchestra as first violin.'

While it is not yet known which violinist Alan Jones thinks would have been able to handle a certain happy-clapper's decision to send all of the homosexuals to hell, it seems the on-field performances in Australian rugby are also a cause of frustration for both fans and the board.

As a former Wallabies coach from an era before the Pacific Revolution, Alan Jones is just one of many silverware winners who can't understand why Australian rugby isn't as successful as it was when our players had Olympic-standard training facilities and the All Blacks were mostly white PE Teachers who lived off potatoes and Waikato Draught.

It is not known who the next scapegoat may be for the dismal state of Rugby Australia, as commentators continue to overlook the issues of 'cattle' – and the fact that the entire code has basically forgotten its working-class grassroots of Western Sydney and South Brisbane, opting to scout mostly from six elite private schools made up of kids who grew up in homes where they were allowed to wear shoes on the couch.

While the board is yet to outline their new direction, any underprivileged kids who wanna be a Wallaby have been told that their best avenue to wearing the jersey is to go viral in a 50-second high-school football video.

Tamworth's Local Rugby League Clubs Quietly Hoping For A Few Isolation Breaches In The Warriors Camp

NORTH-WESTERN NEW SOUTH Wales rugby league clubs are reportedly stoked to have the New Zealand Warriors staying in the epicentre of the New England region for the next few months.

As the first NRL side to begin training after being given exemptions to travel from New Zealand to Australia, the Warriors are currently in lockdown in Tamworth and yesterday were beginning to be put through their paces.

Other clubs weren't due back for physical training until today, but the Warriors' quarantine camp in Tamworth has already fired up at Scully Park.

The squad was split into four groups and shuttled through field and gym sessions with as little contact with each other as possible.

When the mandatory 14-day isolation phase is complete, players will begin contact drills.

Unlike the cowards in Albury Council who voted down the opportunity to host the Melbourne Storm on the New South Wales side of the border, the Warriors were met with cheers upon their arrival in Tamworth, with local clubs saying that having the players there for a couple of months is a great boost for local footy in the region.

However, aside from the joy it brings footy fans to watch superstars like Roger Tuivasa-Sheck running around the oval in their own town, clubs in the region say that there are many other benefits that could come from this experiment.

Namely, a potential boost in talent for the next generation of rugby league players.

North Tamworth Bears CEO Barnaby Windsor says that in the scheme of things, sixteen or so extra single mothers in the region would actually be a net win for local football.

'I mean, ideally, when the competition is under way and the virus is starting to disappear, it'd be great to see the boys firing up their dating apps and making a few isolation breaches,' he said.

'You can just imagine. Haha.'

In fact, the idea of a bit of cross-Tasman interbreeding has been met with so much enthusiasm that isolation breaches are being openly encouraged for Warriors players.

A letter signed by over 50 coaches and administrators from both the Group 4 and Group 19 competitions states that a little bit of fence-jumping couldn't hurt rugby league in the region.

Glen Innes Magpies head coach, Humphrey Archdale, says there is a very real possibility that New England could host a new wave of Pacific Islander talent in the years to come, if the local girls play their cards right.

'Imagine having our very own Vuna playing for the Maggies,' he said.

'We've got the second generation of the Vuna footballing dynasty currently sitting idle in the middle of Tamworth. I mean, I don't know if he has a missus back home or . . . Ya know?

'Or maybe a Tuivasa-Sheck. If we can take anything from this year's NRL season . . . well, anything is possible.'

Miranda Donnelly, CEO of the Gunnedah Bulldogs, agrees.

'Hosting the Warriors in the middle of New England might hold the key to the future of rugby league in north-western New South Wales. I'd love to see these boys sow their oats. And you know what they say about New England . . . very fertile soil.

'Maybe it's time for the food bowl to become the footy bowl? When you consider the indiscretions of our local member, we are already known as a hotspot for Kiwi citizens to spread their seeds.'

Mandatory Flu Shots Somehow The Biggest Concern For Women Married To Rugby League Players

Even with the entire planet locked inside while hundreds of thousands of people die from one particular illness that human civilisation cannot yet vaccinate against, the loudest voices in the room have once again proven to be the most controversial.

IN WHAT IS THE biggest hurdle yet to be faced by the embattled rugby league, there are now reports that several players are refusing to receive flu shots after being pressured by their wives.

While not mandatory, common flu vaccinations are part of the NRL's strict biosecurity protocols in order to restart the competition in May following the coronavirus shutdown.

However, even with the entire planet locked inside while hundreds of thousands of people die from one particular illness that human civilisation cannot yet vaccinate against, the loudest voices in the room have once again proven to be the most controversial.

Several high-profile NRL WAGs have recently taken advantage of the vulnerable position of the organisation that provides their main source of income, and used their equally uneducated husbands as tools through which to spread awareness of a movement that advocates the supposed freedom of Australian citizens to bring back horrible illnesses that have killed millions, such as polio and whooping cough.

With an ingrained culture of very naughty off-field behaviour within the rugby league, it is not lost on the general public that the lives of NRL wives and girlfriends would be very stressful. However, most would have assumed that binge-drinking, drug use and rampant adultery would be their number-one concern.

NRL fans are today surprised that in fact vaccination scepticism appears to be the biggest marital issue faced by some WAGs, who have leveraged the notoriety garnered by their husbands' abilities to run really hard into other large men while carrying an inflated sheath of rubber.

Some anti-WAGxers have since apparently made thousands of dollars running 'vaccination awareness' seminars, profiteering off the fears of young mothers who have experienced traumatic childbirth. The movement has since spread right around the world, causing the drastically low immunisation rates in Samoa that resulted in nearly 83 deaths in last year's measles epidemic.

This growing 'freedom debate' has got so out of control that it has prompted even Prime Minister Morrison to weigh in, saying the NRL should enforce a 'no jab, no play' policy that would ensure players who rejected vaccination would be suspended from competing.

However, several players from clubs that will never ever win a premiership have responded with criticism to the Prime Minister's comments, saying it would be 'coercion', which is a big word their wives learnt on YouTube.

While the anti-vaxxers continue to build their profiles with Israel Folau–like stubbornness, NRL fans and administrators now wait gleefully to see what happens when a movement of conspiracists are faced with the unrelenting ferociousness of Saint Peter V'Landys.

Vaccine Scientists Develop NRL-Friendly Flu Shot That Can Be Sniffed Off An iPhone

LEADING VACCINE AND immunology scientists from Betoota's University of Western Queensland campus have today made groundbreaking developments that could resolve the National Rugby League's newest pre-kick-off hurdle.

The breakthrough research has seen a new variation of the common flu shot, which could be administered to vaccination-sceptic footballers in a way that they are more familiar and comfortable with.

This comes as ARLC chairman Peter V'Landys continues to jump through hoops to restart the rugby league season amid the 2020 coronavirus pandemic. This week, his newest hurdle comes in the shape of a small list of ungrateful players who claim to be smarter than 99 per cent of medical professionals, and are reportedly avoiding their flu shots at the insistence of their anti-vaxxer wives.

Because the general public can't possibly imagine that these NRL players would jeopardise 80 per cent of their own income and risk the possible collapse of the entire competition over some bullshit articles written by bored Byron mums, their opposition to receiving a common flu shot has been put down to a fear of needles.

However, today's discovery in the Betoota science labs appears to have provided an alternate option for these players who are apparently extremely worried about 'putting things into their body'.

The new NRL-friendly flu shot will allow footballers to rack up the immunisation in powdered form off an iPhone screen.

Professor Julian Gower is the leading researcher for the University of Western Queensland's snortable vaccine program. He says this new version of the flu shot should help NRL players through the uneasy process of taking part in the most successful achievement of medical science since the invention of soap.

'Unlike the AFL, a lot of rugby league players are nervous about needles,' said Dr Gower.

'When you pair that fear with a bored wife, you end up with anti-vaxxer conspiracies.

'This new variation of the flu shot should ease NRL players into randomly hoovering whatever is lined up on an iPhone in front of them. We would recommend racking up this flu shot at a strip club after a big day on the pineapple Cruisers.'

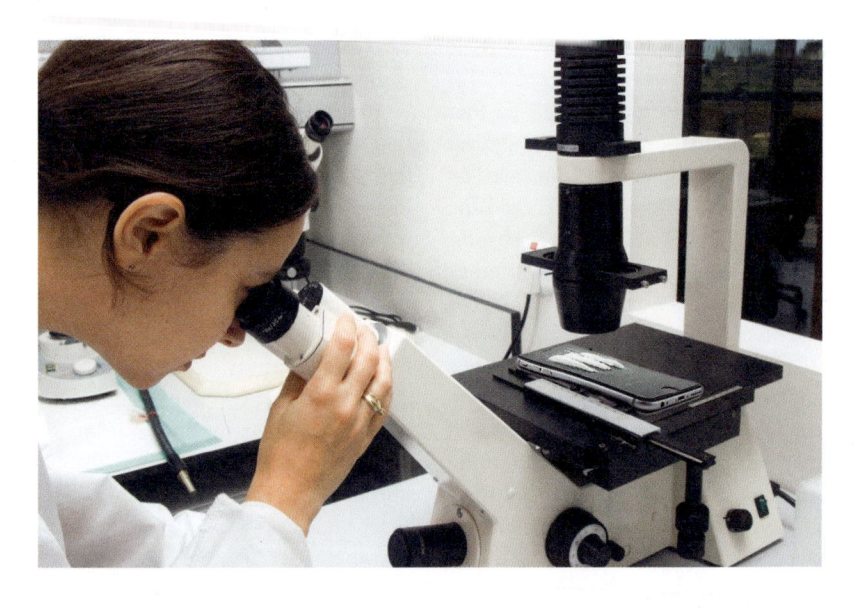

His newest hurdle comes in the shape of a small list of ungrateful players who claim to be smarter than 99 per cent of medical professionals, and are reportedly avoiding their flu shots at the insistence of their anti-vaxxer wives.

Heavily Botoxed NRL WAG Tells Heavily Tattooed Husband To Not Let Those Needles Near Him

PROMINENT RUGBY LEAGUE WAG, Kaylentaya Shayley, has today drawn a line in the sand.

Her husband, Braydeighn Shayley (32), who plays fringe NRL for a club that will never win a premiership, has been told by Kaylentaya to sit out the 2020 football season as the freedom of choice debate fires up among the anti-WAGxers.

Kaylentaya says she's fine with her husband spending ten years in and out of concussions, because that's part of his job. She says she was very supportive when Stephen Dank put her husband on a cycle of legally grey performance supplements while he was on the bench for the Sharks seven years ago, because that's part of his job. She also didn't mind when he had to have three separate shoulder reconstructions and keyhole surgery in his knee, because they're part of his job, too.

But the NRL's new mandatory flu shot protocols, aimed at protecting the welfare of players during the COVID-19 pandemic, is a step too far.

This comes as Queensland's Chief Health Officer Jeannette Young says NRL players will not be exempt from flu vaccinations for philosophical reasons. Meaning they need to talk to another real doctor before they can refuse vaccinations from their club's doctors. That's if they want to maintain employment.

On top of all this, both the Queensland and New South Wales state governments and the NRL have said that Instamunologists citing disproven medical papers do not count as a 'real doctor'.

These new rulings, according to Kaylentaya, are an affront to what she believes are her husband's constitutional rights. That's why she's had to draw the line, and would rather threaten their entire family income than let her husband take the same flu shot he's taken every year since he was a child.

'Baby,' a heavily botoxed Kaylentaya tells Braydeighn, her heavily tattooed husband who earns a quarter of a million dollars a year in his role as a product of medical and sporting science, 'don't let those needles anywhere near you.'

THE SHOW GOES ON

Local Toff Says NRL Matches Would Be More Entertaining With 20 Minutes' Worth Of Scrum Resets

IRWIN PAISLEY-ADAIR SAYS he's not really too sure what all the fuss is about.

The 54-year-old accountant from Betoota Grove says he probably won't bother paying much attention to tonight's return of rugby league, a phenomenon that has plenty around the country and the world intrigued.

This follows the NRL ploughing full steam ahead towards kick-off this evening at 7.50 pm, in a moment that has been likened to the moon landing in rugby league circles.

The die-hard Reds and Churchie rugby fan explained that the only reason he'll be watching is because of his two sons, who are both forced to play rugby at Whooton School, but who love the game of rugby league.

'Rugby league is so symptomatic of the working classes,' explained Paisley-Adair.

'Crass, devoid of intellect and monotonous,' continued the rich old boy who gets his kicks from having enough money to play the housing and share market and chortling about scrum chat with his fellow old-boy mates.

'Run tackle, run tackle, run tackle, run tackle, run tackle, kick, repeat,' said the former prop, who enjoys watching a game where half of the time on the clock is spent watching fat blokes reset scrums.

'Give me a Churchie v Nudgee game any day over rugby league,' laughed the man who thinks the game of rugby is dying in this country because of sports science.

'That's what rugby should be doing,' he finally surmised, referencing the fact that Rugby Australia just announced some plans for a domestic competition in spite of the NRL kicking off their actual game tonight.

'Broadcast the schoolboys!'

NRL Anti-Vaxxer's Love Of Money Actually Stronger Than His Philosophical Stance On Flu Shots

IN NEWS THAT HAS rattled the nation to its very core, some NRL players have chosen to chase a paycheque.

This comes after the two remaining Gold Coast Titans players holding out on the flu shot are reportedly set to get the jab since having their lucrative pay packets threatened.

That threat followed from the Queensland Government refusing to allow any unvaccinated players who didn't have a legitimate reason to refuse the vaccine to play in the NRL, which has moved heaven and earth so the competition can restart and the boys can get paid.

The players' about-face follows weeks of anti-vax WAGs taking to social media to call medical professionals (who are paid far less than their footy-player partners) liars, authoritarian actors, and even Nazis.

However, despite the active social media campaign designed to encourage people not to get vaccinations, despite all of the actual medical advice available, and to boost anti-vaxxers' fledgling social media followings so they can pyramid-scheme other footy WAGs, it can be confirmed that some players don't believe in their alternative truth enough to miss out on getting paid the big bucks.

'Yeah, they've forced us to fall in line with their agenda,' said one prominent anti-vaxxer who could just as easily walk away from the game and go and get a job where a vaccination isn't required, like millions of other people in our society.

'I guess I'll just have to white-ant the game that's given me everything,' he said.

They could easily walk away from the game and go and get a job where a vaccination isn't required, like millions of other people in our society.

Star Casino Prepares For Major Losses After The Entire NRL Develops Autism From Flu Shots

AFTER MONTHS OF HEAVILY botoxed bogans politicising the lives of people with autism to create fear around vaccinations, Star Casino has today made plans to place limits on the number of NRL players permitted in their venue at any time.

This comes as thousands of rugby league footballers began developing high-functioning cognitive skills not often seen in blokes who run as fast as they can into other blokes for a living.

The anti-vaxxer myth that humans are not simply born with autism has once again been peddled through social media by people who think that Bill Gates owns Apple.

Despite the fact that the entire global economy has been brought to its knees by a virus for which there is as yet no vaccine, the anti-WAGxers have used this difficult time to double down on their beliefs that immunisations provided by Australia's free healthcare system actually cause autism in 'normal people'.

However, in a strange turn of events, it seems these uneducated lifestyle influencers may actually be correct.

Since last week's mandatory flu shots, NRL players have begun to show signs of competency in rapid calculation, artistic mirroring, mapmaking and violin.

While the WAGs may now be able to say 'I told you so' about their grave concerns surrounding the suggestion that life-saving immunisations might cause autism, it seems their propaganda isn't entirely accurate.

The Instagram-charged stigmatisation and dehumanisation of autistic people has today been debunked, after Roosters prop Jared Waerea-Hargreaves was able to accurately sketch the entire Sydney CBD, street by street, after only one helicopter ride over the city.

It has also been reported that Bulldogs enforcer Dylan Napa has become a world-champion chess player since contracting autism from his flu shot last Thursday. He is expected to represent Australia in the international chess championships in Yekaterinburg, Russia, later this year, where he will face reigning World Champ Magnus Carlsen.

The anti-vaxxer movement is reportedly furious at the suggestion that autistic people can live normal, and sometimes extraordinary, lives – and have since begun looking for other scarier medical conditions to attach to their money-making bullshit cause.

Star Casino has revealed it is also unhappy at the recent autismification of the new 'rainmen' NRL stars, and have begun preparing for major losses the moment Gladys lets them open up the tables again.

However, NRL fans say this is the best thing that could happen to the game, and are excited to see some actual geniuses take to the field on 28 May, after decades of that word being thrown around a bit too generously.

NRL Star Learns To Read After Developing Autism From Flu Vaccinations

IN YET ANOTHER WIN for the anti-vaxxer movement, it seems the fears of Australia's NRL WAGs have again been proven correct today.

This comes after a 26-year-old Tugun man began experiencing permanent changes in his neurological functions.

Close friends and family of fringe Gold Coast Titans hooker, Wayde Slade, say it is undeniable that the footballer is no longer the man he used to be.

His fiancée, Sianna-Marie, says that her hubby-to-be was absolutely fine until he was forced into the NRL's oppressive COVID-19 quarantine program that asked all players to allow health experts to immunise them against common strains of influenza.

However, in a rare departure from the usual scenario in which heavily botoxed Instagram influencers diagnose the side effects of vaccines themselves based on shit they read on the internet, it seems that Wayde's newfound neurodiversity has also been confirmed by medical professionals.

Club doctors for the Gold Coast Titans have today confirmed Wayde Slade as the latest case of an NRL star developing never-before-seen cognitive skills as a result of contracting autism from their mandatory flu jabs.

'It has today been confirmed that Wayde Slade was seen reading a novel in the club locker rooms,' read a statement from the Titans.

It is believed that medical staff were first alerted to the footballer's autistic mannerisms after learning that Wayde had not only learnt to read, but was also beginning to show an interest in space and planets and shit.

These new behaviours are in stark contrast to his usual post-training activities, which consisted of him filming TikTok videos and DMing sex workers.

'Player welfare liaisons have since been directed to work with Slade and his young family to offer any support needed as they forge a new future with the permanent changes in his brain,' said a club spokesperson.

Sianna-Marie, a former chocolate milk promo girl who met Wayde at a cocaine-fuelled bender 18 months ago, says their family will never be the same.

'First, he started doing our taxes without any hurdles. Now he's reading books. This is not the man I agreed to marry in a viral video at the Ivy rooftop pool bar last year.'

> *Medical staff were first alerted to the footballer's autistic mannerisms after learning that Wayde had not only learnt to read, but was also beginning to show an interest in space and planets and shit.*

NRL Stars Welcome Return To Normal Sex Life After Government Allows Gatherings Of Up To Ten

CURRENTLY, THE ONLY CONTACT sport being played in Australia (or if you live in Queensland, The Only Sport) is NRL, but that's not the only reason players are cheering.

Relaxed COVID-19 restrictions allow gatherings of up to ten, meaning NRL players can finally recommence their sex lives as normal.

'Be they single or taken, this is a welcome announcement for all players,' stated NRL CEO Andrew Abdo.

'We are not sure why they like to do it in such large groups. Perhaps it's the camaraderie of participating in a team sport, or maybe just a general disregard for functional relationships?

'For some, they might be just trying to line up a potential career in porn after footy. The blokes swingin' low are definitely thinking about that.'

When asked if he believed that NRL group sex had continued during restrictions, Abdo denied such behaviour, stating that at the very least it had not been filmed.

'We thank the government for this decision and look forward to relaxed legislation on violent assaults in Bali.'

After 67 Days, Man Can Finally Go Back To Playing On Phone With Footy As Background Noise

FOR JUST OVER TWO months, a Betoota Heights man has tried to play with his phone with Netflix on in the background, or the news, various commercial television programs and even the radio.

But it was never as good as having the footy on, he says.

'Whenever you hear one of the commentators, probably Rabs, start yelling and carrying on, you can just look up from your phone to see some winger getting tackled into touch or scoring a sick try,' said Sam Jensen of Greenbow Street. 'Then Gus will start talking shit and I can get back to my phone.

'There's nothing I like more than curling up on the couch with a full charge and the NRL on the telly. Nothing better. Maybe a bowl of potato gems covered in smoky barbecue sauce. A cold tin of gold.

'It's been a long time.'

Broncos Scramble To Find A Big Room Of Pokies For Last-Minute Warm-Up Before Facing Parramatta

THE BRISBANE BRONCOS ARE back to settle a score with the Parramatta Eels tonight, in their first showdown since last year's humiliating 58–0 flogging in the 2019 finals.

The Broncos and Eels will officially kick off the NRL's season relaunch at 7.50 pm tonight, and are expected to host close to 300 million viewers around the world as the first live sporting match to take place since the 2020 coronavirus lockdown began.

While both teams are looking recharged for their second season launch of 2020, it's clear to all fans that the Broncos have a lot more to lose.

It's for this reason that they are sticking to their tried-and-true playbook when it comes to pre-match preparations.

Starting off the day with a team breakfast of Darling Downs sirloin steak and potatoes with a Milton Mango shandy, the boys from Brisbane have been in and out of ice baths and saunas all arvo.

After a half-hour refresher on their backline plays from coach Anthony Seibold, the team was then sent to the theatre room at the Red Hill leagues club to watch the entire *Austin Powers* trilogy.

There is one ritual, however, that is proving quite hard for the players to undertake, as bans on VIP gaming rooms remain in place due to COVID-19 social-distancing measures. It is believed that players and staff are nervous that superstition will spell trouble if the boys aren't able to feed a few pineapples through the brickies' laptops before kick-off.

Club officials have confirmed that all 30 members of the playing squad have been directed to scour the River City for a publican who is a big enough Broncos die-hard to violate state law and turn on the machines for them.

At time of press, one player looks to have made some progress with the manager of the iconic Paddo Tavern, who was directing the boys round the back to the drive-thru bottle shop entry.

BLACK
LIVES
MATTER
I
WANT
A
HAIRCUT
TRUMP
FOR PRESIDENT
2020
No 5G
Our Kids
Live Here!
SOCIAL
DISTANCING
=
COMMUNISM

GLOBAL UNREST

Being tucked away down here at the bottom of the planet, it's easy for Australians to forget our place in the world. It's even easier to forget that most of our newspapers and news websites have a world news section. From wars and famine to natural disaster, it's easy to see why most Australians don't care. Who wants to read about that stuff? It doesn't really happen here. Sure, we have bushfires and maybe a flood every now and then, but it's not like the earth is quaking or sliding or sinking. Our island is a solid rock.

This year changed all of that. Suddenly, our small colonial hellhole here on the dark side of every classroom globe had to deal with a world news issue.

It wasn't like SARS, Ebola or some other god-awful disease that windrows humans – other, far-flung humans – like they're a shot crop. This thing, whatever it is, made the jump from the world news section to the front pages. It made Australians sit up and take an interest in what was going on beyond their own borders. Their ability to go down to the pub, visit their mates and head up the coast for a holiday was now gone. Gone because of something from China, a country which was formerly known to Australia as that piñata full of coins that we as a nation could thrash from time to time to fill up our coffers. The piñata had come home to roost.

When *The Advocate* was drafting up this book in the Australian summertime, we didn't anticipate that we'd have to include a section about the world. Because here in the Queensland desert, our world starts at Quilpie and ends at Birdsville. It runs as far north as Mount Isa and as far south as the Dig Tree. Coronavirus forced us to look further, into the world that lies beyond even the shores of this nation. And then look back at ourselves again. And maybe draw some parallels between systemic social issues in other countries and our own shortcomings as a society.

But we're richer for it. If this crisis has taught us anything up here, it's that Queensland can handle a crisis when we really want to. The Territory can handle a crisis and so can the West. Tassie can – to an extent. South Australia, yes, but yawn, who cares. This crisis has taught us that Victoria, despite its reputation, isn't that up to handling a crisis and New South Wales, in typical fashion, have managed the virus while simultaneously looking like they've got no idea what's going on.

So enjoy this section, and spare a thought for our reporters overseas who didn't make it home before the borders closed. This is their story.

Western Society Now Dictated By Blokes Who Look Like An Uncle That Starts Shit At Christmas

BORIS JOHNSON HAS BEEN named the next British Prime Minister in what has been described as another much-needed win for husky guys who don't know how to dress that well.

Johnson became the most recent winner in the UK's revolving-door leadership coups after knocking off Foreign Secretary Jeremy Hunt for the top job.

However, Mr Johnson has found favour with one very high-profile TV-star-turned-leader-of-the-free-world: Donald Trump.

The US President said Mr Johnson was a 'really good man' who is 'tough and smart'.

Donald Trump, the original daggy dictator, heaped similar praise on Australian Prime Minister Scott Morrison in the hours after the latter's 2019 federal election win.

Between the three of them, it looks like there could be a lot of stern conversations about the Australian cricket side's batting order over a few too many Crownies this Christmas.

Johnson's appointment now also means ill-fitting suits and messy hair are officially back, as Western civilisation makes it clear that they would prefer to be led by very rich people who look and act like your school bus driver.

Canadian Prime Minister Justin Trudeau has reportedly taken Johnson's win as a clear warning, and has immediately ditched his vegetarian diet for a carb-heavy alternative.

> *Between the three of them, it looks like there could be a lot of stern conversations about the Australian cricket side's batting order over a few too many Crownies this Christmas.*

England Leaves World Cup Empty-Handed Just Weeks Before They Exit Europe With Even Less

ENGLAND HAS COME SECOND IN this year's Rugby World Cup, losing to South Africa tonight in the final at Yokohama Stadium.

The All-Whites leave the competition empty-handed once again, their only solace being the defeat was probably the fault of their Australian coach, Eddie Jones.

It comes as another blow to England, as they and the rest of the nation-states they've tied to the Brexit mast are just weeks away from leaving the European Union with even less.

Disney+ To Create More Realistic Prince Who Mixes With Elite Paedophile Sex Ring

PROVING THEY ARE FOR all children, entertainment conglomerate The Walt Disney Company continues to fill its movies with the most financially viable representation possible.

Once famously white and heterosexual, modern Disney Princesses are known for being more racially diverse as well as, in some instances, just queer enough without pissing off China.

While Disney Princesses have been the company's focus in recent years, little has been done to make Disney Princes more realistic. Until now.

'We are proud to announce that our latest prince will be just like the ones we know and loathe,' stated Disney rep Lilly Tian. 'He is an elitist, privately educated middle-aged man who likes to mingle with other wealthy men among a group of trafficked underage girls.

'Oh, and I forgot to mention, this is on taxpayer money, too!'

This realistic portrayal of princes sets a new standard for filmmakers, who may still be inclined to portray male royalty using the less realistic stereotypes of being honourable warriors with no interest in befriending men who are interested in underage girls.

'He likes to mingle with other wealthy men among a group of trafficked underage girls.'

212 THE BETOOTA ADVOCATE | AUSTRALIA 2020

Elon Musk Unable To Confirm Or Deny Reports He's Taking The Cyber Ute To Deni Next Year

BE CAREFUL WHO YOU throw food dye on next year at Deni, because it could be one of the most successful tech entrepreneurs in the world.

Elon Musk is committed to but unable to confirm whether or not he'll be attending the 2020 Deniliquin Ute Muster with his new Cybertruck – or Cyber Ute, as he's calling it.

Nearly 200,000 people have paid a refundable AUD$150 deposit to secure their own Cybertruck when it hits the market sometime over the next five years. Just over ten thousand of them are in Australia.

Mr Musk spoke briefly to *The Advocate's* motoring journalist, Holden Commofield, about how he's going to launch the world's first all-electric light commercial vehicle in Australia.

'I'm committed to taking the Cybertruck, or as you guys will call it, the Cyber Ute, to the Deniliquin – am I saying that right?'

He wasn't, but our reporter just kept nodding for some reason.

'To the Deniliquin Ute Muster next year. It should be great. I can't wait. It's so great how Australians have such an affinity with the ute slash truck product. Watch this space!'

However, some of the more traditional Deni ute devotees aren't exactly thrilled at the news.

A local man who attends the Muster each year in his WB said that Musk won't be as welcome as he thinks he will be down in the Riverina.

Dale Poncho, who works in some capacity, said the electric ute isn't a real ute and therefore won't be allowed to enter in any events.

'A Proton Jumbuck would be more welcome at Deni,' he said. 'This cyber shit isn't a real ute. At least a Jumbuck burns petrol. The Malaysian billycart had to earn its place at Deni. If Elon thinks he can just come in here and do what he wants, he's got another thing coming.'

Our reporter asked Elon what he thought of the muted reaction from certain members of the ute-mustering community like Mr Poncho, and Mr Musk said they can form a line to 'suck my dick'.

Chinese Comment With Over 11K Likes On Mack Horton's Instagram Must Be A Pretty Good Burn

AUSTRALIAN SPORT HAS TODAY been graced with the most amazing sledge since the days of Merv Hughes, in an Instagram post of one of Mack Horton's most recent photos that has attracted wide praise.

While Australians, as a whole, appreciate a good bit of return fire when it comes to international sporting rivalries, it seems the greatest ever insult directed to an Aussie athlete is one that most of the country is unable to translate.

Anger towards Australian swimmer and prominent gweilo Mack Horton has once again dominated Chinese social media, with millions of people directing their fury at the Rio gold medallist over his refusal to share a podium after being beaten by alleged drug cheat Sun Yang.

Horton has long been critical of swimming authorities for allowing the Chinese star to compete after serving a three-month suspension in 2014 for testing positive to a banned stimulant, and last year smashing a blood vial during a dispute over the process of a random drug test.

Chinese social media users have violated their own country's internet censorship rules to attack Mack Horton on Instagram, with hundreds of thousands of comments taking aim at the Australian swimmer – and also accusing him of being 'the real drug addict' because the 2013 Australian men's swim team admitted to abusing Stilnox when Horton was just finishing high school.

However, unfortunately for us English-speaking spectators of this social media storm, we'll never be able to translate all of this golden banter because most of it is in Mandarin or Cantonese.

One particular comment has rung up 11,063 likes and resulted in a lot of laughing emojis from Chinese Instagram users.

'吃袋鼠狗屎你不敬的白猪', wrote Casaxoxo, in what appears to be a very good call, and one that has triggered nearly one hundred more replies with poo emojis next to the Australian flag.

Australians are rushing to translate this post because it looks like it must have been quite a burn.

> **Meg N Haz Essex**
> Today at 07:33
>
> Getting pretty sick of the drama aye. Not really sure why some ppl feel the need to constantly be chucking their two sense in about other peoples lives... If you've got a problem why don't you be a man and talk to me face to face instead of sayimg shit to other people behind me and Meg's back.
>
> 👍 Like   💬 Comment   ↗ Share
>
> 👍❤️😮 16

Unemployed Prince Harry Takes To Facebook With Vague Status About Being Sick Of The Drama

AS THE ROYAL FAMILY prepares for an 'emergency crisis meeting' convened by the Queen, want-away Prince Harry has thickened the plot with a vague, passive-aggressive Facebook status.

After days of intense scrutiny over his and Meghan's decision to step down from their royal duties and attempt to become financially independent, the young father took to his shared Facebook account to vent.

Aimed at someone who probably 'knows who they are', the popular and unemployed royal posted the status this morning, informing his Facebook friends that he's sick of the drama.

Stopping short of calling anyone a two-faced dog, Harry told *The Advocate* this morning that he just wanted to put everyone on notice.

'Mate, things are pretty tough at the moment, and I don't want to mention any names, but people like my brother saying he won't put his arm around me as a brother anymore are pissing me off,' said Harry.

Like many people angry at those around them, Harry said he felt like blowing off some steam with the vague but targeted status on Facebook.

'I'm over all this drama. I don't need it in my life. I'm done with toxic people, bro,' he said.

Shortly after hanging up the phone, fellow royal defector Meghan posted a photo of a coffee on Instagram with the caption, 'Please lord give me the strength to deal with all these idiots.'

The royal meeting is set to take place later on today.

Stopping short of calling anyone a two-faced dog, Harry told The Advocate *this morning that he just wanted to put everyone on notice.*

REDACTED BY LEGAL

Kevin Rudd Warns Against Upsetting Chi – Blah Blah Blah Blah Blah I'm A Fucken Nerd Blah Blah

FORMER PRIME MINISTER Kevin Rudd has tried to tell us what to think of China again and blah blah yawn, Kevin, find another hill to die on.

Today at some $2000-a-plate lunch for some fucking think tank, Kevin said some things about China and how it's not as bad as the nation's Holden Racing Team shirt owners think it is and so on.

'Blah blah blah blah blah I'm a fucken nerd blah blah,' he said.

The comments come after non-former Prime Minister Scott Morrison has said he wants to get to the bottom of the coronavirus and put his support behind calls for a global investigation into the cause.

China is obviously not stoked about this investigation, said Rudd, which means we should support the investigation.

Rudd was, for the third time in his life, thrown under the bus by Opposition leader Anthony Albanese, who said he supports Scott Morrison's push for the investigation.

'I support this investigation,' said Albo.

Kevin then said a few things in Mandarin, which failed to lift the crowd.

'You'll be sorry when China starts to boycott us. No more tourists, no more students. No more trading partners.'

A visibly intoxicated mining executive then took it upon himself to stand up on his chair, exposing the piss dribbling down the right leg of his beige moleskins, cup his hands together around his mouth and tell the former Prime Minister what he really thought.

'Neeeerrrrrrrddddddddd,' he said. 'Shut up, Kevin!'

Kevin finished his speech and gestured for the bloke to follow him.

They went outside and Kevin slapped the mining executive into next Thursday. As the big mining executive tried to get back on his feet, Kevin put one of his size-five Hush Puppies across the iron ore cowboy's jaw then watched him fall back onto the cement.

Mr Rudd then left the scene on foot.

> *A visibly intoxicated mining executive then took it upon himself to stand up on his chair, and tell the former Prime Minister what he really thought. 'Neeeerrrrrrrddddddddd,'*

Bloke Who Tells Traffic Cops To Fuck Off And Catch Real Criminals Disgusted By US Protestors

PROTESTS OVER THE DEATH in custody of George Floyd are continuing in over 50 major cities across the United States.

In some areas the riots have descended into looting as law enforcement loses the ability to de-escalate the demonstrations that were ironically kickstarted by law enforcement's inability to de-escalate the routine ID check of an unarmed black man who was murdered by police on live video in Minneapolis six days ago.

However, it appears that the frustrated crowds are now turning their attention to the political class that has provoked this volatile underclass to the point of complete civil disorder.

Police have marched on large crowds of protesters gathering near the White House, and National Guard members have been deployed to protect town halls in Minneapolis and other cities around the country as the protests begin to get a bit scary for the political elite.

14,772 kilometres away from the Minnesota capital, Betoota local and Quiet Australian Tony Bishop (54) says that these bloody protestors need a good clip around the ears.

It's a sentiment echoed right across the country through conservative news channels like *The Australian* and Sky News.

The Betoota Heights–based tractor retailer says you can tell all of these protestors received a trophy in team sports, because this kind of disrespect for authority only comes from a childhood of never hearing the word 'no'.

Despite the fact that Tony nearly lost his entire franchise after comments he made about Julia Gillard on local talkback radio in 2011, the father-of-three says this kind of civil disobedience towards government is a worrying trend that never existed before Waleed Aly was on TV.

> *14,772 kilometres away from the Minnesota capital, local Quiet Australian Tony Bishop (54) says that these bloody protestors need a good clip around the ears.*

Tony's new-found respect for law and order also comes as a stark contrast to his habit of routinely telling traffic police to fuck off and catch real criminals every time he gets pulled over for speeding or driving erratically while arguing with his wife.

'It's not the same,' he says, when asked to compare Americans protesting the systemic racism ingrained into law enforcement and the time he nearly got taken to the watch house for telling a 60-year-old Queensland police officer to suck his cock during a random breath test.

'These people are snowflakes.

'Andrew Bolt is right. This is just an opportunity for minority groups to steal free stuff because they weren't raised properly.'

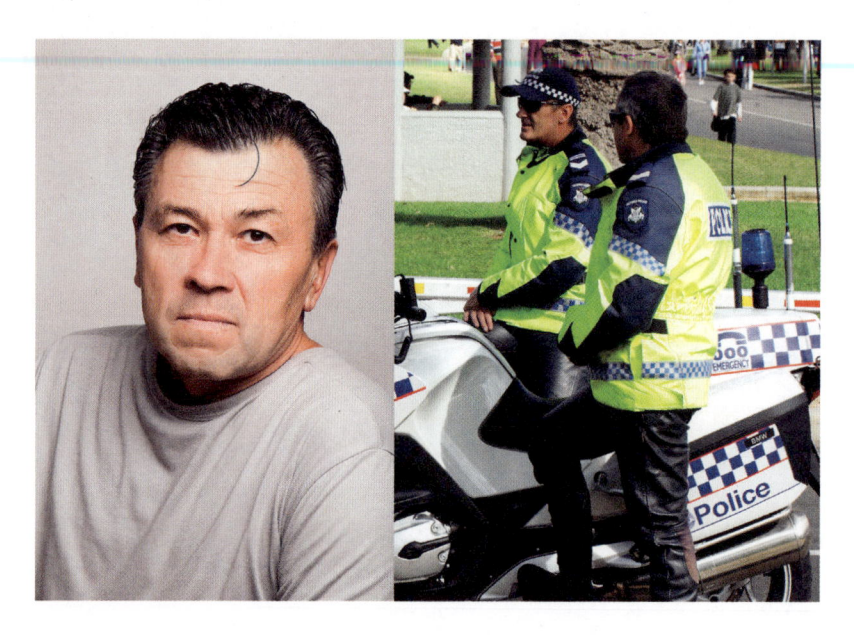

'Donny, Mate, I'm Telling Ya. Hawaii.'

AS CIVIL RIGHTS PROTESTS continue in nearly 80 major cities across the United States, President Trump has today called the only man who can give him advice on what to do when your country is on fire.

Sources said Mr Trump rang Mr Morrison this morning to enlist his support in how to manage his own self-care in such a troubling time.

In between phoning Mr Morrison and tear-gassing protestors so that he could prove he didn't need a bunker to be safe, Mr Trump inflamed the situation in the US by threatening to call out the military to suppress the unrest.

It is believed that Mr Morrison was unaware at the time of the phone call that a Channel Seven cameraman had been insulted by DC riot police – not that he would have confronted his political idol about it anyway.

The PM's office has today clarified that the phone call was mostly Trump asking for pointers on how to manage his work–life balance during the unprecedented civil unrest.

With his country continuing to descend into an unflattering display of public disorder, it appears that Trump is starting to get a bit tired and grouchy.

Morrison had the answer for him.

'Donny, mate, I'm telling ya. Hawaii.

'You aren't the first bloke to experience a shock to the approval ratings because of your inability to handle a crisis. Take it from me, the best thing you can do right now is park your arse in Waikiki and ride this thing out.

'I'll get Jenny to send Melania the name of the place we stayed at.'

GLOBAL UNREST

FBI Arrests Bill Gates For Biological Terrorism After Tip-Off From Melbourne 5G Protestors

THE BILLIONAIRE FOUNDER OF Microsoft, Bill Gates (64), has been arrested by the FBI today on charges of biological terrorism after it was revealed he created the coronavirus so that he could control us because he's always had an interest in that kind of thing.

Over 1000 FBI officers surrounded his high-security underground Seattle science bunker earlier today, where they told him to come out with his hands up, and to bring the cure for COVID-19 with him, if he could.

The arrest of Bill Gates is reportedly the result of a tip-off from the Melbourne conspiracy theorists who breached Victorian lockdown restrictions yesterday to spread 'the truth' about this so-called pandemic.

According to the 100 or so freedom fighters who gathered at the steps of Victorian state parliament yesterday, the truth is actually a lot different from what Australia's 32,000-plus medical practitioners are suggesting, which is that COVID-19 is a highly contagious respiratory illness that appears to have crossed over from wildlife to humans in the Wuhan region of China late last year.

Instead, those who can 'see through the media' say that it is actually a combination of villainous pharmaceutical companies working with both the Orwellian scientists behind the 5G cellular technology network and tech billionaire Bill Gates to control our minds and ruin our economy.

The brave protestors also believe this evil coalition of authoritarian billionaires is working alongside Australia's commercial TV networks to lie to the general public about this messy and highly inconsistent combination of authoritarian agendas.

Ten people have been arrested for breaching government social-distancing measures and physically clashing with the police at the rally.

Protesters chanted slogans criticising Victorian Premier Daniel Andrews and demanding that stay-at-home restrictions be lifted, while also calling for Bill Gates to be arrested.

It is not yet known how Bill Gates has become public enemy number one for our nation's coronavirus conspiracists, especially after his recent donation of $10 million to Australian disease researchers working to prevent severe cases of COVID-19 in at-risk groups such as healthcare workers and the elderly.

Regardless, it seems that their brave efforts to spread the truth have paid off overnight, with the FBI finally arresting Bill Gates on charges of biological terrorism and the recently invented crime of coronavirus-making.

Speaking to *The Betoota Advocate* today, leading Victorian anti-5G-anti-vaccine-anti-lockdown protestor, Keith (49), says while he appreciates seeing Bill Gates arrested, this is just the tip of the iceberg.

'You can't arrest Bill Gates while David Koch and Karl Stefanovic get to walk free,' said the prominent YouTube user and retired roofer who has been on compo for two decades.

'We need the FBI to arrest the hosts of both the *Today* show and *Sunrise* for lying to us. As well as the blokes who keep building these phone towers. Telstra, Vodafone, Optus. Them too. They are all complicit.

'ScoMo should also be brought to justice for peddling the advice of these so-called medical experts. This is just the beginning. The truth is out there.'

The brave protestors also believe this evil coalition of authoritarian billionaires is working alongside Australia's commercial TV networks to lie about this messy and highly inconsistent combination of authoritarian agendas.

US Government Deploys Military After Oil Was Discovered Beneath Dozens Of Protests

US PRESIDENT DONALD TRUMP'S idle threat to deploy the military to help quell scores of protests around the country has all but been guaranteed after large deposits of oil were discovered beneath the protests themselves.

Speaking in the White House's Rose Garden earlier today, Trump explained that he's putting America first and securing their oil supply long into the future.

'These protests are a weapon of mass destruction,' he said.

'They threaten the security of the United States and our way of life. For the benefit of the global community, we are going to remove these protestors … and secure the energy assets beneath them. Thank you.'

The President concluded the press conference without taking any questions.

The news that the military is going to be deployed against US citizens has been met with widespread criticism – but many other leaders around the world have joined Trump in saying action needs to be taken.

Prime Minister Scott Morrison and his British counterpart Boris Johnson phoned Donald early this morning to congratulate him on the strong stance he's taking on national security and to pledge their support.

Speaking begrudgingly to our newspaper this morning, the Prime Minister said he and the other leaders of the English-speaking world have joined a 'coalition of the willing' of sorts.

'We wanted to let the people of America know that we stand with them,' said Scott Morrison.

'I want the people of Betoota to know that this newspaper is trash and they should be reading *The Betoota Bugle*, which is edited and managed by Col Allan's dachshund, Persephone. But I don't need to tell you that. The articles in her paper aren't very disparaging of me.

'Together, we'll all get through this.'

Boycott Heats Up As China Now Threatens To Stop Buying Australia

THE RELATIONSHIP BETWEEN China and Australia is at an all-time low today as Beijing has threatened in a tersely worded statement that if relations do not improve, China will immediately cease purchasing Australian companies, houses, resources and vast swathes of prime Australian agricultural land.

Chinese entities currently own (or have 99-year leases on) the Port of Darwin, an airport in Western Australia, a few coalmines and wind farms, 732 gigalitres (2%) of Australia's fresh water supply and nine million hectares of farmland, which represents 2.3% of Australia's agricultural land. Around 5% of Australian houses are owned by foreign nationals and one-third of residential development sites in Australia are sold to Chinese companies alone.

In comparison, China does not allow foreign investors to purchase land in China.

'We'll do it!' said a spokesminion from China's Ministry of Commerce. 'We'll say come on, chaps, head home, our money's not welcome in Australia. I guess they think they can run their own country without us. Good luck!'

Following the statement, most Australian politicians were in damage control as they desperately tried to keep the money rolling in to make all the balance sheets look pretty for the next election.

No members of the Australian public were available for comment as they were all online, trying to insult as many Communist Party of China officials as possible.

NBA Facing Pressure From Netflix Viewers To Please Bring Back Those Nineties Dress Codes

THE NATIONAL BASKETBALL Association is being urged by both fans and non-fans to please re-implement the dress code standards that once saw Michael Jordan wearing a skivvy with a blazer and beret in post-match press conferences.

This follows the success of the new Netflix isolation blockbuster *The Last Dance* – a new ESPN production that has introduced an entire generation to the 1990s Chicago Bulls fashion sense.

The ten-part documentary chronicles Michael Jordan and the Bulls' two separate championship three-peats, with never-before-seen dressing room footage that highlights the glorious outfits of that era.

The since-discarded NBA dress codes once stipulated that all players must dress in business or conservative attire while arriving for and departing after a scheduled game, on the bench while injured, and when conducting official NBA business (press interviews, charity events, etc). The dress code banned fashions most often associated with hip-hop culture, specifically: jeans, hats, do-rags, T-shirts, large jewellery, sneakers and Timberland boots.

Understandably, the dress codes were eventually thrown out for being a little bit too elitist and military for a game based around throwing a rubber ball through a hoop, with players now opting to wear their warm-up kit and game jerseys for pre- and post-match functions.

While both basketball fans and distant observers have always been aware of the eccentric fashion sense of Bulls legend Dennis Rodman, this new documentary has given Netflix viewers an even better look at Jordan and Scottie Pippen's 1990s drip, as well as those white boys who used to dress like Bruce Springsteen.

The NBA has released a statement today in response to the growing social media campaign calling for the game to re-implement the dress codes under the hashtag #DressLikeMike.

'The NBA understands the nostalgia associated with seeing Michael Jordan in jet-black country club attire,' read the statement.

'Unfortunately, we have no plans to reintroduce player dress codes at this time. Seriously, do you think those baggy cream suits would hold up in 2020? Nowadays the stars wear whatever their Kardashian girlfriends tell them to, which is usually something designed by Kanye West, which is usually quite aesthetically unpleasing.'

> *This new documentary has given Netflix viewers an even better look at Jordan and Scottie Pippen's 1990s drip, as well as those white boys who used to dress like Bruce Springsteen.*

GLOBAL UNREST

Americans So Mad They Might Even Consider Thinking About Possibly Voting

> *'I don't need to vote; I made a sign instead,' said a protestor at a rally held inside a burning Target store. 'That way, other people at this protest will realise how important this issue is, which should be easy since they are there for the same reason I am. Then, if they decide to vote, they will vote for the person I would have voted for anyway.'*

AS THE US COMPLETES the transition from a dangerous place full of guns into a dangerous place full of guns and riots, some protestors have signalled that they are so dissatisfied with how their country is being run that they might even vote if they get around to it.

Unlike Australia, where voting is compulsory for everyone over the age of 18, the United States does not compel citizens to vote, resulting in a much lower voter turnout.

As a consequence, in the 2019 Australian federal election, 96.8% of eligible voters were enrolled to vote and, of these, 91.9% exercised their democratic right to vote for the party that they considered the least likely to totally fuck up the country.

Meanwhile, in the US 2016 presidential elections, a mere 58% of eligible voters bothered to vote, possibly because nobody seriously believed the winner would be someone who at the time was famous for firing people and giving Macaulay Culkin directions in *Home Alone 2*.

'I don't need to vote; I made a sign instead,' said a protestor at a rally held inside a burning Target store.

'That way, other people at this protest will realise how important this issue is, which should be easy since they are there for the same reason I am. Then, if they decide to vote, they will vote for the person I would have voted for anyway. So it all works out.'

However, voter turnout for the 2020 presidential election is predicted to be the highest in a century, as public dissatisfaction drives non-voters to register. As young, non-white and low-income groups are over-represented among non-voters, and over-represented in the protests, it could be bad news for Team Trump if all of these groups get around to possibly thinking about maybe registering to vote.

But the world will have to wait until the end of the year to find out if elderly white upper-class Trump serves another term or if he will be ousted by elderly white upper-class Joe Biden.

What a time to be alive.

> *Some protestors have signalled that they are so dissatisfied with how their country is being run that they might even vote if they get around to it.*

China Threatens To Boycott Kangaroo Scrotum Coin Purses

AS TENSIONS BETWEEN Australia and China escalate, Beijing has released a statement threatening to ban Australia's fourth most valuable export.

The iconic kangaroo scrotum coin purse ranks just behind coal, iron ore and other tourist trinkets which are technically made in China as a critical cornerstone of the export economy and a key indicator of economic stability ever since they were invented by kangaroos millions of years ago.

Made by multiple companies, the coin purses are inexplicably popular tourist souvenirs, and are sold at tourist attractions and on eBay.

In 2008, it was estimated that more kangaroo scrotums existed outside of Australia than within, attached to the undercarriage of kangaroos.

Minister for Finance Mathias Cormann said it was critical that China–Australia relations improve immediately to prevent the collapse of the vital kangaroo scrotum coin purse industry.

'Kangaroo scrotum coin purses currently make up over 80% of our manufacturing output,' explained the nervous Finance Minister this week.

'If we can't sort this situation out then we'll have to switch our focus back to trying to smuggle methamphetamines into China, and that hasn't been going so great lately either.'

Although multiple kangaroos were contacted for comment, none was prepared to speak on the matter except one who mentioned something about Timmy being stuck down a well or something.

PM: 'Killing Unarmed Black Men Is One Thing, But Don't You Dare Touch The *Sunrise* Cameraman!'

FOR THE FIRST TIME since Minnesota law enforcement officers killed the unarmed black man George Floyd live on camera seven days ago, Prime Minister Scott Morrison has today suggested that maybe American police are a little heavy-handed.

This comes after a Channel Seven cameraman was punched by riot cops outside the White House last night while the latter were clearing the vicinity with tear gas so that President Trump could get a photo in front of a church across the road.

The incident comes amid a string of police attacks on members of the media during the nationwide protests triggered by the most recent murder of a black man by police, who then released a tampered autopsy absolving themselves of blame – despite being caught on video pressing a knee into his neck for nine minutes.

However, unlike the incident that actually caused these protests, the attack on a white cameraman for a conservative Australian news channel has finally forced the Prime Minister to confront the issue head-on.

It's for this reason that Morrison has instructed Australia's embassy in the US to investigate the incident.

'Look, I usually stay out of America's volatile culture of systemic racism in their police forces and industrial prison system,' said Morrison.

'Do they have a horrible culture of killing unarmed members of minority groups and not prosecuting the cops involved…? That's not my place to say. But what I saw today on *Sunrise*, between the Cash Cow segment and the weather report – what we all saw – sent chills through my body.'

Morrison says that he can only imagine the fear felt by the cameraman in that moment, knowing that he was completely powerless to stop the assault, even though he was a correspondent for the Liberal Party's propaganda arm.

'I will say this to the American police force, and the American government as a whole: Killing thousands of unarmed black men is one thing, but don't you dare touch the *Sunrise* cameraman.

'I saw a good meme on the weekend – Ronald Reagan didn't change anything by brutalising white men,' he told 2GB this morning.

'Hopefully the President can schedule in another phone call with me over the next few months so we can talk about this.'

Anti-Fascist Punk Takes Break From Smoking Bongs In Grandma's Basement To Mastermind Race Riot

OHIO-BASED ANTIFA MEMBER, Marshall Kent (24), says he was never really that political in college.

That was until he saw Hillary Clinton undermine Bernie Sanders' chance of winning the Democratic presidential nomination, in turn handballing the White House to a white supremacist.

After that, he started going to protests. Some of them were violent, but he always knew he was never going to be arrested because of his white privilege.

It wasn't long until he was sneaking out at night to vandalise Confederate statues in his small university town.

Fast forward an entire presidential term, and Marshall is now a full-blown domestic terrorist. Not the type that takes a loaded AR-15 into a black church and kills nine elderly worshippers before getting a ride to Burger King on his way to the police station. He's not the type that bombs abortion clinics and synagogues after months of polluting the internet with Nazi propaganda without raising any suspicion from the police. In fact, those guys are his enemies, because Marshall is an anti-fascist terrorist.

'I'm more into the false-flag operations,' he says. 'You know, like organising the destruction of over 75 major US cities with race riots by masterminding 400 years of systemic racism and generational inequality among black people. That's my specialty. You might have seen some of my stuff in the news.'

Unfortunately for Marshall, he's not gonna get away with this kind of stuff for much longer, after President Donald Trump tweeted that he is going to designate self-proclaimed anti-fascists as a terrorist organisation.

Trump has pointed the finger for the current US riots at 'Antifa' – which is a loose title for anti-fascist radicals who fight against the same kind of people that the US Army used to fight against when the country still had a bit to be proud of.

With the FBI now placing bugs in the underground marijuana-cloaked man cave out the back of his grandmother's house, Marshall says it feels like the end is near for his cause.

'I've stocked up on some cyanide. I'm gonna go out a martyr,' he says.

'I hope that America's minority underclass can continue to mobilise against police brutality and white supremacy without my help.'

Study Into Free Trade Deal With UK Concludes They Have Nothing We Actually Want Or Need

WHILE THE BRITISH PRIME Minister continues to spruik the potential economic bonanza that awaits a post-Brexit Britain, a study into the proposed trade deal with Australia has yielded a different sentiment.

The study, conducted by the Diamantina Chamber of Commerce, has found that Britain doesn't make anything Australians actually need or want.

Conversely, there are many things that Australia produces and exports that the Brits want to get their filthy little unwashed hands on.

'It's a bit of a one-way street,' said DCC Chairman Darcy Tuckwell.

'The only thing Britain really offers Australia is a constant supply of mediocre, largely inbred people to be used as unskilled labour. We've all seen those roly-poly English blokes on their Australian odyssey, half rooted before 9 am and carrying a bucket of busted bricks from an upstairs shitter down to the skip bin.

'Or you've got the token office Pom. Huge underbite. Big St George Cross up on the pillar nearest their cubicle. Water cooler conversations about Everton and why David Warner is a bender. There's really not that much else.'

Conversely, there are many things that Australia produces and exports that the Brits want to get their filthy little unwashed hands on.

Trump Tells Supporters He's Gonna Need Another Four Years To Really Make America Great Again

US PRESIDENT AND FORMER host of *Celebrity Apprentice*, Donald Trump (74), famously won the 2016 presidential election running on the promise to 'Make America Great Again'.

Due to the USA having a history of massacres, slavery and something called the McBiscuit, Trump failed to win over minority voters by promising to restore things to how they once were.

Yet, the man who opened the only casino that has ever lost money won the election by ranting at mass rallies and berating the media, who actually really enjoyed the ratings boost they got from relaying his bigotry into very watchable soundbites.

After about three minutes in office, it became clear that President Trump would prefer campaigning to making the changes he promised, which seems to be the case again this time round as he takes time off his busy golfing schedule to start campaigning for 2020.

At a recent rally in Bigotsfield, Mississippi, Mr Trump spoke honestly with his supporters and told them he'd need another four years to really make America great again.

'People say that I was going to do everything in one year. I never said that, you filmed it, I didn't say it,' stated Mr Trump in an assembly room which literally contained more Nazis than Paris in 1941.

'You take the four, minus the one, that's three, math, very smart. Now we're going to make America really great again in just four years, numbers, that's my thing.

'The wall is going to be made of guns, it will protect itself, that's jobs!'

Critics of Trump and other people who don't have fucking rocks in their head have criticised the President's first term for inciting multiple counts of race violence, normalising sexual assault and threatening mass global conflict every time he takes his phone with him to do a Diet Coke-powered shit.

'Even Webster's has a better definition of "great" than Donald Trump,' stated CNN reporter and known Antifa member Anderson Cooper.

'He has fanned the flames of a second civil rights movement. This is definitely someone who is taking our country back more than a few years.'

Trump has, however, insisted that he's not far off that greatness he promised, but he's obviously met a few hurdles with the whole COVID-19 pandemic and nationwide civil unrest.

'I'm gonna need four more years,' he says.

'Bigger job than I thought.'

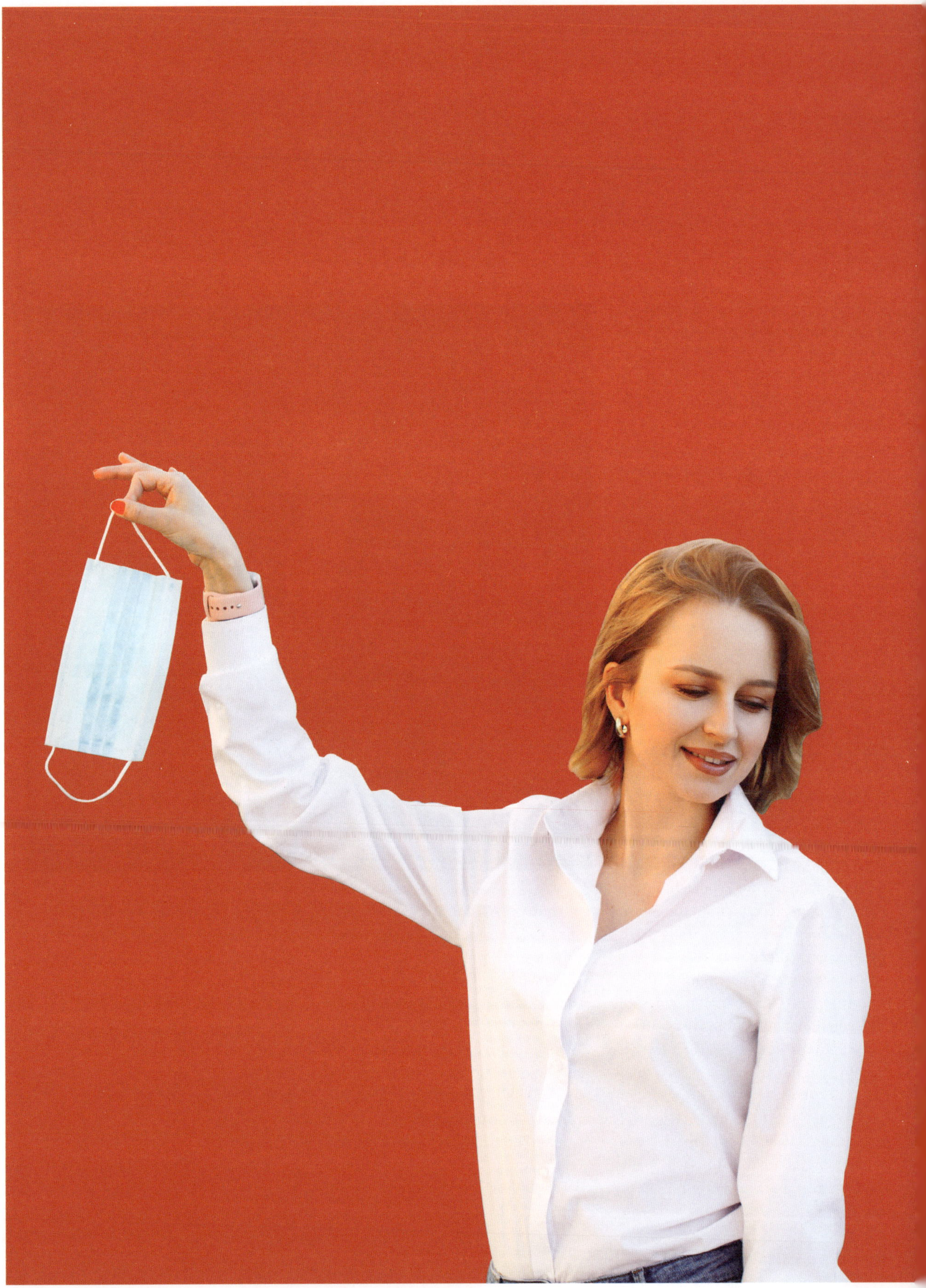

LIKE NOTHING HAPPENED

After the walls came down and we could hold hands once more, it became clear that Australians weren't going to take any of their freedoms for granted again.

As the restrictions gradually loosened, Australians returned to the streets with renewed enthusiasm.

Going to the pub or a restaurant is no longer viewed as 'something to do' – it's now something we *must* do. Weekend sport has never been more important, and it's a great time to be dating. Plus, the once unappreciated road rage incident or a run-in with parking rangers is now an experience to be cherished, because any human contact is better than none.

While the global COVID-19 lockdown gave nature a chance to heal without the ubiquitous smog and pollution, the post-isolation period has given our communities a new lease on life.

Australians now associate a quiet weekend watching Netflix and working on the backyard with that horrible time we spent hiding from the virus. With that (mostly) behind us, it's time to get out and about. The economy is limping along, but our appreciation for one another has never been more evident. The only reason anyone should be watching TV is if they couldn't get tickets to the footy. Even the flakiest of flakes are turning up to parties to celebrate non-milestone birthdays.

In this chapter, we are taking a break from the politicians that have undeservedly become household names due to Australia's celebrity deficit. It's time to focus on the way things were and shine a spotlight on the mundane situations and yarns that tell the tale of this crazy thing called life, from the local men and local women, mums, dads, sisters, brothers, boyfriends, girlfriends, wives, husbands, pops, nans, kids, pets, enemies, mentors, rivals, heroes, villains and strangers that glue us together.

The world may be burning and coughing, but at least now we can hug.

We have love affairs, we have scandals, we have big losses and big wins. This is your community, and these are your stories.

Pork Chop Denies Carrying On

A MEAT RAFFLE AT the iconic Betoota Hotel has ended in a brawl after a pork chop started carrying on.

Although accounts of the night vary due to the differing amounts of alcohol consumed by those present, the pork chop claims he is not to blame.

'Yeah, it's unfair, mate. Everyone goes yeah, he's carrying on like the pork chop that he is, but that's actually a really offensive stereotype and there's no need for that sort of shit in 2020.'

Derek Ralstone, who was the bouncer on the night as part of his Year 10 work experience placement, said the pork chop really was the instigator of the ruckus.

'He just wouldn't shut up, everyone was like, get over it mate, it's just a joke, but he kept saying that it was his right to make a scene and he wasn't prepared to cool off in the coolroom.'

However, the pork chop disagrees.

'Yeah, things got pretty wild for a bit. Some guy made a pig joke, but I responded like anyone in my position would, and then it was on for young and old. I did tenderise a few blokes, that's true, but they had it coming, for sure.

'What, you don't believe me? Bullshit, mate, I saw you smirking, smartarse, what's so funny? You think this shit is funny, bro? Put up or shut up, mate.

'No, fuck you, I won't calm down, I've had a gutful of pricks like you thinking I'm carrying on like a pork chop, like it's my destiny or some shit.

'Fuck you, bring it on! Let's go, mate. Let's go, come on. Bring it on, brother!'

Further details were not available as the recording device was damaged at this point.

Derek Ralstone, who was the bouncer on the night as part of his Year 10 work experience placement, said the pork chop really was the instigator of the ruckus.

Local Man Thinks He Might Let The Dogs Out Tonight, Just Quietly

A LOCAL CITY WORKER immediately cleared his evening schedule the moment an ice-cold schooner touched his lips this afternoon.

Mickey De Santis, a local graphic design and signage specialist from Betoota Plains, has just felt a thick plume of steam roll up the back of his shirt and out his collar.

'AAHHHHHHHHHHHHHH,' he says. 'That's pretty fucking good.'

With maybe a few half-hearted social events lying there in wait with different friends and family, Mickey has already fired off a few texts to the mates he knows will be down.

'Well, the post-silly season lull is over, I guess,' he says to one of our reporters.

'I went pretty straight for a while there. Like a week or so. I've got a bit of a sting, aye.'

While his first schooey this arvo was actually with his work colleagues, he's pretty willing to bet that if he buys his boss another one of those tasty craft beer things he likes, they are all gonna be given the rest of the day off.

This means Mickey can jump ship and meet his mates at a pub that he actually likes drinking at.

'Who's on?' he says to his mates in their Friday arvo group chat.

'I reckon I might let the dogs out tonight, just quietly.'

> *'I went pretty straight for a while there. Like a week or so. I've got a bit of a sting, aye.'*

City Dog Visiting The Bush Disgusted By Dry Dog Biscuits She's Served

A CITY DOG HAS entered her fourth day of a hunger strike today after she's once again served a bowl of dry dog biscuits.

The strike is particularly worrying for Christine Iskender as she's dog-sitting Ruby the pug for her cousin while she's holidaying in Europe.

'She just won't eat, at one point she even started dry retching. I thought she was dying,' said a desperate Christine to our reporter.

In an effort to keep Ruby alive for her cousin, Christine hired Betoota's best dog behavioural expert to see if she could communicate with Ruby and see what the problem was.

'Yes, yes, the issue is completely clear to me,' she said.

'Ruby hates what you're feeding her.

'She usually has brown rice and poached chicken twice a day, darling.'

The expert pressed her face into Ruby's for a deeper reading.

'She's now telling me that you haven't even been massaging her paws. And that her anxiety is through the roof because you haven't been playing her meditation tracks as she goes to sleep.

'Ruby's asked me to tell you to pull your head in and start treating her properly or she'll bite you.'

It's believed Christine was unsure how to respond to the expert's reading.

On one hand, she was concerned that the dog wasn't eating, but on the other, it was a fucking dog and it would eat what it was bloody well given.

---

234   THE BETOOTA ADVOCATE | AUSTRALIA 2020

Local Derro Puts Holden Badge Back On His Chevrolet Commodore In Touching Display Of Respect

A BETOOTA HEIGHTS petrolhead has announced this afternoon that he plans to put the Holden badge back on his Chevrolet Commodore today in order to pay respect to the Australian carmaker who earlier this week decided to pull out of the right-hand-drive market.

Awash with feelings of guilt and pangs of regret, Damien Leary admitted he swapped out Holden's iconic lion badge for Chevrolet's creepy gold cross motif a few years ago because he saw a few other people do it and thought it looked cool.

Now he feels he's played a part in GM's demise on this hellish planet we have all helped destroyed in some way.

'Like, aw fuck, mate, I feel heaps bad about Holden and that,' he said.

'But, like, the Chevvy badge looks fucken sick but like you got to pay your respects to Holden now. Like, that was Aussie. Nothing more Aussie than a Commodore. Like yeah, that 3.6 litre engine or whatever it was had heaps of grunt for towing things.

'I'm putting the Holden badge back on. It's the least I can do.'

> 'Like, aw fuck, mate, I feel heaps bad about Holden and that,' he said.

Bloke With Weeping Muffler Burn Says What Ya Wanna Do Is Go Straight To Kuta Beach

LOCAL GOLD COAST MAN Broadie Cavill (39) knows all the good shit to do in Bali, if you were ever thinking of going. He just got back.

With his right arm strapped in cling wrap and his triplet daughters rocking the cornrows, Broadie is trotting around his local tavern in the canal district of the Glitter City talking about how fucking good his fifth trip to Indonesia was.

'What ya you wanna do is go straight to Kuta,' he says while scratching his chest through his 'tang singlet.

'There's this joint there called Potato Heads. Fuck it's good.'

Broadie's wife Anastaysha, who is covered from head to toe in a brightly coloured muu-muu, disagrees.

'Seminyak is pretty good too, wouldn't you say, love?' she overrides. 'Great shopping. Don't bother with any of those other hippie islands. They are just full of locals. There's a few great Aussie spots near Seminyak. It's pretty much the new Kuta.'

Broadie, a FIFO formworker out of Mount Isa, says you don't wanna go any longer than a week before the locals get a bit too annoying.

'The resorts are all right. We pretty much only stayed in the resorts at night,' he snorts, while sucking back a clovey. 'Make sure you stay in a resort because the street food is fucken crook.

'Oh, and get yourself a scooter. But watch out [laughs]. They'll try and sting you for it if you come off.'

Girlfriend Rattles Off Last-Minute Panic Order Despite Studying Menu Online Days Prior

A LOCAL WOMAN is this evening seething in her seat after she ordered fish fingers at 14 Wilson St, one of Betoota's top Italian restaurants, despite spending the best part of the last three days studying the menu.

'I don't know what happened,' says a distraught Claire Dougham.

'I have been looking at the menu for the past three days, I'd even decided what I wanted. I don't know what came over me.

'Oh well, I'll just have some of Jim's.'

However, upon speaking with Jim, *The Advocate* can confirm that she'll only get a mouthful of his feed.

'This is her bed, she can lie in it. She has been studying this menu like it's her HSC or something. If she can't make a decision then that's her problem.'

At the time of print Claire had just placed a second order of garlic bread in hopes of filling up on that scrumptious delicacy and fending off the pain and regret she feels from ordering what is basically a frozen meal.

236　THE BETOOTA ADVOCATE | AUSTRALIA 2020

Local White Guy Only Has Like Three Cousins

A LOCAL ANGLO-AUSTRALIAN has today revealed that he doesn't relate to big family events, because he only has like three cousins that he only sees once every three years.

Ethan Brendan (25) has taken things to a new level of whiteness today by saying he doesn't understand why woggy weddings are so big, because, like, why would you get that worked up by your mum's sibling's daughter getting married?

'I think my cousin Michael got married a few years ago … I'm not sure. I had my girlfriend's netball final on that weekend, from memory …

'But, yeah, there was no plate-smashing or people being lifted on shoulders. Haha. That stuff is so weird.'

As a sales rep for a new brand of superannuation software, Ethan quite often meets a lot of people from a lot of different backgrounds – so it's not like he only hangs out with white people.

'The guy I sit next to is Indian,' he says, referring to his Sri Lankan sales manager. 'And there's heaps of chicks and stuff in the office too. Like 50 per cent women,' he says, somehow insinuating that white women aren't white.

'But yeah, the whole cousins thing is weird to me. I can't even remember who belongs to which aunt or uncle. There's just three only-children. On both sides of my family.

'I reckon any more than that'd be a handful, haha.'

> *He doesn't understand why woggy weddings are so big, because, like, why would you get that worked up by your mum's sibling's daughter getting married?*

LIKE NOTHING HAPPENED

Man Unfit To Operate Barbecue Posts Picture With Baby Niece

'I haven't seen him this happy since he got all four limbs taken out of a cast on the same day.'

AN EERIE SILENCE HAS swept through a small-town social media bubble today as social media user Dazza Noble (32) uploaded a picture of himself holding his baby niece despite the fact he cannot even be trusted to operate a barbecue.

Although he's holding down a job as a fulltime drummer, Noble has something of a reputation for being a clown's clown, and is the only person to date in Australia to be charged with attempting to drive using his scrotum.

'Aw yeah, that was funny as fuck,' laughed Noble, who for public safety reasons, we must repeat, really shouldn't be allowed near infants.

'Nut drives! Yeeeew!'

Thankfully having not reproduced himself, Noble has limited experience around newborns, which makes it all the more troubling that his sister Shannel would allow her firstborn child to be held in the hands of a man who once tried to grubber-kick a kebab.

'He's really excited to be an uncle. I haven't seen him this happy since he got all four limbs taken out of a cast on the same day.'

At time of writing, Noble states he is hosting a sausage sizzle for his new baby niece, as soon as he can figure out how to connect the gas canister to his barbecue, which he has put off cleaning for the past 12 years.

Local Apprentice Bolts Toolbox To Centre Of His Already Impractical Flat Tray Ute

LOCAL APPRENTICE HAMISH Hickley has today shocked his entire worksite by debuting a customised toolbox in the centre of the flat tray of his lowered 2004 Toyota Hilux.

After finally securing an apprenticeship with a local builder, the aspiring chippy got overexcited after receiving three separate paycheques in as many weeks.

'I just took out a personal loan. It's only had one owner before the guy I bought it off,' he says.

'It's mad, hey.'

Having already learnt that his modified vehicle is unable to carry wheelbarrows or shovels without using straps, the 18-year-old is about to realise just how inconvenient it is having to climb onto his ute tray every time he wants to grab something from the toolbox.

'He'll still be paying this thing off well after he's got his ticket,' says one of the foremen on the South Betoota residential development.

'By the time he's fucked up his cab with cement shovels, no one will ever look at this thing for resale ever again … unless he can find some other moron schoolie to buy it off him in the next six months.'

> *The 18-year-old is about to realise just how inconvenient it is having to climb onto his ute tray every time he wants to grab something from the toolbox.*

LIKE NOTHING HAPPENED

Local Dad Hoping Inferior Dad Next Door Heard Him Start Mower In One Pull

A SUNNY AFTERNOON JUST got a little brighter for local dad Wayne Crocker (48), as he started his lawnmower in just one pull, and is pretty confident the inferior man next door saw him do it.

'Was he looking? He was? Haha, classic.'

Usually a fan of besting his neighbour, Arnie Dale (35), in other ways, such as with extravagant Christmas decorations and having a bigger barbecue, Crocker made sure to wait for Dale to step outside before starting his lawnmower in a single stroke.

'Got him! Don't even really need to mow!'

Crocker used this opportunity to showcase his exceptional mowing skills to his neighbour, pointing to his ability to mow easily beneath the trampoline and the immaculate edges he cut that separate the two properties to the millimetre.

'Yeah, you can borrow this one once I'm done, if you like? I hear you're still on a Parklander! This ought to do the trick a bit better. Here, come and try it out.'

Upon showing Dale the intricate pull-string method that starts his mower, Crocker found himself becoming slightly aroused as his less masculine neighbour took two pulls to start the engine.

'Did you see that? Bet you he didn't get his licence on the first go either! Probably drives auto!'

From there, Crocker proceeded to show Dale the ease with which his Honda HRU196M1 Buffalo Classic can handle rough terrain by mowing Dale's front lawn.

'You don't mind me cutting your grass, do you, Arnie? Haha!'

Speaking privately with *The Advocate*, Arnie Dale shared with us his thoughts on his neighbour's dazzling lawnmower skills.

'One stroke every time? How does he do it? Fucking hell.'

One Night Stand's Dog Looks Up At Local Man With A Vacant Look Of Disgust

WITH HIS PONYTAIL FLAPPING playfully in the warm desert breeze last night, a mildly unpopular accountant threw caution to the wind and followed his friends from a suburban pub to a famous inner Betoota nitespot.

Coming clean to our reporter this morning on the D45 bus from the French Quarter up the hill to Betoota Heights, Boris Watson said he was kind of glad he did follow his mates to the Fitzrovia Club on Rue de Putain last night, because he ended up going home with a perfect stranger.

'It was kind of weird,' said the directionless 32-year-old.

'Come to think of it, it was pretty fucking weird. I told myself I wasn't going to get pissed last night. I even took my work shit to the pub so I'd have a reason to leave. But yeah, it was stinking hot yesterday out in that beer garden and long story short, I reckon I must've inhaled five schooners of heavy in one hour on an empty stomach. The only smart thing I did was put my work gear behind the bar.

'Then, yeah, it's all a bit of a blur until we got down to the Fitz. We had some shots then me and another mate decided to cut the rug for a bit downstairs in that part, you know, just as you walk in?'

Judging from the reactions he received from other bus passengers as he continued with his yarn, the rest of the story has been omitted from today's edition of *The Advocate*.

Nevertheless, around 6 am this morning, he left the bedroom of an Old City-district leasing agent, had a drink of water from her share house kitchen tap and ran into the dog.

'He just kind of looked up at me, stared right into my eyes,' said Watson.

'I wondered if he was hungry or something but he wouldn't let me near. He wouldn't even take a pat. He just looked at me with this knowing but ultimately disgusted look. It was quite confronting. This hasn't happened to me before. I said goodbye to him and walked out the door.

'When I said it was a weird night, that's what I mean. I mean the dog.'

Childless Couple Think They'd Never Use A Tablet To Distract A Toddler For Five Minutes

A YOUNG BIRKENSTOCK-WEARING couple, Bindi Aye and Archie Freeman, are this afternoon treating themselves to a nice lunch.

After enjoying their entrée, the couple began to let their judgemental eyes roam around the restaurant. It's believed it was at this point that they noticed the Kelly family, a slightly older couple with a five-year-old boy who was playing a game on a tablet.

Bindi and Archie's eyes immediately darted back to one another, looks of disgust radiating from their faces.

'That poor child, it doesn't stand a chance,' said Bindi, leaning over the table so only Archie could hear.

'That thing is frying that poor kid's brain,' replied Archie. 'There's no way I'm letting our kids go anywhere near a screen.'

'Did you know none of the creators in Silicon Valley will let their kids have phones or tablets?' parroted Bindi, repeating a fact she'd heard from someone who might have read it somewhere.

While they say they're not snobs, Bindi and Archie continued to hypothesise the horrible life they foresee in the child's future.

The Advocate is waiting to see if Bindi and Archie will still be on their tech-denying high horse when they've got a snotty, screaming, misbehaving child doing everything it can to ruin their attempt at a nice meal out.

Cashed-Up Tourist's Inability To Reverse With Trailer Brings Joy To Locals

'LEFT HAND DOWN, MATE,' HE yelled from the jetty.

'Yeah, keep going. Nah, go back up and straighten out, mate. Yeah, woo! Now come down slower.'

Nat Wilmott is trying to keep the peace down at the Betoota Sailing Club boat ramp – but he's having a little bit of trouble.

The line this morning was nearing ten trailers as a sunburnt Betoota Grove financier was trying and failing spectacularly to launch his boat into Lake Yamma Yamma.

In the dry desert heat, people were getting frustrated.

But not everyone.

Those not in the line, the jetty fishermen and the like, were all laughing at the expense of Peter Mantis, a somewhat likeable private fund manager at Debit Ecosse Private Wealth in the French Quarter.

'Mate, you're fucking useless!' screamed one bloke from beside the boat ramp. 'Do you want me to do it? I've never driven a Merc before, but. Is the big silver cunt an auto or what?'

That was when Nat, the owner-operator of the Betoota Sailing Club Tackle Shop, stepped in to help.

Peter had fallen into the trap of boat ownership without first mastering the art of reversing down a boat ramp – something he regrets now.

'It looks easy enough, to reverse a trailer, but it's not,' said Peter.

'Then this nice old man, Nathan I think his name was, coached me through it and I ultimately got the thing in the water.

'The whole damn episode certainly entertained these South Betoota mouth-breathers. Leering at me from the edge of the boat ramp.'

242 THE BETOOTA ADVOCATE | AUSTRALIA 2020

Spunky Italian Barista Sends Hot Flush Through Local Mum By Remembering Her Name And Order

USING ALL OF HER primary school Italian in saying thank you to local barista Giovanni 'Jack' Chapmanio, a South Betoota mother of four asked for the air conditioning to be turned on after being personally greeted by the Italian national with her order ready to go.

'*Grazie*, Jacko! *Come è ora?*' said Angela Ikona, the owner–operator of Jim's Hairdressing on Lewis Parade.

'*Grande! E come su di te, bella ragazza?*' replied Jack.

Realising she'd hit the bottom of her Italian vocabulary, the 43-year-old said thank you once again in her thick Caboolture Catholic mother tongue, took her coffee and left.

Speaking to *The Advocate* just moments ago from the car park in front of Tom's Cash'n'Carry Cafe and Toastie Bar where the Italian works, Ikona said she just couldn't handle being in the same room as him any longer.

'God, every time he says my name in that accent, it's like being dipped in hot water,' she said.

'Similar to what I imagine one of those acid attacks you read about would feel like.'

> *Realising she'd hit the bottom of her Italian vocabulary, the 43-year-old said thank you once again in her thick Caboolture Catholic mother tongue, took her coffee and left.*

LIKE NOTHING HAPPENED

'Make Some Mothafuken Noyazz!' Says Unknown Local Hip-Hop Group Three Acts Before Touring DJ

THE BETOOTA ENTERTAINMENT Centre was last night treated to an array of international musicians, and some incredibly shit local ones, as part of the opening acts for touring big-beat electronica artist DJ Howsyafather from Manchester, UK.

While a Thursday night blowout is not ideal for the greying Gen X ticketholders that fit into that weird Fatboy Slim-esque demographic, the vague start time of the main act meant that they had to sit through every nameless act the promoter had slapped together during the frantic two weeks prior.

'When's he coming on?' asked local contract lawyer, Emily (39).

'The gates have been open since 7 pm. It's 10 pm and we still haven't seen any of the touring acts.'

The fact that DJ Howsyafather had brought two other DJs with her from northern England was also quite concerning for the prudes who used to do ecstasy at uni in 1999, as it looked very much like no one was getting out of the venue until at least 1 am.

Andrew (42), a local digital content director for some shit News Corp–affiliated online media company, was similarly ropeable.

'Who the fuck are these guys on stage now?'

Andrew was of course talking about VIN SENSE & CORE LEONE, two of Betoota's most social media–heavy local barbecue rap rappers.

Colloquially referred to as VS&CL, it is not known how many of tonight's concertgoers would actually call themselves fans of western Queensland's skip-hop heavyweights.

In fact, it seems that a large majority of the two-thousand-strong crowd of largely late-30s corporate creatives have no idea who on earth VS&CL fucken are.

This hasn't stopped the rap duo from trying to lift the roof, a good 90 minutes before the main event. Which is a DJ who makes very different music from this poorly-booked opening act.

'Everybody make some mothafuken noyazz!' shouts VIN SENSE as loudly as his over-exaggerated Aussie accent will allow.

The crowd kind of yells back with guarded enthusiasm.

CORE LEONE is inspired by the rapport they are building with this largely sober crowd, most of whom are constantly checking on the babysitter.

He decides to get political.

'When I say FUCK! You say TRUMP! 'FUCK!'

The crowd doesn't give him an inch, so VIN SENSE has to fill the gaps.

By the end of the chant, it's just CL saying FUCK and VS saying TRUMP.

The awkwardness of their failed crowd integration is immediately buried by the soft opening hook of their 2003 Triple J classic 'Australian Men Sometimes Suffer from the Pressures of Everyday Life'.

'Yeah, this is a serious one,' says VIN SENSE, in a sombre tone.

'Yuh-huh,' says CORE LEONE.

'Listen up …'

It is not known how many of tonight's concertgoers would actually call themselves fans of western Queensland's skip-hop heavyweights.

LIKE NOTHING HAPPENED   245

'My Tiny Penis Grew Eight Full Inches After I Bought This Very Loud Motorbike'

THERE IS A MIRROR opposite Ben Tyler's shower.

Each morning, the 32-year-old Gemini stands in that shower, the warm water crashing into his supple body.

Up until a week ago, just when he thought he was happy, when he felt that everything was in its place, he'd catch a glimpse of his tiny penis staring back at him.

Last Friday, he thought to himself, 'Man, I've got to do something about my tiny dick. I'm not getting any younger.'

Wrapped in his towel and sitting on the end of a single bed, Ben began googling motorbikes.

He visited one in Betoota Heights on Sunday, where he made a purchase.

The man who sold Ben his new motorbike is Darcy Pearson.

'He came in and asked for the loudest bike we had,' he said.

'Which is a pretty common request. Lots of young blokes come in here and want a really, really loud motorbike. It used to be the fastest motorbike, now the trend is that the louder ones fly off the showroom floor. Some even take the baffles out of the muffler, so they're extra loud. Loud enough to physically injure pedestrians.'

Our reporter met with Ben this morning at a Betoota Grove park. He could hear him well before he could see him.

At great speed, Ben tore up the road into the park, taking no notice of the 10 kph speed limit signs.

The pace proved to be too great.

Ben left the road and collided with a barrier, sending him sailing through the air and into the gravel on the other side.

Our reporter rushed over to the lifeless bone bag that was once Ben's body and asked him if he was okay.

'Mate, don't move. I'm calling an ambulance,' he said.

'I'm okay, bro,' coughed Ben.

'Is my bike okay?'

Local Girl Shares Extravagant Travel Plans As RSVP To Low-Key Birthday Drinks Back Home

BAZZA'S 30TH WAS SUPPOSED to be just a relaxed Friday afternoon drinks at his favourite pub. It was one of those things where, if you can make it, good … if you can't, oh well.

But his girlfriend's work friend's girlfriend must have missed how casual it was going to be.

Despite being at the level of friendship where she is not even expected to RSVP whether she is going or not, Sally has jumped at the chance to be clear about why she won't be able to attend this event.

By offering her current international travel itinerary to the entire invitee list, Sally has also invited Bazza to share anything he might know about a tourism hotspot he's never been to.

Sorry Baz. Can't make it – Jamie and I will most likely be drinking cocktails in Phuket on the 30th. Let us know if you have any suggestions for Thailand. Will have to catch up when we get back. landing the weekend after xx

The post was joined by several other oversharing friends who posted similar excuses – none quite as indulgent as Sally's – however, some did explain that there was another social event on that night for some reason.

Slly Alcorn ▶ Bazza's 30th
2 mins

Sorry Baz. Can't make it - Jamie and I will most likely be drinking cocktails in Phuket on the 30th. Let us know if you have any suggestions for Thailand. Will have to catch up when we get back. landing the weekend after xx

👍 Like   💬 Comment

LIKE NOTHING HAPPENED

Local Fuckwit Buys Himself A New Pair Of Fuckwit Shoes

A LOCAL FUCKWIT DECIDED overnight that he deserves to give himself a present after resisting the urge to buy a small bag of cocaine over the weekend.

Conor Royd-Ross, who is someone's son, purchased some woven leather shoes from the popular Diamantina-based online fashion aggregation shop, Autofellatio, in the dying sunlight of yesterday afternoon.

'They were only $250, which is basically half what a bag costs in the Simpson Desert these days,' he told our reporter.

The 25-year-old spoke candidly to *The Advocate* after our publisher told the editorial team to find something other than the pandemic to report on.

'So I'm saving money buying these shoes. I might even have a bit left over to buy a linen polo shirt or some linen trousers. I'm probably going to do that every weekend from now on.'

When asked by our reporter what he meant by 'do that' every weekend, Conor threw his head back in a sharp, forced laugh and scratched his limp, dull penis.

'Just have a few little liney-linies from some other cunt's bag, brother!'

Conor Royd-Ross, who is someone's son, purchased some woven leather shoes from the popular Diamantina-based online fashion aggregation shop, Autofellatio, in the dying sunlight of yesterday afternoon.

248 THE BETOOTA ADVOCATE | AUSTRALIA 2020

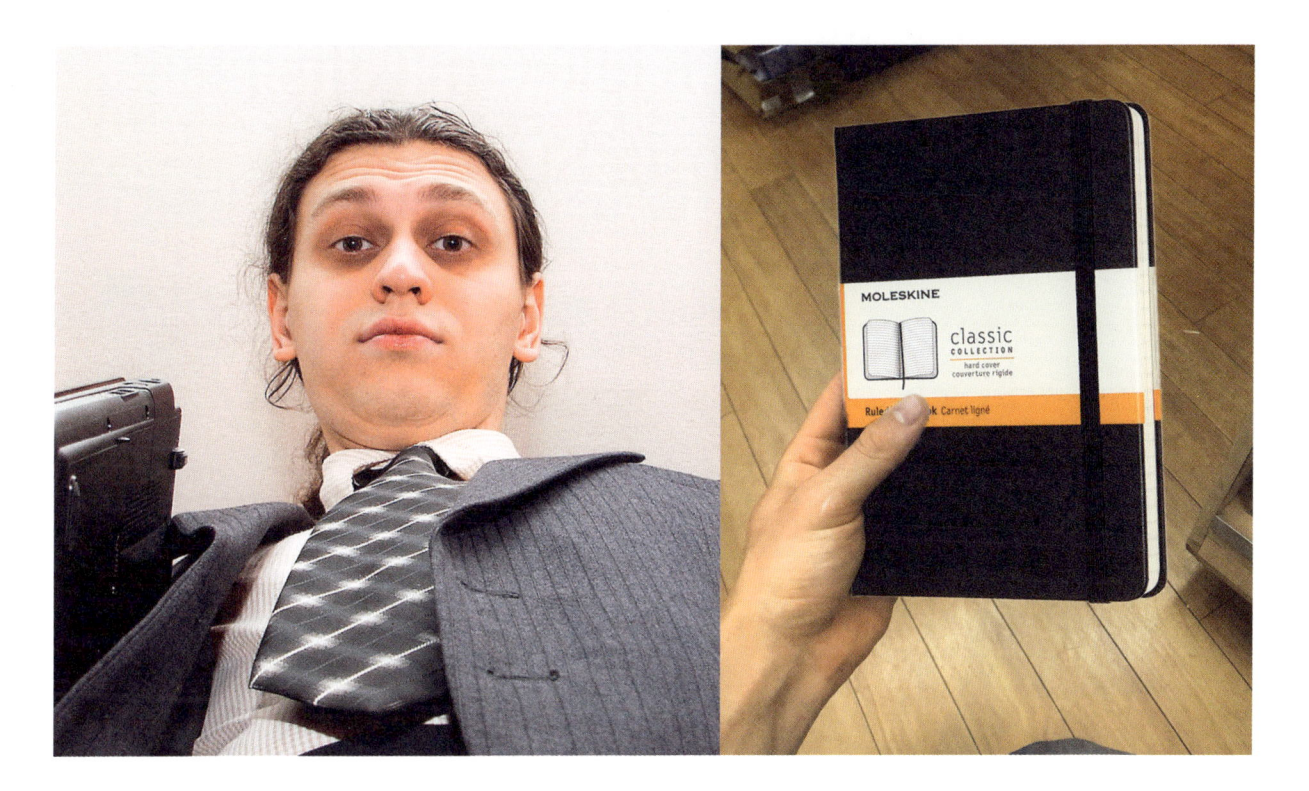

Local Man Who Enjoys Throwing Money In The Bin Buys Moleskine Diary

A LOCAL PIECE OF sun-dried devon has bought himself a needlessly expensive diary today in the hope that it'll turn his pointless life around.

This year marks the first year that Oliver O'Reardon's mother hasn't purchased a Moleskine diary for him. He says it's because he's an unmarried 34-year-old with the lung function of someone twice his age.

She says it's because she forgot.

One thing that Oliver enjoys doing more than most things is to go and find an ATM, put his card in and withdraw some cash, then throw the money on the footpath and walk away.

Another thing he likes doing, but not as much, is putting cash directly into a bin. Any bin, it doesn't matter.

Oliver spoke briefly to our reporter after wrapping up a conversation he was having by himself in the Rover Road public toilets.

'You want to know why I bought this?' he asked our reporter at the urinal.

He held out a fresh 2020 Moleskine diary with the plastic wrap still intact. After a pause, he took the plastic off with his teeth and threw the diary into the trough.

'Wee on it,' he said.

Oliver and our reporter wee'd on the diary for about a minute, then Oliver bent over to pick it up.

'Perfect,' he said softly to himself as he put the soaking diary into his briefcase.

He then left without saying another word.

One thing that Oliver enjoys doing is to go and find an ATM, withdraw some cash, then throw the money on the footpath and walk away.

Random Bloke At Kick-On Tells Uncomfortably Long Story With No Climax

Dan (or Dane?) is excused for his behaviour – as it is quite clear that he completely forgot what he was talking about halfway through that piece-of-shit story.

A RANDOM BLOKE WHO has somehow got a bait to an intimate bender kick-on has just spent the last twenty minutes telling a story that is designed purely to keep people listening for as long as possible.

The story, which started with a bit of momentum, has spiralled off into a bizarre lengthy anecdote with no real punchline or climax.

In fact, there doesn't seem to be any form of ending to this yarn at all.

The bloke, whose name might be like Dan or Dane (?), has already been twice reprimanded for trying to talk about politics and other deep shit like war – so this most recent fuck-up marks a third strike.

However, as the sun begins sizzling through the window and the birds begin chirping, Dan (or Dane?) is excused for his behaviour – as it is quite clear that he completely forgot what he was talking about halfway through that piece-of-shit story.

As the host of the house begins texting his cab driver mate to drop off some more grog, Dan (or Dane?) makes the absolutely truly abhorrent suggestion that they play a drinking game.

'Mate, it's like six o'clock in the morning and we've got a couple of tickets en route. We aren't playing drinking games. What the fuck?' says the least sympathetic guest, Dixy. 'How old are you?'

Luckily for Dan (or Dane?) all is forgiven once he reveals that he's about six years younger than everyone else and therefore completely out of his depth.

Local Bachelor Insists His Bed Is More Comfortable Without A Bed Frame

LOCAL BACHELOR AARON WELLS has been a little out of touch with the ladies since his breakup and has reportedly regressed to his teenage ways.

The heartbroken uni student recently moved his belongings to an on-campus share house and is rumoured to have only left his room to use the toilet or to heat up some two-minute noodles.

However, Aaron insists that he's fully committed to his new low-budget bachelor lifestyle and loves that he has 'a space for himself'.

'I feel like I can finally be myself,' Aaron says.

'And do whatever I want, WHENEVER I WANT.'

'Nobody's going to complain about me being on the Xbox now, HAHA!'

Despite being a solid 6'4, our reporter notes that the majority of Aaron's furniture is at floor level.

This includes a slightly cracked plasma TV and a smelly bean bag chair which he uses to store the same three shirts he wears on rotation.

'I guess you could say I'm a minimalist,' says Aaron, gesturing to a double mattress with mysterious brown stains on it. 'No bells and whistles here.

'I just prefer it without a bed frame,' he insists, without provocation.

'It's more comfortable.

'… I don't have time to look for one anyway.'

Our reporter attempts to quiz him further but Aaron begins to absent-mindedly pluck at his out-of-tune acoustic guitar, signalling that he's bored with the conversation.

Despite being a solid 6'4, our reporter notes that the majority of Aaron's furniture is at floor level. This includes a slightly cracked plasma TV and a smelly bean bag chair which he uses to store the same three shirts he wears on rotation.

Local Community Figure Does A Burnout For The Kids

A LEGENDARY LOCAL MAN has today done a burnout on request.

In what is often viewed as a bit of a treat in small towns and suburban outskirts around the country, local community man Eric (31) didn't even hesitate to drop it when a bunch of local townie kids yelled at him from the school bus.

As the nation's truckies gradually respond less and less to kids doing the 'honking' hand sign, and coppers and fireys are even less likely to bung on the siren just for the fuck of it, Eric's illegal behaviour comes as a refreshing and heartwarming change for the children from Betoota City Limits Primary.

Local kid Timmy (10) says that all he had to say was, 'Oi, do a burnout!' before the local landscaper absolutely lit it up.

'It was a real smoke show. I think he did it in like third, because it was loud as. So sick.'

While the teachers present on the school excursion appeared less than impressed by their students' interactions with the local degenerate, the bus driver (Kenno, 68) says he thought it was grouse.

'Good to see a few blokes still treatin' their Commodores like Commodores in this day and age,' said Kenno.

'Sends a real good message to these young ones.'

As the nation's truckies gradually respond less and less to kids doing the 'honking' hand sign, and coppers and fireys are even less likely to bung on the siren just for the fuck of it, Eric's illegal behaviour comes as a refreshing and heartwarming change.

Local Girl Posts Heartfelt Mother's Day Tribute To Mum She Refuses To Friend On Facebook

LOCAL SOCIAL MEDIA oversharer Clare Pinnington (22) has posted an emotional tribute to her mum on several different channels this Mother's Day.

It is believed that Clare's write-up about 'the special woman in her life' was so emotional and kindly worded that many of her friends on social media initially thought that her mother had been diagnosed with a terminal illness.

Captioned with a 70-word paragraph that includes very strong terms such as, 'My one and only' and 'Love you more than anything', the photo has since notched close to 200 'likes' across both Facebook and Instagram.

Unfortunately, Clare's mum Janet will never know this, because Clare has yet to accept her requests to connect on social media.

'She's just so nosy!' says Clare, who has left her mum's friend request in the backlogs for two years now.

'She can't be trusted with all the stuff she sees on there. I fucking hate how snoopy she is. She needs to get a life.

'I hate her!'

Unfortunately, Clare's mum Janet will never know this, because Clare has yet to accept her requests to connect on social media.

Local Girl Sends 83 Drunken Texts Explaining She Doesn't Need Toxic People In Her Life

AFTER MAKING EXCUSES to get out of an arranged dinner date, Sally Westington (27) sits in her Betoota Cove apartment drinking alone and scouring social media. Unfortunately, her moment of bliss was cut short when the Virgo saw a photo of two of her best friends having dinner together – the very friends she'd blown off.

Immediately screenshotting the Instagram post, Sally sent the photo to her third, fourth and fifth best friends, expressing her dislike of the image. Monique, the fifth best friend, was the only one who replied.

'Can you believe these two?' Sally had captioned the photo in a text message.

'What's the big deal?' replied her filler friend, Monique.

'I was meant to be there!' said one message.

'I can't believe they went without me,' said another.

'We are 27 now,' said the next.

'I don't need to be dealing with these toxic bitches anymore.' And another.

Familiar with Sally's loose-lipped track record, Monique knew better than to agree with her friend's bitching, so she replied with a neutral, 'Mhmm'.

The following week, Monique alerted our reporters to an Instagram post of Sally's, a boomerang that sees Sally and her two aforementioned best friends cheersing their Aperol Spritzes with the caption 'T H E S E T W O <3'.

Monique then went on to explain that Sally was in fact the most toxic person in their friendship group, often letting her jealousy get in the way of common sense and rationality and to 'not trust a word she says'.

PICTURE CREDITS

Page 2 Ashley J Nixon; 4 Nic Walker; 9 Ashley J Nixon; 12 Shutterstock; 15 Shutterstock; 16 Shutterstock; 17 Shutterstock, AAP/James Ross; 18–20 Shutterstock; 21 Diamantina Consolidated Holdings Pty Ltd; 22 Shutterstock; 23 Diamantina Consolidated Holdings Pty Ltd; 24 Shutterstock, Diamantina Consolidated Holdings Pty Ltd; 25–26 Shutterstock; 27 Mark Cranitch/Newspix; 28–31 Shutterstock; 32 AAP/James Ross, Shutterstock; 34 AAP/Lukas Coch; 36 Shutterstock; 37 AAP/Steven Saphore; 38 Instagram/@conniefinlay; 39–40 Shutterstock; 41 AAP/Lukas Coch; 42 Selina Miles; 43 AAP/Joel Carrett, AAP/Mick Tsikas; 44 AAP/Joel Carrett, Shutterstock; 45 Shutterstock; 47 AAP/Dave Hunt; 48 Gregory Nelson, Diamantina Consolidated Holdings Pty Ltd, Shutterstock; 49 AAP/Mick Tsikas, Shutterstock; 50 AAP/James Ross, Shutterstock; 52 AAP/James Ross, Diamantina Consolidated Holdings Pty Ltd; 53 Diamantina Consolidated Holdings Pty Ltd, Shutterstock; 54 AAP/Mick Tsikas; 55 Shutterstock; 56 Alex Ellinghausen/Sydney Morning Herald; 59 Diamantina Consolidated Holdings Pty Ltd; 60 AAP/Lukas Coch; 61 AAP/Mick Tsikas, Shutterstock; 62 Diamantina Consolidated Holdings Pty Ltd, Shutterstock; 64 Shutterstock; 65 AAP/Lukas Coch; 66 Shutterstock; 67 Alex Ellinghausen/Sydney Morning Herald, Shutterstock; 68 Diamantina Consolidated Holdings Pty Ltd, Shutterstock; 70 Facebook/Scott Morrison MP; 71 Shutterstock; 73 AAP/Dave Hunt, AAP/Cameron Laird; 74–79 Shutterstock; 80 Diamantina Consolidated Holdings Pty Ltd; 82–84 Shutterstock; 85 AAP/James Gourley, Shutterstock; 86–87 Shutterstock; 89 Lisa Clarke/Newspix, Shutterstock, Diamantina Consolidated Holdings Pty Ltd; 90 Janie Barrett/Sydney Morning Herald, AAP/Joel Carrett; 91 AP/Lukas Coch, Shutterstock; 92–99 Shutterstock; 100 AAP/Rebecca Le May, Shutterstock; 101–107 Shutterstock; 108 AAP/Lukas Coch, Shutterstock, Diamantina Consolidated Holdings Pty Ltd; 109 Shutterstock; 110 Diamantina Consolidated Holdings Pty Ltd; 111 Shutterstock; 113 Shutterstock; 114 Diamantina Consolidated Holdings Pty Ltd; 115 Shutterstock; 116 AAP/Paul Miller; 117–125 Shutterstock; 126 AAP/Lukas Coch; 130 AAP/Mick Tsikas; 132 AAP/Steven Saphore, Asylum Seeker Resource Centre; 133 AAP/Mick Tsikas, Shutterstock; 134–137 Diamantina Consolidated Holdings Pty Ltd; 138 Shutterstock; 140 AAP/Lukas Coch, Diamantina Consolidated Holdings Pty Ltd; 141 Diamantina Consolidated Holdings Pty Ltd; 142 AAP/Lukas Coch, Shutterstock; 143 Shutterstock; 144 AAP/Mick Tsikas, Shutterstock; 145 Shutterstock, Diamantina Consolidated Holdings Pty Ltd; 147–148 AAP/Mick Tsikas; 162 Shutterstock; 165 Shutterstock; 167 AAP/James Ross; 168 AAP/Lukas Coch; 169 AAP/Mick Tsikas; 170 AAP/Paul Braven; 171–172 AAP/Mick Tsikas; 173–174 Shutterstock; 175 AAP/Alex Ellinghausen, Shutterstock; 176–177 Shutterstock; 178 AAP/Lukas Coch, AAP/Dean Lewins; 179 AAP/Joel Carrett, Shutterstock; 180 Shutterstock; 184 AAP/Joel Carrett; 187 Shutterstock; 188 AAP/Dan Himbrechts, Shutterstock; 189 Shutterstock; 190 AAP/Peter Rae, AAP/Joel Carrett; 191 AAP/Joel Carrett, Shutterstock; 192 AAP/Dave Hunt, Getty Images Sport/Mark Evans; 193 AAP/Lukas Coch, Diamantina Consolidated Holdings Pty Ltd; 194 AAP/Joel Carrett; 195 AAP/Scott Barbour; 196 AAP/Joel Carrett, Mike Brett/Popperfoto; 197 AAP/Darren Pateman, Shutterstock; 198 Shutterstock; 200 Shutterstock, Diamantina Consolidated Holdings Pty Ltd; 201–206 Shutterstock; 207 AAP/Jono Searle, Wikipedia Creative Commons BY–SA 3.0; 208 Shutterstock; 211 AAP/Lukas Coch, Shutterstock; 212 Shutterstock; 213–215 Diamantina Consolidated Holdings Pty Ltd; 216 AP/Gerald Herbert via AAP, Shutterstock; 217 AAP/Joel Carrett; 218 Shutterstock; 219 PA/AAP/Pete Marovich, Shutterstock, Diamantina Consolidated Holdings Pty Ltd; 221 AAP/Scott Barbour, C Brendan Mcdermid/Reuters; 222 Shutterstock; 223 Getty Images National Basketball Association/Rocky Widner; 224 Shutterstock; 226 AAP/Mick Tsikas, Shutterstock; 227–230, 233–238, 240–243, 245–246 Shutterstock; 247 Diamantina Consolidated Holdings Pty Ltd; 248–249 Diamantina Consolidated Holdings Pty Ltd, Shutterstock; 250–253 Shutterstock

First published 2020 in Macmillan
by Pan Macmillan Australia Pty Limited
Level 25, 1 Market Street, Sydney, New South Wales
Australia 2000

Text copyright © Diamantina Consolidated Holdings Pty Ltd 2020
Cover art copyright © Ashley J Nixon 2020

The moral right of the author to be identified as the author of this work has been asserted.

All rights reserved. No part of this book may be reproduced or transmitted by any person or entity (including Google, Amazon or similar organisations), in any form or by any means, electronic or mechanical, including photocopying, recording, scanning or by any information storage and retrieval system, without prior permission in writing from the publisher. The author and the publisher have made every effort to contact copyright holders for material used in this book. Any person or organisation that may have been overlooked should contact the publisher.

A CIP catalogue record for this book is available from the National Library of Australia:
http://catalogue.nla.gov.au

Cover design by Trisha Garner
Text design by Susanne Geppert

Colour + reproduction by Splitting Image Colour Studio
Printed in Singapore by 1010 Printing International Limited

10 9 8 7 6 5 4 3 2 1